THE APOSTATES

SIMON COTTEE

The Apostates

When Muslims Leave Islam

HURST & COMPANY, LONDON

First published in the United Kingdom in 2015 by
C. Hurst & Co. (Publishers) Ltd.,
41 Great Russell Street, London, WC1B 3PL
© Simon Cottee, 2015
All rights reserved.
Printed in the United Kingdom

The right of Simon Cottee to be identified as the author of
this publication is asserted by him in accordance with the
Copyright, Designs and Patents Act, 1988.

A Cataloguing-in-Publication data record for this book
is available from the British Library.

ISBN: 978-1849044691

www.hurstpublishers.com

In memory of Irtaza Hussain—ex-Muslim, sceptic and freethinker
1991—2013

Change only the name and this story is about you.

Horace

CONTENTS

CONTENTS

PREFACE

Irtaza Hussain was just 22 when he died. His body was found in Hainault Forest in Chigwell, Essex, at 4.20pm on Wednesday, 11 September 2013. He had hanged himself. And he wanted the whole world to know it, posting a picture of himself on Facebook only moments before. The picture was entitled 'Just a Jump Away' and shows Irtaza sitting in a tree. The camera lens is pointing downward, rope ominously in view.

I first met Irtaza in March 2012. He had agreed to be interviewed for the research study on which this book is based.[1] It wasn't an easy interview. Not because Irtaza was reticent—on the contrary, he was talkative, vocal and often trenchant in his opinions—but because he was initially emotionally distant and ill at ease discussing his personal life. He talked extensively about what he saw as the dangers of Islamism and passionately defended the principles of secularism, religious tolerance and science, describing himself as 'a staunch atheist'. But I had to repeatedly press him about his family life. It was obviously a difficult subject for him.

My interview with Irtaza runs to just over two hours. And for most of that time Irtaza is cool and detached. Except for when he touches on his first suicide attempt, which he does only once and towards the end of our interview. Here his voice is raw and throbbing with emotion. It is hard to listen to.

In the months after our interview I stayed in contact with Irtaza, mainly through email, but we gradually lost touch. The last time I saw him was at a Council of Ex-Muslims of Britain (CEMB) lunch in November 2012. Most of us went to the pub afterwards, but Irtaza didn't join us. He seemed distant and left soon after the meal.

Born in Islamabad in 1991, Irtaza moved to Britain with his family in 2008, when he was sixteen, first to Cardiff and then to Dagenham in east London. Moving to Britain had a profound impact on him. By the time he began his A-levels, in Cardiff, Irtaza was having 'strong doubts' about Islam.

On 21 October 2010, Irtaza made his first post on the CEMB forum, announcing that he had recently left Islam 'because of its inability to justify the restrictions it imposes on me', elaborating that 'I had a lot of trouble trying to make sense of what my parents had enforced upon me and I had quite a lot of difficulty trying to find out why it would be a good thing to call myself a Muslim'.

Unlike many ex-Muslims I have interviewed, Irtaza was open about his apostasy and had told his family about his atheism. He said that the relationship with his father was especially turbulent and that leaving Islam made it all the more so. Indeed, according to Irtaza, his father had threatened to disown him over the matter.[2] Despite this, they had reached an agreement: they were not to talk about faith.

Irtaza also had difficulties at college. Despite his intelligence, he had performed poorly in his A-levels in Cardiff and was unable to secure a place at university. This made him despondent. That his brother, Ijtaba, was academically very successful would only have amplified Irtaza's crushing sense of underachievement: he had to settle for working at his father's furniture store in Romford.

To read the scores of condolences on his Facebook page, Irtaza was well-liked and admired. 'You were a caring, sensitive soul with a brilliant mind,' said one acquaintance, echoing a common sentiment. Andrew Copson, chief executive of the British Humanist Association, described him as 'an intelligent and thoughtful young man'.

Irtaza had 290 friends on Facebook, yet he was profoundly lonely. He had few friends outside the virtual world of the internet. As he remarked on the CEMB forum, 'I hate not having physical company' and 'I hate how I'm completely alienated from society and will never find a way to fit in'. In one post Irtaza alluded to the 'minor heckling or snarky comments' he would encounter on the street in Dagenham. It is not difficult to imagine the tenor of these.

Irtaza especially wanted relationships with women. It pains me to know that these never went anywhere. Recalling one particular rejection in a forum post in January 2013, Irtaza said that 'I cried my eyes out'. It was over the cancellation of a second date—a *second* date. It is heart-breaking now to think just how vulnerable Irtaza was and how deeply he felt every disappointment and setback.

Reading his online postings, which became progressively more desperate towards the end, it is clear that Irtaza's problems started to crowd in on him and that he couldn't see a way out. In one of his last CEMB forum posts Irtaza said he felt 'detached from reality...Life just seems incredibly difficult and I don't want to spend the rest of my life like this'.

In another post Irtaza said that he hated 'how people just ignore me even when I have something useful to say'. This was a persistent theme in our interview. And it was a theme in Irtaza's suicide note, which he posted on Facebook. It was addressed to all his friends and family. In the note, Irtaza speaks of his pain and his desire for an 'ultimate liberation' from his torment. He speaks, too, of the indifference of friends and family alike, of 'the fools' who 'will hold a candle saying that they missed me enough to mourn yet stand by doing nothing'. And how 'ultimately no one cares'.

Irtaza had an Islamic burial on Friday 13 September 2013, in accordance with his family's wishes. A week later, Irtaza's friends held a secular memorial service for him in Kentish Town Community Centre. The turnout was good and many warm and affectionate tributes were made. Irtaza's family was also present. Just as the event was about to end, Irtaza's father rose to his feet and made an impromptu speech. By all accounts it was deeply moving, relaying memories of happier times, when Irtaza was a young child in Pakistan.

Irtaza's apostasy was clearly a decisive event in his life, but so, too, was moving to Britain as an immigrant and the challenges of growing up as a stranger in a strange and not entirely hospitable land. In another poignant tribute to Irtaza, one friend and fellow ex-Muslim reflected: 'We all recognize ourselves in him... Irtaza was just like us, a young person growing up in an adopted country, with sometimes difficult situations at home, financial issues, problems with career and employment, loneliness, heartbreak, sometimes stress, frustration, depression and despair.'

There is a lot of pain and torment in the lives of ex-Muslims. This is to do, in part, with feelings of shame: the sense that they've failed their families and the wider Muslim community, that they're not right, that they're wrong. Not normal. To do, also, with feelings of alienation, a sense of being out of place. Not belonging.

PREFACE

This book is about the experiences of ex-Muslims not unlike Irtaza. One interviewee, a young Sudanese woman, told me that leaving Islam is 'such an intense journey and you go through so much...but to everyone else it's just another story, people don't really care'. This interviewee was referring to her non-religious friends. But to this woman's family it isn't just another story. It is a calamity. The aim of this book is to document the difficulties and challenges which ex-Muslims face in traversing these two opposing worlds of care and concern.

The overwhelming picture which emerges from the stories recounted in these pages is that ex-Muslims in the west feel marginalized not only from their families and the wider community of Muslim believers but also from a predominantly white and non-believing secular world which shows little interest in, still less understanding of, their situation. The argument in this book is that ex-Muslims deserve better. Irtaza deserved better. It is dedicated to his memory.

* * *

The book is organized as follows. Chapter 1 is an exercise in throat-clearing and spells out what this book is and is not about. Chapter 2 provides an overview of the sociological study of apostasy. Chapter 3 explains the process of exiting Islam. Chapters 4 and 5 address the issue of disclosure, documenting the various challenges and consequences associated with, respectively, the confession and the concealment of apostasy. Chapter 6 explores the various problems of adjustment involved in leaving Islam. Chapter 7 offers a conclusion.

All Arabic words in the text have been italicized. The glossary contains their English translations.

PRINCIPAL CHARACTERS

Aisha: lives in Greater London (UK), where she is taking a degree in history. She was born in London in 1992. Her family are Sunni Muslims of Somali origin. Atheist. Closeted.

Nubia: lives in London (UK), where she is taking a degree in physics. She was born in 1993 in Saudi Arabia to Sudanese parents. Describes her family as 'strict Wahhabis'. Atheist. Closeted.

Alia: lives in South Yorkshire (UK), where she works as a programmer in web development. She was born in Pakistan in 1987, and moved to the UK with her family shortly after her birth. Describes her parents as 'traditional Sunni Muslims'. She is an atheist and is open about this to her family, from whom she is estranged. She lives with her boyfriend, who is also an atheist.

Omar: lives in West Yorkshire (UK) with his wife and children, where he works in information technology. He was born in 1974 in Britain to a Sunni Muslim family from Pakistan. Identifies as an atheist and secular humanist. He is open about his apostasy to his family, but remains closeted in the community where he lives.

Azhar: lives in Vancouver, where he is taking a degree in philosophy. He was born in London (UK) in 1987, and moved to Canada when he was twenty. His family are Sunni Muslims with roots in Pakistan. Describes himself as 'neither theist nor atheist but Platonic Idealist', and is open about his apostasy to his family. He lives with his wife, with whom he has been married for over six years.

Wahid: lives in the East Midlands (UK), where he has recently completed a degree in computer science. He was born in Pakistan in 1990 and moved to the UK with his family when he was four. He grew up in London and has disclosed his apostasy to his mother and siblings.

Tasnim: lives in London (UK), where she was born in 1991 to Bengali parents. She has a degree in politics and describes herself as a 'Muslim atheist'. Her family, who are Sunni Muslims, are devout and remain unaware of her apostasy. She lives at home.

Farhad: lives in London (UK) with his family, where he is taking a degree in information technology. He was born in 1991 in Bangladesh to Sunni Muslim parents, and moved to the UK when he was four. Describes himself as an 'ex-Muslim atheist'. Closeted.

Hanif: lives in the West Midlands (UK) with his wife and family, whom he describes as 'typical Pakistani' and Sunni Muslim. He was born in 1988 in the same area and works in catering. Atheist. Closeted.

Salim: lives in the south east of England, where he works for a tech startup company. He was born in 1989 in a mountainous area on the Eastern shores of the Mediterranean, and moved to the UK when he was two. Describes his mother's side of the family as 'secular Sunnis', his father's as a 'devout Sunni with traditional Naqshbandi leanings'. He is an atheist, 'with a small "a" and a humanist'. His mother and brother are aware of this, but not his father, from whom he is estranged. He is single and lives alone.

Masood: lives in the north of England with his parents, who are Sunni Muslims with roots in India and Pakistan. He was born in 1975 in Scotland, but has lived most of his life in West Yorkshire. Describes himself as 'an ex-Muslim, secular humanist and atheist'. He is *single*— Masood's italics—and is currently between jobs. His siblings are aware of his apostasy, but his parents are not.

Luqman: lives in the East Midlands (UK), where he works as a software engineer. He was born in 1982 in Kenya to Indian parents, and moved to the UK with his family when he was fourteen. Describes his family as 'religious Deobandi, Sunni Muslims' and himself as an 'atheist, sceptic, secularist, liberal ex-Muslim'. He is open about his apostasy. Lives alone and has minimal contact with his family.

Nabilah: lives in London (Ontario) with her children. She was born in Lebanon in 1975 to Sunni parents, and moved to Canada with her family before her first birthday. Works in a shelter for battered women. She is an atheist and is open about her views. Divorced and single.

Khadija: lives in south west London (UK) with her children, and is taking a degree in politics. She was born in London in 1976 to an English mother and Moroccan father. She is an atheist and is open about her views. Divorced and single.

Yasmin: lives in Toronto (with her partner), where she works in web design. She was born in Pakistan in 1979 and moved to North America with her family when she was twelve. She is open about her atheism to her family, half of whom identify as Sunni, the other half Shia.

Abdullah: lives in a city on the south coast of England, where he is taking a degree in mathematics. He was born in Germany in 1992 and moved to the north of England with his family when he was seven. His parents are Sunni Muslims from Afghanistan. He identifies as an atheist but has not disclosed this to his parents.

Amina: lives in East Anglia (UK), where she is taking a post-graduate qualification in a science-based subject. She was born in Bangladesh in 1987 and moved to Britain soon after with her family. Atheist and closeted.

Mustafa: lives in a city in the north of Britain, where he works as a medical doctor. He was born in the early 1980s in Iraq. His parents, with whom he does not live, but with whom he has regular contact, are 'practising Shiite Muslims' and know about his apostasy. Describes himself as 'Atheist, Iraqi, Arab'. Unmarried and single.

Ahmed: lives in Toronto, where he is taking a degree in political science. He was born and raised in the Arabian Peninsula to a Sunni Muslim family and is irreligious. He is unmarried and lives away from his family, to whom he has yet to disclose his apostasy.

Maryam: lives in the north east of England, where she is training as a medical doctor. She was born in 1988 in West Yorkshire to Malaysian Sunni-Muslim parents. She has disclosed her apostasy to her mother, but not to her father. Atheist.

Ramesh: lives in Ottawa with his wife and children. He was born in London (UK) in 1974 and moved to Canada with his family when he was fifteen. From a Hindu background, he converted to Islam in his early twenties. He works as a graphic designer. Identifies as a humanist. He is open about his views to his wife and children, but not to his wife's family and friends.

Amir: lives in Toronto, where he works in the field of mechatronic engineering. He was born in Pakistan in 1988 and moved to Canada when he was eleven. He lives away from home, but visits his family, who are Sunni Muslims, frequently. Atheist. He has disclosed his apostasy to his father, but not to his mother.

GLOSSARY OF ARABIC AND ISLAMIC TERMS

abaya	a garment of clothing for both sexes, covering most of the body
alhamdulillah	'thanks and Praise to God'
ameen	agreement with God's truth
bismillah	'in the name of Allah', followed in its fullest form by 'most Gracious, most Compassionate'
dawah	the proselytizing or preaching of Islam
deen	religion or belief
dhikr	remembrance of God; devotional act involving the repetition of the names of God, phrases from the Quran etc.
fajr	the first of the five daily prayers offered by practising Muslims
fatwa	an authoritative statement on a point of Islamic law
hadith	reports relating to the sayings and deeds of the Prophet Muhammad; some of the various collections are considered more authentic and reliable than others
hajj	the annual pilgrimage to Mecca in Saudi Arabia, which every adult Muslim of either sex must make at least once in their lifetime
halal	religiously permitted
haram	religiously forbidden
hijab	covering; a veil that covers the head and chest
iftar	the evening meal when Muslims break their fast during the Islamic month of Ramadan
imam	leader in prayer; leader of the Muslim community
iman	faith; belief

GLOSSARY OF ARABIC AND ISLAMIC TERMS

inshallah	'if God wills'
jihad	struggle for the sake of God (including military engagement)
ka'bah	a small shrine located near the centre of the Great Mosque in Mecca and considered by Muslims everywhere to be the most sacred place on Earth
kadi	a judge
kāfir	an unbeliever
mashallah	'whatever God wills'
nafs	self; psyche; soul
rakah	a part of the *salat*, the prescribed prayers said five times a day
rawda	a part of the Great Mosque in Mecca
salafi	a term used to denote those who rigorously follow the example of the companions (*Salaf*) of the Prophet Muhammad. Salafis tend to be conservative and puritanical and are often Wahhabi affiliated.
shariah	Islamic law
sheikh	an elder or leader
subhanallah	'glory be to God'
sufi	a branch of Islam, defined by adherents as the inner, mystical dimension of Islam, but considered heretic by some others
sunnas	the body of Islamic custom and practice based on the Prophet's words and deeds (as recorded in the *hadith*)
sura	a chapter of the Quran
surah yusuf	the story of the Prophet Yusuf, as relayed in the Quran 12:1–7
takbeer	'God is [the] Greatest' or 'God is Great'
taraweeh	extra prayers performed at night in the month of Ramadan
tawhid	oneness or unity of God
ummah	the community or nation of Islam, composed of all Muslims worldwide
umrah	a pilgrimage to Mecca, performed by Muslims that can be undertaken at any time of the year
witr	a prayer performed at night before dawn prayer

INTRODUCTION

The Sociological Unimagination

Apostates are marginal people and apostasy is a marginal sociological subject. In 1969 Armand L. Mauss remarked that the sociological literature on religion contained hardly more than 'an occasional oblique mention of religious defection'.[1] Over a decade and a half later little had changed, as Stuart A. Wright observed in his ground-breaking 1987 study *Leaving Cults*: 'Though empirical work on conversion and recruitment to social and religious movements abounds in sociology, there exists relatively little systematic investigation of defection, deconversion or disaffiliation.'[2] But by 1998, with the publication of David G. Bromley's edited volume on apostasy from 'new religious movements' (NRMs) or cults, entitled *The Politics of Religious Apostasy*,[3] Mauss's complaint was no longer valid. There was now a rich, if rather narrow, body of scholarly literature on religious exiting. However, since then, and despite the publication of a few notable studies,[4] sociological interest in apostasy has considerably waned. Wright's prediction, expressed in *Leaving Cults*, that 'in the coming years the volume and depth of research on disaffiliation will rival the research on conversion',[5] was premature to say the least.

Islamic apostates or ex-Muslims are not merely marginal in sociology; they are non-existent. Indeed, there is not a single sociological study, in either article or book form, on the issue of apostasy from Islam. This is puzzling, especially given the substantial and growing sociological interest in conversion into Islam.[6] Perhaps it is related to sensitivities around religion and Islam in particular. Perhaps sociologists are wary of inviting the charge of Islamophobia. Or perhaps they are anxious that by attending to voices critical of Islam they will be giving ammunition to the political right. Muslims in Europe, as Ian Buruma writes, are 'an already embattled minority'.[7] Why add to their woes by focusing on those who leave? Far better to attend to those who *join*, because the joining act is also a vindicating act. People *not* raised as Muslims *wanting* to join the Islamic faith: this affirms Islam. This shows not a dark side but a positive side. Or perhaps, more straightforwardly, it is because Islam is tangential to the concerns of mainstream sociology, although this doesn't quite explain the interest in conversion into Islam.

This book is intended as a corrective to the neglect of Islamic apostasy in sociology. It is also intended as a corrective to existing sociological studies of religious apostasy, where the focus is commonly on leaving cults, as opposed to conventional or mainline religions.[8]

Politics and Theology

Writing about Islamic apostasy is difficult—and not just because the stories one uncovers are often so full of emotional pain and suffering. It is difficult because the issue has become so intensely politicized and polarized. This is directly related to the contested status of Islam in western democratic secular societies.[9] Is Islam a religion of peace or is it a religion of conquest and oppression? This is the debate—often crude and reductive—currently raging in Europe and North America. Because apostasy in Islam is intimately connected to the question of tolerance and freedom of conscience, it has become conscripted into this wider public reckoning over the political identity of Islam.

On one side, moderate Muslims insist that Islam endorses the modern liberal concept of religious freedom and is hence perfectly compatible with secular democratic values. Nearly always, the advocates of this view appeal to Chapter 2: verse 256 of the Quran: 'There is no compulsion in religion.'[10] Mustafa Akyo, for example, argues that although 'most classical schools of the *Shariah* consider apostasy from Islam a crime punishable by death', the Quran 'decrees no early retribution' for apostasy and contains 'verses that seem to suggest that rejecting Islam is a matter of free choice'.[11] By way of illustration, Akyo cites 2: 256.[12] Shaykh Ibrahim

Mogra, the assistant secretary general of the Muslim Council of Britain, is more forthright: 'The position of many a scholar I have discussed the issue with is if people want to leave, they can leave. I don't believe they should be discriminated against or harmed in any way whatsoever. There is no compulsion in religion.'[13]

Against this, militant secularists contend that Islam, far from embodying a liberal philosophy of religious freedom, is in fact a religion of intolerance.[14] Like their Muslim adversaries, these critics invoke Islamic scripture to substantiate their case. Invariably, the following accredited *hadith*—from Sahih Bukhari, Volume 9, Book 84, Number 57—is summoned: 'Whoever changes his religion, kill him'. Sam Harris, for example, cites this *hadith* in his critical discussion of tolerance in Islam[15] and concludes that 'the justice of killing apostates is a matter of mainstream acceptance, if not practice' in Islam.[16] It also appears in Ibn Warraq's 2003 collection of ex-Muslim testimonies *Leaving Islam*, alongside many other incriminating scriptural sources, in a chapter entitled 'Islam on Trial: The Textual Evidence'.[17]

Neither of these contrasting positions is convincing. Yohanan Friedmann advises that 'rather than denying the existence of certain intolerant elements in medieval Islamic thought, modern Muslims might instead admit that such elements exist, while at the same time exercising their power to reject these and embrace the more liberal and tolerant principles of their tradition'.[18] Here is the essential point: the Islamic tradition contains both intolerant and tolerant elements. This may sound like an utterly banal statement. But it is a vast improvement on the polemical grandstanding on both sides of the divide in this polarized and now tiresome debate. Friedmann convincingly argues that 'the real predicament facing modern Muslims with liberal convictions is not the existence of stern laws against apostasy in medieval Muslim books of law, but rather the fact that accusations of apostasy and demands to punish it are heard time and again from radical elements in the contemporary Islamic world.'[19] The real problem, in other words, isn't Islam. It's demagogues like the Egyptian cleric Yusuf al-Qaradawi, who regards apostasy as a capital offence punishable by death,[20] condones suicide attacks on Israelis and condemns homosexuality.[21]

The previous three paragraphs notwithstanding, I have deliberately avoided theological discussion of apostasy in Islamic jurisprudence in this book, because it isn't a work of theology and because I'm not a theologian. And because it's a grave error to make assumptions about the situation of ex-Muslims on the basis of selective theological readings.

Still less is this book a polemic against Islam or religion in general. Nor does it trespass on the terrain of Islamic studies or the broader discipline of political science. It is, rather, a work of qualitative sociology—although I even hesitate to call it sociology since I've tried to write it without recourse to jargon and with the expectation that people will actually want to read it. Its focus is centrally on the social situations, experiences and self-understandings of ordinary ex-Muslims in the western context. Instead of asking 'What do the Quran and the *hadiths* say about apostasy?', I ask 'What do Islamic apostates say about apostasy in Islam?' Instead of asking 'What actions constitute apostasy?', I ask 'How does one leave Islam and become an apostate?' Instead of asking 'What is the punishment for apostasy in Islam?', I ask 'What challenges and difficulties do apostates encounter in leaving Islam?' The focus, in other words, is on the lived realities of apostates and how they subjectively make sense of their situation and the world in which they live.

Even when public discussion of Islamic apostasy shifts away from the theological to the material, there is a marked tendency toward polarization. On the right, Islamic apostasy is widely viewed as a serious global human rights problem and apostates are portrayed as brave dissidents who live in fear of violent reprisal from fanatical Muslims. For example, Susan Crimp and Joel Richardson's 2008 collection of personal testimonies *Why We Left Islam* praises the courage of the 'men and women who have left Islam—*at the risk of death*' and condemns Islam as a 'barbaric and repressive' religion.[22] On the left, by contrast, the question of Islamic apostasy barely registers and is seen at best as a diversion from more pressing issues, like the emancipation of Palestine. On the occasions when it is discussed, concern over apostates is typically derided as 'Islamophobic'[23] and activist ex-Muslims are attacked in an *ad hominem* register as charlatans out for their own ends. Consider, for example, the wildly emotional and intemperate reaction to Ayaan Hirsi Ali among many liberal-leftists. Brian Whitaker's polemic, published on the *Guardian* website, in which he castigates Hirsi Ali as a 'native informant' and mockingly categorizes her as a 'courageous reformist Arab personality (CRAP)',[24] is emblematic of this. It is also only the tip of a very toxic iceberg.

The argument in this book is that neither of these viewpoints is persuasive. No doubt apostasy from Islam is a fundamental human rights problem in Muslim-majority societies.[25] But apostasy from Islam is not a fundamental human rights problem in the secular west, where the principle of religious freedom is inscribed into law and people are free to join or leave religious groups without threat of violence. However, it is wholly unwarranted to suggest that concerns over Islamic apostasy are misplaced, still less that they are necessarily motivated by 'Islamophobic' enmity toward Muslims and Islam. This book strongly counters this, arguing that ex-Muslims in the west must manage the moral stigma attached to apostasy within their own communities and the many emotional difficulties and challenges involved in leaving Islam.

A Methodological Note

Between September 2011 and February 2013, I conducted life-history interviews with thirty-five ex-Muslims.[26] Interviews lasted between 2–3 hours. Some subjects were interviewed more than once. I also engaged in written correspondence with many respondents after they had been interviewed and traced some of their online footprint, where this was possible.[27] In addition to this, I attended numerous ex-Muslim 'meet-ups' in both Britain and Canada over a two-year period.

About the sample: all respondents, except one, were born and raised as Muslims. Eight had been Shia Muslims, while the remainder had been Sunni. All self-identified as 'ex-Muslims'—though not without reservations—and all were non-religious, defining themselves as either agnostic or atheist. Fifteen were women, twenty men. The youngest was eighteen, the oldest forty-eight. At the time at which they were interviewed nine were based in Canada, twenty-six in the UK.

Assembling even this modest sample was not an easy task. Apostasy is a stigma and ex-Muslims tend to be highly secretive. Indeed many are 'closeted' and actively conceal their disbelief. I had to go online to find them. This wasn't difficult, but persuading people to talk to me *in person* was, because they didn't know who I was (was I a jihadi in disguise or some nut-job out to do them harm?), whether I could be trusted or whether I had an 'agenda' (was I some right-wing douche-bag out to demonize Muslims? was I some religious apologist douche-bag out to demonize ex-Muslims?). In addition to this, not a few respondents told me they suffered from acute social anxiety and felt uncomfortable meeting and talking with strangers. They had spent a long time ruminating over whether to do the interview and had had to summon up the courage to do it. One respondent told me that she would almost certainly have backed out had I not travelled such a long distance to meet her. (Luckily for me—or unluckily—I was living in Bangor, north Wales, at the time, a city not famed for its travel connections, still less for its ethnic and cultural diversity.) And this was not uncommon: that I would arrange an interview and the subject would back out at the last minute.

There are two principal groups for ex-Muslims: the CEMB, founded in 2007 by Maryam Namazie, and Faith Freedom International (FFI), launched by Dr. Ali Sina in 2001. I recruited respondents exclusively from the online forum of the former. This in part is because the CEMB is based in Britain, as indeed are most of its forum users, although there are many living outside the UK, most notably in Canada. It is also because the CEMB forum is primarily a self-help refuge for secular and non-religious ex-Muslims, whereas the FFI online forum, which is based in the US, is more squarely a site for political engagement and discussion. Since, as I explain below, I am interested in the emotions and not the politics of Islamic apostasy I focused my attentions on the CEMB forum.

In several posts on the CEMB forum, between May 2010 and February 2012, I advertised my interest in speaking with ex-Muslims, explaining that I was a sociologist and that I wanted to know what it was like to leave Islam, how this occurs and with what consequences. I also said that my study was the first of its kind and made it clear to interviewees that my aim was to understand the dynamics of apostasy and not to criticize Islam, still less Muslims.

At first, my advert attracted curiosity but no participants. I then spoke with a prominent and well-respected member of the site. We discussed the study and its aims at length and after satisfying him that I was neither a douche-bag of the right nor a douche-bag of the theistic left he agreed to lobby for participants on my behalf, expressing his support for the study on the CEMB's forum. Soon after, several forum members contacted me and offered to participate in the study. Some of these respondents knew other ex-Muslims and through them I was gradually able to 'snowball' a larger sample of respondents. A good number wrote positively about their interview experience on the forum, encouraging other members to participate in the study.

Aside from the difficulty of finding participants, there was the logistical challenge of carrying out the interviews. The majority of respondents lived with their families and so, with a few exceptions, I could not interview them in their homes. Some interviews were done in cafés; most were carried out in hotel rooms, which introduced a different order of anxiety altogether, partly related to perceptions about what hotel staff thought we were up to.

All respondents signed a participant consent form promising confidentiality: hence all respondents have been given pseudonyms to protect their identities. Respondents in most cases chose these themselves.

Assembling the sample through an online self-help group may invite the suspicion that it is unrepresentative, since, it might be supposed, ex-Muslims who seek out a forum like that of the CEMB are more troubled than those who do not. My response to this is twofold: clearly not everyone who goes online and seeks out a forum for ex-Muslims is troubled. Equally clearly, there must be many troubled ex-Muslims who haven't even heard of the CEMB or similar groups. Many respondents undoubtedly were troubled, but some were not—or rather not any more averagely troubled than anyone else. It is also important to clarify that some forum members I interviewed had only the most fleeting engagement with the forum, whereas others were long-time, although not necessarily active, participants in its life. More practically: good luck to anyone who wants to find ex-Muslims without the aid of anonymous online ex-Muslim groups.

A Cautionary Note

Apostasy as a subject is full of interest and drama. Leaving a religion can be a difficult and fateful decision: the catalyst for a storm of conflicting emotions, ranging from exhilaration, joy, relief and ambivalence through to guilt, anguish and loneliness. It can also be the catalyst for irreconcilable conflict, estrangement, pain and grief. Were it not for the tumult in the lives of apostates, apostates might be happier. But they wouldn't be nearly as interesting.

'Happiness writes white,' Henry de Montherlant wrote. 'It doesn't show up on the page.'[28] Or as Mickey Sabbath, the fictional protagonist of Philip Roth's *Sabbath's Theatre*, puts it:

> For a pure sense of being tumultuously alive, you can't beat the nasty side of existence. I may not have been a matinee idol, but say what you will about me, it's been a real human life![29]

Apostates are neither idols nor demons, but their lives are certainly real.

Apostasy is a large subject, but the canvas of this book is deliberately narrow. Its focus is on the life-experiences of a small group of non-religious self-avowed ex-Muslims in Britain and Canada.

Among non-believers, non-religious ex-Muslims are a unique category: they were not born into unbelief, but determinedly exiled themselves into it and away from their former faith. Acquiring disbelief was typically an active process of self-transformation, the culmination of struggle, self-examination and self-doubt. It was also often traumatic, because in abandoning the guidance and consolations of faith they had put into question the very foundations of their identity and indeed the very basis of their existence. As one interviewee put it, speaking of the first few months after losing her faith, 'I felt lost...as though I don't know who I am anymore'. For those who have never believed, creating and preserving meaning in a rapidly changing and indifferent universe is an ongoing challenge; for non-religious ex-Muslims that challenge is felt all the more acutely, given the memory of who they were and how they once believed.

Non-religious apostates are also unique in the sense that they deviate not only from the faith into which they were born or converted, but also from the widely shared cultural assumption that one must invest in *some* notion of the divine.[30] This makes them doubly deviant—and doubly interesting.

This book is an exercise in qualitative social research and is correspondingly subject to all the limitations inherent in that methodological approach. It is not concerned to explore macro sociological questions. It does not, for example, address the 'background' structural conditions of Islamic apostasy in the western secular context, not because I think this is an uninteresting or unimportant question, but because the more pressing task is first to capture what it is or means to apostatize from Islam in this setting.

It is not body-guarded with an emollient foreword by a secular or moderate Muslim figure,[31] because no amount of kowtowing to the closed-minded would convince them that this book is a good idea.

It does not offer a comparative analysis of how the experiences of ex-Muslims living in secular western societies differ from those of ex-Muslims living in Muslim-majority societies, although it briefly touches on this question in the conclusion. It does not offer a comparative analysis of how the experiences of ex-Muslims in the UK differ from those in

Canada, because the data I have collected isn't wide-ranging enough to yield any reliable comparative insights.[32]

It does not offer an account of why and how Muslims convert to other religions: that is for others, no doubt the earnestly religious, to worry about. My interest, rather, lies in the varieties (to invert William James)[33] of *non-* or *irreligious* experience and what it means to renounce religion *in toto* and to live a life beyond religious belief and practice. This subject-area remains neglected in the social sciences.[34]

It does not focus on the lives of politically active ex-Muslims, like Ayaan Hirsi Ali or Ibn Warraq. Not because I find these people or their activism uninteresting, but because the central concern of this book is to explore the social situation of *ordinary* non-activist ex-Muslims. This is in sharp contrast to existing sociological studies of apostasy, where the dominant focus is on the role of 'career apostates' and their crusading activities against their former groups.[35]

It does not address empirical questions like 'how many ex-Muslims are there in the UK or Canada?', 'What is the median age at which ex-Muslims apostatize?', 'Are Shia Muslims more or less likely to apostatize from Islam than Sunni Muslims?', 'Are women more or less likely to apostatize than men?', 'Do ex-Muslims share certain characterological traits and drives?' It does not address these issues because empirically, right now, they are intractable. Apostasy from Islam is a potent stigma. Few people are willing to discuss it openly and honestly. Conducting large social surveys on apostasy would thus be deeply problematic from a practical point of view.

It does not say things like '75 per cent of respondents said...' or 'five respondents reported...', because that, frankly, would be idiotic—and both pedantic and unenlightening. My sample is just too small to warrant such statistical precision. So instead I say things like 'some respondents' or 'many respondents'. In any case, my concern is to identify and understand what is special in the structure of the apostate's life, not to quantify the percentage of respondents who said this or that.

It does not use insipid and opaque sociological terms like 'exiter', 'dis-affiliate' or 'leave-taker', opting instead for the term 'apostate'. This is primarily because 'apostate' is the more readily understandable term and conveys not merely loss of faith, but its active rejection. I recognize of course that the term may carry a negative connotation,[36] but this depends entirely on how it is used. Indeed many ex-Muslims I have met and interviewed referred to themselves as 'apostates'. Their objection wasn't to the term itself, but to the moral condemnation of their apostasy by others, especially loved ones.

I did not speak with the families of ex-Muslims nor to members of the faith communities in which they were or are living. This would have been fascinating, but not directly relevant to the specific research aims of this study.

I do not address the question of how apostasy from Islam can be reduced or eradicated, because I do not see apostasy from Islam as a moral problem in need of correction, still less do I see apostates as sinful delinquents in need of correction. However, there can be no doubt that apostasy *is* a moral problem: *for the apostate*.[37] The nature of this problem and how it is subjectively experienced and managed by the apostate is what this book is centrally about.

But neither do I see apostasy from Islam as a moral achievement, as something to be celebrated or encouraged. This study is not a moral defense of the particular choices, actions and outlooks of ex-Muslims, although it nonetheless tries to understand these from the perspective of the apostates themselves. Indeed, my aim is not to engage theologically, morally or intellectually with what ex-Muslims say about Islam, but, rather, to focus on what they say about themselves and their emotional experiences of leaving Islam. This book is of course about Islam, but it also not about Islam.

To echo Dostoevsky, to understand is not necessarily to excuse or justify and in recovering the experiences of ex-Muslims I have tried to maintain an objective spirit. To anyone coming at this issue with a fixed political agenda I can only offer my sincerest apologies, because the experiences relayed in this book are complexly real and cannot be reduced to any given ideological narrative. You will need to go elsewhere is search of rhetorical ammunition, so on you may kindly stroll. For all others, I implore you to stay the course and to lend an empathetic ear to the voices expressed in these pages.

2

ASPECTS OF APOSTASY

For it would have been better for them never to have known the way of righteousness than, after knowing it, to turn back from the holy commandment that was passed on to them.[1]

2 Peter, 2: 20–1

The Offence of Apostasy

'People get very emotional about it.' This is Hanif, an ex-Muslim in his mid-twenties from the Midlands. Hanif is talking about apostasy and why he thinks it's such a sensitive issue for Muslims. 'It's not just that you're criticizing Islam in some way,' he elaborates, 'you're actually criticizing the very foundations of it and people take it as an attack on their identity, not just their belief.' Wahid, from east London and slightly younger than Hanif, would no doubt concur with this, as indeed would many of the ex-Muslims I have interviewed:

> To them [Muslims], it doesn't really matter if you do the praying stuff, because to them it seems that you just don't care. But it's a big deal if you say, 'Yeah, I'm not a Muslim'. It changes nothing in your actions or in what you do. But to them, it means everything. Because it's an attack on their life. It's not, 'Oh, he's just a bad Muslim' kind of thing. It's like, 'Shit, he doesn't believe'.

For some Islamic jurists, apostasy is at least as grave an offence as murder, since it threatens the very unity of the Muslim community—the *ummah*—from within. Yusuf Al-Qaradawi puts it like this: 'Waging war against Allah and His Messenger by speaking openly against them is more dangerous to Islam than physically attacking its followers...moral mischief in the land is more hazardous than physical mischief.'[2]

'The apostate', wrote the classical Muslim jurist al-Samara'i, 'causes others to imagine that Islam is lacking in goodness and thus prevents them from accepting it.'[3] But that is not why apostates arouse disquiet among Muslims. Apostates arouse disquiet because it is *Muslims* they confound. Because if one person can be persuaded to leave Islam, then why not all?[4]

There is nothing peculiarly Islamic about any of this. Apostates of all religions arouse disquiet in believers and among the devout they are the object of particular fascination and contempt. 'Neither Judaism nor Christianity,' Yohanan Friedmann remarks, 'treated apostasy and apostates with any particular kindness.'[5] Indeed, as early as the fifth century the Theodosian Code ruled that 'it is graver than death and crueler than massacre when someone abjures the Christian faith and becomes polluted with the Jewish incredulity'.[6]

Nor is there anything peculiarly religious about this: apostates from secular groups are distrusted and condemned with equal vehemence. The hardest and most perceptive thinking on this matter has been done by the great German sociologist Georg Simmel. 'In-group conflict,' Simmel contends, is more intense than 'out-group conflict.' The more the conflicting parties have in common, the more intemperate the quarrel:

> People who have many common features often do one another worse or 'wronger' wrong than complete strangers do...We confront the stranger, with whom we share neither characteristics nor broader interests, objectively; we hold our personalities in reserve...The more we have in common with another *as whole persons*, however, the more easily will our totality be involved in every single relation to him...[7]

Simmel makes particular reference to the 'renegade' and explains how their previous allegiance with group members increases the scope for conflict:

> The recall of earlier agreement has such a strong effect that the new contrast is infinitely sharper and bitterer than if no relation at all had existed in the past...And where enough similarities continue to make confusions and blurred borderlines possible, points of difference need an emphasis not justified by the issue but only by that danger of confusion.[8]

But it is the perception that the renegade threatens group unity, Simmel observes, which explains why they provoke such intense hostility and distrust among group members.

In his book-length treatment of Simmel's work on conflict, *The Functions of Social Conflict*, Lewis A. Coser reinforces and refines this fundamental observation. 'Groups', he says,

> when threatened by other groups, may be forced to 'pull themselves together'. Here we note that a similar reaction occurs in the defence of the close group against a danger from within. Indeed...the reaction may be stronger under these conditions because the 'enemy' from within, the renegade or heretic, not only puts into question the values and interests of the group, but also threatens its very unity. Renegadism signifies and symbolizes a desertion of those standards of the group considered vital to its well-being, if not to its actual existence.'[9]

'Renegadism', Coser goes on, 'threatens to break down the boundary lines of the established group,' and hence 'the group must fight the renegade with all its might.'[10]

According to Coser, the renegade does not act alone: he is aided. And he in turn aids: he transfers his allegiance to a rival out-group. Because he cannot return to his former group, 'he will be more firm in his loyalty to the new group than those who have belonged to it all along'.[11] He also strengthens the out-group, Coser suggests, by increasing its sense of ideological rectitude.[12] Just as the renegade's departure serves to lower the values of the in-group,[13] the renegade's defection to the out-group serves to elevate those of its own.[14] 'This', Coser writes, 'makes him more dangerous in the eyes of his former associates than any other member of the out-group'.[15] Renegades, Coser adds by way of a footnote, arouse even greater fear and revulsion in groups which are weak and insecure about their continued survival: 'As long as the group is still struggling for acceptance, it must mobilize all its energies against the dangers threatening from within. This means that the sharpness of the reaction to the "inner enemy" is in proportion to the sharpness of the conflict with the outer enemies.'[16] By contrast: 'Once a group is well established and its continued existence is no longer in question, it can afford to take a milder view of renegadism.'[17]

Neil Vidmar, discussing the social-psychological dynamics of retribution, similarly lays great emphasis on group unity and the threat in-group deviance represents to this:

Social harm to the community is far worse when the deviant acts are committed by those who are in-group members than when they are committed by outsiders. The acts are not only viewed as a violation of rules, but an explicit rejection of the norms and values by one who is required by group membership to adhere to them. Thus, the acts are far more threatening to the members of the community who subscribe to the values. The reaction is further exacerbated when the acts come to the attention of outsider groups that are viewed as competing with the in-group, because the deviance lowers the in-group values relative to those of the out-group.[18]

The apostate's offence, in other words, is to cause remaining members of the group to reflect on their *own* commitment to the group. This can be unsettling and explains why apostates excite such intense retributive sentiments among those they have departed.

'Crime', Emile Durkheim famously wrote, 'brings together upright consciences and concentrates them'.[19] Crime, that is, provides a pretext for the group to unite and reassert its values. It is the darkness against which virtue can better define itself. Thus crime is 'an integral part of all healthy societies'.[20] So it is, too, with apostasy. It offends and unites the righteous. And because it strikes at the very symbolic heart of the group, it demands a forceful punitive response: ritual degradation; shunning; 'correction'; banishment. Or worse: imprisonment; torture; death.

Apostasy and Related Concepts

Apostasy is a type of exit. But not all (non-trivial) exits are like apostasy. It isn't, for example, like leaving a marriage, even though the leaver's actions may be perceived by the deserted party as a form of betrayal.[21] Nor is it like resigning from a job or giving up a hobby. Apostasy, rather, is an exit from a group or collective and is informed by a self-conscious renunciation of the group's foundational beliefs and values.

It goes without saying that the exited group must have been a previous source of belonging or identity for the leaver: one cannot apostatize from a group to which one did not belong or with which one did not identify.[22]

Apostasy is thus by definition a confrontational act, whereby the exiter disavows the very epistemological and moral tenets of the group. It is also by definition an act of personal transformation: the leaver's sense of self—their very identity—undergoes a dramatic change and they become, as a matter of self-definition, an ex- or former member of the group from which they exited.[23]

To exit a group is to withdraw from it, but this need not imply actual physical separation. It is perfectly possible to publicly renounce the norms of a group and still live among, or in close proximity to, its members as an outcast. Diogenes of Sinope is a good example of this. Although he sharply distanced himself from the social conventions of the Athenian society in which he lived,[24] he did not remove himself from its public setting and did little to conceal his scorn for its norms: indeed, he would fart loudly in crowded places, defecate wherever he chose and masturbate in the marketplace, knowing full well that these activities would scandalize the Athenians who witnessed them and invite their public censure.[25] Diogenes thus fits into that category of persons whom Robert K. Merton describes as '*in* the society but not *of* it'.[26] He is like 'the stranger', whom Simmel describes as 'near and far at the same time'.[27]

It is also possible to withdraw from a group and yet remain an outwardly compliant participant in its practices and life-world. That is, it is possible to privately reject the fundamental beliefs and values of a group and still involve oneself in its affairs to the effect that one fully subscribes to them. The experiences of 'closeted' apostates directly speak to this,[28] where outward adherence to group beliefs and practices indicates not fidelity, but a pragmatic concern to avoid censure or even banishment from the group. There are even cases of, to annex the title of an article by Daniel C. Dennett and Linda LaScola, 'Preachers Who Are Not Believers': pastors who continue in their clerical role despite their mounting disbelief.[29] Merton's description of the 'ritualist' is also pertinent here. The ritualist, Merton argues, relinquishes the conventional aspirations of the wider culture and in this sense he is deviant.[30] But he does not reject the 'institutionalized means' for achieving conventional aspirations: on the contrary, he continues to adhere 'almost compulsively' to these.[31] This 'clinging' to 'safe routines' Merton characterizes as a form of self-protective '*private* escape from the dangers and frustrations' inherent 'in the competition for major cultural goals'.[32] Thus outwardly the ritualist is conformist, but inwardly he is deviant. All this strongly suggests that exits can be emotional as well as physical and that one can simultaneously be both tied to and distant from a group.

In the sociological literature on religion, apostasy has been defined in a variety of ways. C. Kirk Hadaway and Wade Clark Roof suggest that an apostate is someone 'who held a religious identity at one time, but who now has rejected that identity' and chosen 'not to identify with any religious group'.[33] An apostate, that is, is someone who not only disaffiliates from their former faith, but from organized religion altogether. Apostates, Hadaway and Roof clarify, belong to the 'the unchurched' population, as do 'nones',[34] but they are distinctly unlike 'invisible affiliates', who while rarely if ever attending religious services may still retain a religious identity.[35] Nor are they synonymous with nones, since the 'none' category 'contains persons who have never had a religious identity'.[36]

David G. Bromley specifies a more restrictive definition of apostasy. The apostate, he suggests, not only renounces his former religion; he *opposes* it. Indeed, he is at war with it: 'Apostate refers not to ordinary religious leavetakers but to that subset of leavetakers who are involved in contested exit and affiliate with an oppositional coalition.'[37]

Stuart A. Wright similarly enforces a distinction between 'the typical *leavetaker* and the *apostate*'.[38] Whereas the former 'decides to terminate his or her commitment and disaffiliate in a non-public act of personal reflection and deed',[39] the latter is 'a defector who is aligned with an oppositional coalition in an effort to broaden a dispute, and embraces a posture of confrontation through public claimsmaking activities'.[40]

Anson Shupe echoes this. Apostasy, he argues, is not just 'a loss or wilful abandonment of faith'; it is an act of political opposition; and the apostate is 'an outspoken, visible critic' of their former group.[41]

This emphasis on rejection and rebelliousness is no doubt well-placed. An apostate does not merely challenge or critique their faith; they reject it. Apostasy is an act of disavowal. This, indeed, is its core definitional feature. But it is unduly narrow to stipulate that apostasy is *necessarily* a political act of rebellion, since this excludes the many personal and private apostasies which are not politically shaded.[42] Bromley prefers to categorize these apostasies as acts of 'leavetaking', but 'leavetaker' is vague and unhelpful. It is more useful and sensible to talk of public and private apostasies. A silent apostasy is no less an apostasy than a loud one—and is certainly no less interesting.

Nor is it quite right to suggest, as do Hadaway and Roof, that apostasy is necessarily synonymous with irreligion, since it is eminently possible to exchange one religious faith for another.[43] That a person has joined another religious group doesn't alter the fact that they have apostatized from their former group.[44]

For the purposes of definition, it makes better sense not to prejudge the issue of the apostate's motivations and destination. In deciding whether someone has apostatized, the essential question to ask is, 'Did they reject the faith into which they were born or converted so that they no longer subscribe to its core beliefs nor personally identify with it?' If yes, the person counts as an apostate.

Apostasy must be distinguished from conversion, although the two can be deeply entangled. As already suggested, one can exit a group to join (or rejoin)[45] another: in this case the act of joining (or rejoining) is simultaneously an act of apostatizing. That is: 'someone could be an apostate and a convert at much the same time, and the motives for leaving one group might largely overlap with those for joining another.'[46] But it is also possible to exit a group without joining another: one may leave and remain *un*affiliated or independent. For example, none of the ex-Muslims interviewed for this book converted to other groups; many, in fact, remained within—but at a vast emotional distance from—the Islamic fold as 'closeted' apostates. Indeed, and as will become apparent in later chapters, one of the greatest challenges non-religious ex-Muslims face is adapting to a life *apart*: not only from their former co-religionists, but also from non-Muslims who show little interest in, or understanding of, their situation. Scot McKnight and Hauna Ondrey are thus assuredly wrong: not all apostasies are, as they insist, conversions.[47]

Connectedly, apostasy is not defection: not necessarily. Defection refers to the act of exiting a group for another.[48] It implies a realignment of allegiance, a switching of sides in a competitive struggle. To defect is thus necessarily to apostatize, but, as we have just seen, to apostatize is not necessarily to defect (i.e. to transfer one's loyalties to another group). To put it more succinctly: all defections are apostasies, but not all apostasies are defections.

One must also sharply distinguish apostasy from heresy. The heretic does not renounce the group.[49] Quite the contrary: the heretic professes to embody its highest and truest ideals. As Coser puts it, 'Unlike the apostate, the heretic claims to uphold the group's values and interests, only proposing different means to this end or variant interpretations of the official creed'.[50] Or, to use Albert O. Hirschman's terminology, the heretic chooses *voice* over exit, fighting to change their organization from within.[51] Also unlike the apostate, the heretic continues to compete for the loyalty of existing group members.[52] This, Coser argues, makes him a more ambivalent figure than the apostate: 'in his conflict with the group he still maintains the group's basic values' and thus 'is apt to create more confusion in the group' than the person who outright rejects them.[53] Self-perception, in other words, is the crucial determinant: whereas the apostate ceases to view himself as a member of the group, the heretic grandiosely self-identifies as the group's true guardian of orthodoxy.[54] Indeed, the heretic, as G. K. Chesterton observed, furiously denies the charge of heresy, redirecting the self-same accusation against his condemners.[55]

The terms 'disengagement' and 'disaffiliation' frequently recur in the sociological literature on religious exiting. Whereas the former refers to minimal participation in the routinized activities of a religious group,[56] the latter refers to termination of organizational identification with a religious group.[57] Neither disengagement nor disaffiliation is proof-positive of apostasy. For example, there are Mormons who, despite becoming inactive in the life of the church, 'retain an organizational identification with Mormonism and would, if queried, define themselves as a member of that church'.[58] (Conversely, and as has been suggested already, active religious practice isn't necessarily an index of piety.) There are also ex-Mormons who terminated their organizational identification with the Mormon Church and yet continued to adhere to certain Mormon beliefs.[59]

Dimensions of Apostasy

Apostasy is a multifaceted social phenomenon and it is instructive to think of it in terms of the identity of the exited group; the group's reaction to the apostate's exit; how the exit occurs; the reasons for its occurrence; the profundity of the exit; and the moral shading of the exit from the perspective of the exiter and the exited.

As regards to the identity of the exited group, this can take either a religious or a secular form and thus one may speak of either religious or secular apostasies. Twentieth-century 'ex-communists',[60] for example, as much as ex-Catholics, can be classified as apostates. Hence apostasy is not an exclusively religious phenomenon.

The reaction of the exited group can be understood in terms of a continuum between acceptance and resistance. Two variables are crucial here: (1) the nature of the group; and (2) the status of the leaver. Invariably: pluralistic groups permit defections, whereas totalistic groups forbid them;[61] and the higher the leaver's status within the group, the less accepting group members will be.[62] Totalistic groups are especially hostile toward formerly high status ex-members, fearful that they may be used by their enemies as symbolic capital against them. In some cases, totalistic groups will grudgingly accept the ex-member's decision to leave, but only after a process of negotiation.[63] In other cases, group custodians will employ a variety of control measures to convince the ex-member to reconsider, ranging from emotional blackmail to the use or threat of physical violence.[64]

In respect to how the apostate carries out their exit, there are at least seven 'ideal-type' binary possibilities: (1) they may leave *voluntarily*, with full intent and awareness of what they are doing or they may leave *unwillingly*, having been coerced into disavowing their former group;[65] (2) they may leave *secretly* by concealing their exit[66] or they may leave *openly* by announcing it; (3) they may leave *suddenly* or they may leave *gradually*;[67] (4) they may leave *aggressively* by castigating their former group, fully intending to antagonize its members[68] or they may leave *pacifically* by expressing their disavowal in a more circumscribed way and with a desire to remain on good terms with former group members;[69] (5) they may leave *decisively*, certain and comprehensive in their disavowal, or they may leave *tentatively*, with self-doubt and mixed feelings toward their former group;[70] (6) they may leave *cleanly*, with minimal emotional fuss, or they may leave *messily*, in a vortex of turmoil and high drama; or (7) they may leave *jubilantly*, with feelings of relief and even euphoria, or they may leave *mournfully*, with a sense of pained regret that things didn't work out or won't ever be the same again.

The reasons for apostasy are clearly many and varied and can only be hinted at here.[71] One may apostatize from a group for principled reasons: that is, out of intellectual or moral opposition to its fundamental beliefs, values and practices.[72] Or one may apostatize from a group for pragmatic reasons: to 'save one's skin' or to further one's material interests in some way.[73] In his fascinating research on conversion and apostasy in the Late Ottoman Empire, Selim Deringil refers to many instances where Christians apostatized and became Muslims in order to advance in the social hierarchy.[74] Deringil also suggests that many apostasies occurred out of the subtle dynamics of indirect social pressure:

> There is also that grey area, the small insults of everyday life: being referred to as mürd rather than merhum when you die, not being allowed to wear

certain colours or clothes, not being allowed to ride certain animals. These little barbs, endured on a daily basis, must have been the basic reason for many a conversion to Islam.[75]

Another possibility is that one may apostatize from a group for existential reasons: because the group's values and worldview are profoundly at odds with one's fundamental sense of oneself and how one must live.

'The profundity of the exit' refers to the emotional and intellectual distance travelled from the point of departure to the point of exit. Fervent believers who become apostates travel far indeed,[76] whereas formerly moderate or nominal believers cover markedly less ground, their point of departure being closer to the point of exit.[77] It is likely that the process of exit for the latter is less protracted and tumultuous than it is for the former. As Toch tersely puts it, 'defection is an easy process only for members who have been lightly or tangentially committed'.[78]

In his research on interpersonal conflict Roy F. Baumeister argues that there is a vast discrepancy between victim and perpetrator accounts of wrongdoing.[79] Generally, those who commit wrongs construct them as 'meaningful and comprehensible', whereas those who are on the receiving end tend to depict them 'as arbitrary, gratuitous or incomprehensible'.[80] Specifically, in the case of perpetrators, wrongs are framed as accidental or beyond their control, justifiable or at least 'understandable' and relatively inconsequential. Victims, by contrast, are unequivocal on the matter of the essential wrongness of the perpetrator's behaviour, often viewing it as deliberately malicious or arbitrary and lastingly harmful. Baumeister comments that 'the victim stories generally reshuffled and twisted the facts to make the offence seem worse than it was, whereas the perpetrators reshuffled and twisted things to make it seem less bad'.[81] Another way of putting this is to say that perpetrators of wrongdoing tend to minimize the moral significance of their wrongdoing, whereas their victims tend to amplify it.

A similar discrepancy exists between how apostates account for their exit and how the departed group accounts for it. In apostate account-making, the exit is explained and justified: that is, it is morally shaded in a positive light. Indeed in some accounts the exit is presented as a triumph of human spirit over adversity, a story of courageous self-liberation from mental and physical enslavement.[82] In others, the narrative is more nuanced and ambivalent. But in virtually all apostate accounts there is a concern to insist that the exit was not a selfish or ill-considered act.[83]

The exited group almost always sees things differently: that is, negatively. From the group's vantage-point, the apostate's exit is a straightforward betrayal and the apostate's character and motives are vehemently condemned.[84] A persistent theme invoked by the custodians of the departed group is that the apostate, being essentially venal and weak of character, has been seduced by worldly concerns. Another theme strongly recurrent in the group's account-making is that the apostate is cognitively impaired or emotionally damaged in some way, since had they 'truly' understood and exposed themselves to the faith they would never have contemplated leaving it.

Apostasy as a Label

In *Outsiders*, a classic work in the sociology of crime and deviance, Howard S. Becker argues that deviance is 'created by society':

> Social groups create deviance by making the rules whose infraction constitutes deviance, and by applying those rules to particular people and labelling them as outsiders. From this point of view, deviance is *not* a quality of the act the person commits, but rather a consequence of the application by others of rules and sanctions to an 'offender'. The deviant is one to whom that label has successfully been applied; deviant behaviour is behaviour that people so label.[85]

Rule-breaking, says Becker, occurs all the time, but only some of it comes to be officially labelled as 'deviant'.[86] Whether or not the label is applied, Becker argues, will depend on how the act is interpreted by the audience. This in turn will depend on who commits the act and when and where it was committed. By way of example, Becker invokes the case of working-class juvenile delinquency and remarks that unlike the working-class juvenile offender, their middle-class counterpart is 'less likely, when picked up by the police, to be taken to the station; less likely when taken to the station to be booked; and it is extremely unlikely that he will be convicted and sentenced'.[87] Becker's fundamental point—and the central theme of *Outsiders*—is that the social audience plays a decisive role in deciding what is deviant and how deviant behaviour should be dealt with.[88] Drawing on his own empirical research on the use and social control of marijuana, Becker shows just how contingent and arbitrary this can be.[89]

Becker's insights into crime and deviance can be usefully applied to apostasy.[90] Just as deviance is 'behaviour that people so label', so, too, is apostasy: that is, social groups define the range of acts which can be included under the rubric 'apostasy'. In Islam, for example, it is commonly agreed that retraction of the two declarations of faith, or of one of them, counts as apostasy.[91] Indeed, denial of the *shahada* is the foremost indication of apostasy.[92] But it is not the only one. In his compendium of Hanbali jurisprudence, Ibn Qudāma provides a long list of transgressions which amount in his view to apostasy. To the retraction of the *shahada*, he adds:

> vilifying Allah the Exalted or His Prophet, falsely impugning the honour of the Prophet's mother, denying the Book of Allah or a part of it, (denying) one of His prophets or one of His books, rejecting a manifest and agreed upon commandment such as the five pillars (of Islam), or making licit a well known and agreed-upon prohibition, such as wine, pork, carrion, blood, illicit intercourse and the like. If these occurred because of the person's ignorance, his being a recent convert to Islam, or his awakening from insanity and the like— he does not become an unbeliever but is apprised of the law (concerning these matters) and of its proof. If he persists, he becomes an unbeliever, because the proofs of these manifest matters are evident in the Book of Allah and in the *sunna* of His Prophet. The denial (of these matters) does not come forth except from someone who gives the lie to the Book of God and to the *sunna* of His Prophet.[93]

Beyond this, there is a broad range of disagreement among Muslim jurists over what additionally is to be classified as apostasy.[94] It is a general rule of thumb that the more radical—or should that be reactionary?—the Muslim jurist the more extensive will be his list of apostasy-confirming acts. As Patrick Sookhdeo remarks, 'In recent decades, as Islamists have gained in strength, they have increasingly widened the definition of an apostate to include anyone who disagrees with what they consider to be orthodox Islam'.[95] Al Qaeda in Iraq has taken this even further: in their eyes, any Muslim in Iraq who isn't also an insurgent is effectively an apostate and is thus a legitimate target for slaughter.[96]

And just as prohibitions on unlawful behaviour are selectively enforced, so, too, are prohibitions against apostasy. The following two examples, also from Islam, illustrate the range of possibilities.[97] In May 1992, the late Egyptian academic Nasr Hamid Abu-Zayd, then working in the Department of Arabic Language and Literature at Cairo University, submitted an application for promotion to full professor. In considering his application, the tenure committee assessed his published work, including two books and eleven journal articles. The committee solicited the advice of three referees. Two recommended promotion. One did not: indeed this referee, Abdel Sabour Shahin, declared that Abu-Zayd's work was an affront to Islam no less.[98] Shahin's report proved decisive: the committee voted seven to six that Abu-Zayd should be denied promotion. The Council of Cairo University accepted this decision. Abu-Zayd appealed to the administrative court to overturn it but lost his appeal in 1993. This should have marked the end of the affair, but shortly afterwards a pro-Islamist newspaper, in a front-page article, accused Abu-Zayd of abandoning his faith. The heat was now on. At the end of 1993 a lawsuit was filed against him demanding the annulment of his marriage, since in Islamic law it is forbidden for a Muslim woman to marry a non-Muslim.[99] On 27 January 1994 the Giza Personal Status Court rejected the suit, but on 14 June the next year the Cairo Appeals Court overturned this decision, affirming that since Abu-Zayd was an apostate his marriage was therefore null and void. Six days later a group of Al-Azhar scholars lobbied the government to compel Abu-Zayd to repent by applying the legal punishment for apostasy. On 21 June 1995 Islamic Jihad declared that, under Islamic law, Abu-Zayd should be killed. In view of this, and other threats to his life, Abu-Zayd left for the Netherlands.

Two things stand out here. First, Abu-Zayd had not at any point renounced his belief in Islam; that is, he was not, by his own lights, an apostate. Second, the social classification of Abu-Zayd as an apostate and the demand that he should be punished accordingly was a direct consequence of the aggressive crusading activities of the Islamist establishment in Egypt. It had little if anything to do with Abu-Zayd's actual writings.

An altogether different case, discussed by Deringil in his research on the Late Ottoman Empire, concerns a man by the name of Damascinos, who, after apostatizing and becoming a monk on Mount Athos, was brought before the local *kadı* to repent:

> [The *kadı*] offered him coffee which he proceeded to throw into the official's face and started declaiming against Islam as a false religion. He seemed to want to attract the worst punishments the Turks could inflict upon him. But he was taken for a madman and simply given a severe beating. Yet he kept trying, and only after publicly insulting Islam three times in front of Turkish soldiers was he executed.[100]

What is striking here is that, despite the unequivocal classical Islamic ruling that unrepentant apostates are to be killed,[101] Damascinos's prosecutors initially went out of their way to *avoid* imposing that sanction, and were more than willing to honour the face-saving narrative that he was insane.[102] Abu-Zayd, despite his protestations that he was not an apostate, was granted no such leniency by his prosecutors.

In studying apostasy one must therefore be sensitive not only to the deliberate and self-conscious *performance* of apostasy on the part of individuals, but also to the collective *production* of apostasy on the part of social groups.[103]

Apostasy and Social Control

Beckford relays a 'curious fact' about the sociology of religion: namely, 'the relative lack of concern with the process of joining and leaving *conventional* religious groups'.[104] Rather, the dominant focus in sociological research on entry into and exit out of religion has been on 'marginal' or 'deviant' religious groups—commonly referred to among sociologists as NRMs.[105]

A strong theme in studies of exit from NRMs is what Bromley describes as the 'social construction' of 'subversive evil'.[106] NRMs, because they 'contest the established order and sacralize resistance' to it,[107] are subject to 'counter-subversion campaigns' on the part of that order: they are ritually denounced and demonized,[108] put under surveillance and railroaded in various ways. Apostates, Bromley argues, play a crucial role in legitimizing this, since as former members of the demonized group they possess a special moral and epistemic authority to comment on its essential 'evil'.[109]

This account draws strongly and self-consciously on Coser's work on social conflict, which itself finds inspiration from Max Scheler's classic work on ressentiment. The apostate, Coser argues, is not simply one who has experienced a dramatic change in conviction; rather, he is 'a man who, even in his new state of belief, is spiritually living not primarily in the content of that faith, in the pursuit of goals appropriate to it, but only in the struggle against the old faith and for the sake of its negation'.[110] The debt to Scheler is obvious:

> The true 'apostate' is not primarily committed to the positive contents of his new belief and to the realization of its aims. He is motivated by the struggle against the old belief and lives only for its negation. The apostate does not affirm his new convictions for their own sake; he is engaged in a continuous

chain of acts of revenge against his own spiritual past. In reality he remains a captive of this past, and the new faith is merely a handy frame of reference for negating and rejecting the old. As a religious type, the apostate is therefore at the opposite pole from the 'resurrected', whose life is transformed by a new faith which is full of intrinsic meaning and value.[111]

Bromley writes that although Coser and Scheler adopt a social psychological orientation that is a variance with his own 'structural perspective', 'their emphasis on the negation of former beliefs and commitments and the continuing implications of the past relationship for subsequent behavior goes to the heart of the matter'.[112]

Wright agrees. The apostate, he insists, is 'a defector' who 'capitalizes' on 'opportunities of status enhancement' provided by the 'countermovement coalition' and 'carves out a moral or professional career as an ex'.[113] Echoing Scheler, he asserts that 'the intensity and zeal in which the apostate embraces the new moral vision, seeks atonement through public confession and testimony, and makes salvific claims of redemption suggests that the ex-member's new affiliation may be analyzed as a type of quasi-religious conversion in its own right'.[114]

To summarize: the apostate is a prototypical 'true believer',[115] a person 'whose socialization has led them to develop a strong need for comprehensive absolutes, such that when their beliefs are brought into question, a complete new set must be immediately substituted'.[116] He is also a patsy, whose status as an ex-member and 'inside knowledge' is exploited by the enemies of his former group for the purposes of repressive social control.[117]

This is a one-sided account. It suggests that apostasy is not a willed and highly personal act of individual self-transformation, but is merely an epiphenomenon of hegemonic political organization. It suggests that the stories or 'tales' of apostates are not their own, but are 'constructions' of the organization to which they have been 'recruited'.[118] It suggests that the apostate is a dupe, without agency. But it goes even further than this. It suggests that the apostate is not only venal, avaricious and mentally unhinged, but also a liar and a loudmouth. Bromley and his colleagues do not use these morally charged words, preferring instead to euphemize and obscure their scepticism through the abstract, bloodless language of contemporary sociology.

Even if this account presents an accurate picture of apostasy from NRMs, it is wholly inapt as a description of apostasy from mainline religions, where apostates find themselves marginalized and silenced within conventional circles. It is decidedly not helpful for making sense of the exits detailed in this book, many of which were conducted alone and in silence and remain hidden.

Indeed, far from being a tool of social control, many apostates find themselves as its primary *target*: as objects of condemnation, even demonization and coercion.[119] They appear in degradation ceremonies[120] alright, not as hostile witnesses, but as stigmatized 'others', ritually vilified for their insubordination and 'treachery'.

In approaching apostasy, it is undoubtedly important to recognize the legitimatory role of activist apostates. But it is also essential to attend to the lived experiences of the ordinary men and women who apostatize independently and whose aim is not to take on, still less to 'take down', their former groups, but to live autonomously beyond them and on decent terms with their members, as far as this is possible.

Apostate Narratives and Anti-Apostate Narratives

A central question in the sociology of apostasy is how apostates retrospectively make sense of and account for their experiences as former group members. Typically, research on this area has focused on activist apostates and the 'social production' of their testimony against their former group. This takes the form of an 'atrocity narrative' and is worked up in close collaboration with a rival out-group.[121]

An atrocity narrative recounts and rhetorically enlarges, where it doesn't simply invent, abuses which the apostate personally suffered or witnessed during their time in the group. Its purpose or 'social use' is to: (1) justify the apostate's exit; (2) legitimize the use of repressive control against the former group; and (3) rationalize the apostate's former group membership.

Elaborating on this, atrocity narratives construct the apostate's exit as an essentially moral act and hence serve to protect the apostate from possible feelings of guilt at leaving their former co-religionists, from whose perspective the apostate's actions will be seen as treacherous and unconscionable. This is accomplished by amplifying the group's negative features or record: atrocity narratives consist of 'loosely connected accountings of one atrocity after another, containing a substantial amount of violence and sexual allusions'.[122] In the light of this, the apostate can establish not only that they had to leave, but that they left for fundamentally good reasons and that their leaving wasn't selfishly motivated or due to personal ill-feeling. What Wilson says of Pagan defectors in the ancient world undoubtedly applies to apostates from all groups and historical eras: 'It would not be unknown for them to attribute their defection to grand motives when the reality may have been more mundane'.[123]

Grand motives, expressed in the form of an atrocity account, also serve to legitimize social control efforts against the apostate's former group, either in the form of retributory punishment or preemptive coercive restraint. As Shupe states:

> While opponents may suspect the worst of a group, they can only relate what they at best know secondhand. Apostates, however, can claim to have seen firsthand and often personally participated in various horrors. Their testimony is that of the insider and as such provides an apparently irrefutable confirmation for the propaganda of a group's opponents.[124]

Atrocity narratives also serve to protect the apostate from confusion and self-doubt. One obvious counter-riposte to apostates is that if their former group *really* was as bad as they now maintain, why did they join it in the first place or, after having joined, remain for as long as they did? The atrocity narrative supplies the answer: they were coerced—'brainwashed', 'seduced', 'mislead'—into joining or remaining.[125] Had they been acting autonomously or objectively/rationally they would never have joined or stayed. In this way the group can be characterized as uniformly and irredeemably bad: there were never any good reasons for joining or remaining in it. Indeed, there were only ever bad reasons, owing to the apostate's former indolence, naivety, temporary mental retardation or cowardliness—deficiencies from which they have now triumphantly escaped. This narrative is clearly intended to reinforce the resolve and self-confidence of the apostate, as well as to condemn the group.

A no less central question in the sociology of apostasy is how group members make sense of and account for the apostasies of former group members. This, commonly, takes the form of an 'anti-apostate narrative', the main subject of which is the apostate's dubious moral character and, connectedly, their lowly motives.

Anti-apostate narratives construct the apostate's exit as an essentially immoral act and hence serve to protect the group from possible feelings of confusion or self-doubt in the wake of the apostate's departure. This is accomplished by amplifying the group's positive features or record and involves relaying triumphant stories testifying to the truth and ineffable beauty of the group's beliefs and values. Against this background, the group can establish that the apostate was driven, indeed could only have been driven, by fundamentally bad reasons. The following remarks, made in 1635 and in reference to Jewish apostates, are emblematic of the standard critique: 'Everyone knows that most apostates convert only so that their appetites may be satiated, to allow them to steal, to have illicit sexual relationships, and to eat forbidden foods in public...'.[126] From this, it is concluded that the apostate him or herself—in terms of their 'true' moral character—is selfish or debased. Thus defined, the apostate becomes a legitimate target for group hostility and punishment.

Anti-apostate narratives materialize a possible confusion or contradiction: if the group really is as luminously and unimpeachably wondrous as its custodians proclaim it to be, how could anyone possibly contrive to leave it or, after having left, not found their way back to it? The anti-apostate narrative furnishes the explanation: exiters are coerced—'brainwashed', 'seduced', 'mislead'—into leaving. Had they been acting autonomously or objectively/rationally they would never have left. In this way the group can be characterized as uniformly and irredeemably good: there can never be any good reasons for leaving it. Indeed, there can only ever be bad reasons, owing to the stupidity, venality or mental deficiency of the leaver—deficiencies to which they shamefully succumbed. As Susan Rothbaum summarizes it, 'from within the group, leaving is simply inconceivable unless one is either ensnared by delusion or wilfully doing wrong, capitulating to such unflattering motives as fear, greed, laziness, lust or hunger for power'.[127]

Thus the anti-apostate narrative is the mirror image of the apostate atrocity narrative and serves to: (1) condemn the apostate's exit; (2) legitimize coercive control against the apostate; and (3) rationalize the apostate's exit or defection to another group.

Anti-apostate narratives have thus far received little or no sustained attention in the sociology of apostasy. This may in part reflect a systematic religious bias in this sociological sub-specialism, in which all the critical hermeneutic energy is focused on demystifying the rhetoric of apostates and their sponsors. The counter-rhetoric of religious groups is alas neglected and marginalized to the periphery of scholarly concern. This gives the unfortunate impression that it is only apostates who are in the business of constructing 'narrative tales' for the purposes of condemnation and that it is only religious groups which are on the receiving end of moral crusades. But the reverse is also undoubtedly true, as Stephen A. Kent has convincingly argued. The sociological literature on NRMs, Kent says, 'has focused almost exclusively on the construction of 'atrocity tales' by members and organizations in the 'countercult' movement'.[128] Missing from this literature, however, is any systematic examination of the efforts of religious groups to 'portray their opponents as intolerable deviants'.[129] Kent's argument is that the condemnatory rhetoric of religious groups against their former members is as much a legitimate area of scholarly concern as the condemnatory rhetoric of apostates.

Bringing Reality Back In

Sociology once aspired to 'tell it like it is', but now the dominant trend in the discipline is to focus on 'narratives of experience', as if the raw experiences themselves are essentially unknowable or uninteresting. How people tell stories and for what purposes is clearly an important area of research.[130] But what they experience and the nature and consequences of these experiences are equally, if not more, pressing scholarly concerns. People tell stories. 'Man,' as Salman Rushdie observes, is indeed 'the storytelling animal.'[131] And the stories we tell often perform vital moral work, like justifying a course of action or, at the other extreme, condemning it and so can't be taken at face value.[132] But neither can stories be dismissed at face value as pure fiction. Stories, certainly, can mislead: man, as Rushdie would no doubt agree, is also the bullshitting animal. But stories can also enlighten and shed a profound insight into other people's lives and the texture of their subjective experiences. And stories are all we have, the only means by which we can understand one another, so we must attend to them with the greatest possible care.[133]

3

BECOMING AN APOSTATE

FROM ISLAM TO UNBELIEF

I think it was the most difficult decision I've ever had to make.

Tasnim

I always had doubts. In fact, that seems to be the one sort of constant in my life: doubts about myself, doubts about my religion, doubts about everything.

Masood

The How of Apostasy

If you want to know why, don't ask why. Ask how.[1] And let your interviewees speak. These are the two core methodological axioms on which this study is based. So not once in the course of my field-work did I ask why. I asked how. And I bit my tongue.[2]

To ask why is to invite self-justification:[3] ask an ex-Muslim why he or she left Islam and they will invariably respond by explaining why it was *right* that they left Islam. 'Islam is full of indefensible moral commands and judgments'; 'Islam makes large and empirically implausible claims about the world and human existence'; 'Islam is inherently undemocratic and illiberal.' And so on. One need not doubt the sincerity of ex-Muslims who echo these words. But it is a fatal error to assume that what they say in self-justification is necessarily illustrative of why they left Islam. 'Sometimes,' as Stephen Holmes sagely comments, 'people do what they do for the reasons they profess. But private motivations cannot always be inferred from public justifications.'[4]

The crucial question to ask, rather, is *how*. How did ex-Muslims come to reject Islam as a set of beliefs and mode of personal self-identification? What experiences, situations or discoveries led them to reflect on and to ultimately reject their Islamic faith and Muslim identity?

My aim in this chapter is to suggest that leaving Islam for disbelief is a cumulative process which occurs over a period of many months or even years and involves certain common biographical experiences. Pre-eminently, it is a situation of moral jeopardy, where the integrity of the self is put into question and the most fundamental questions to do with human existence are confronted and addressed: 'what do I believe in?', 'what is my purpose?', 'how should I live my life?', 'whom can I trust?', 'with what or whom should I identify?', 'what should I most value?', 'who am I?'

The process of becoming a nonreligious apostate consists of three main phases: the period leading up to the renunciation of Islam, which I shall call the 'pre-apostasy phase'; the 'apostasy phase', where the act of renunciation is mentally registered and ritualistically marked; and the period after the ritualized renunciation of Islam, where the meaning and implications of the apostate's mental metamorphosis are confronted and managed, namely the 'post-apostasy phase'. In this chapter, my concern is to describe the first two phases.

The Pre-Apostasy Phase

Doubt

This is how it begins: with the feeling that something 'isn't right', 'doesn't make sense' or 'doesn't add up'. All respondents felt it: the stab of doubt. And in many cases, they felt multiple stabs of doubt, not always at the same time nor with the same intensity, but in a cumulative sequence which varied from person to person.

Doubts typically centred on one or more of the following: (1) the truth-claims of Islam; (2) the morality of Islamic commands or prohibitions;[5] and (3) the utility of Islamic commands/prohibitions. I consider each of these below, classifying them, respectively, as epistemological, moral and instrumental doubt.

- Epistemological Doubt

Many respondents said their doubts centred on misgivings related to the intellectual architecture of Islam: that is, they suspected that Islam's cognitive claims about how the world is or came to be are not true. Among the various objects of epistemological doubt reported, the existence of God was predominant. This is how Omar, a man in his late thirties, expressed it:

> The problem I had was when I started doubting the existence of God. What if this is just bullshit, what if it's just nonsense? And when that thought occurred to me, I knew I was on a slippery slope. I never recovered from that thought. I never recovered.

For many respondents, it was obvious: there is just too much misery and arbitrary injustice in the world for there to be a divine creator. As Masood remarked, echoing a common theme in the interview testimony, 'If there was a God, why would he allow such an enormity of suffering in the world?' And why, moreover, would he be so human-like? Maryam put it this way: 'The Muslim God is a jealous, vain and insecure God, demanding worship all the time. Even at a very early age I just couldn't conceive of a being that wasn't human that would be like that.' Azhar similarly told me: 'My main doubt was basically the idea that if there is a God he would be far more wondrous and beautiful and amazing than the God of the Muslims and that's what it came down to for me'. 'I cannot with full faith,' Azhar added, 'believe in a God that creates a Hell.'[6]

Another variant of epistemological doubt centred on the divinity of the Quran. Amir, for example, couldn't help noticing this: 'that many of Prophet Muhammad's revelations were conveniently revealed when he wanted something'. 'Slowly', he said, 'I began to realize that Islam was man-made.' In Yasmin's case, it was her discovery of alternative religions which lead her to question the Quran's exclusive claim to epistemic authority: 'I remember some of the questions I had were just very basic, like how do we know we are right, that we have the right religion?'

A yet further variant of epistemological doubt concerned the Islamic creation story: they didn't buy it. All respondents said this. For many, this was a direct consequence of their exposure to evolutionary theory: if that was true, as they suspected, then the Islamic creation story couldn't be. Working this out was often a protracted process, as Luqman explains: 'I never rejected evolution. But I just knew that there was a conflict with

Islam. So I put it to the back of my mind. It's only later when I looked into it that it became a problem.'

● Moral Doubt

Nubia says that 'it was less the intellectual arguments and more the ethical issues that did it for me. At some point, it just felt wrong to believe in all of this.'

Respondents reported four kinds of moral doubt: four different ways in which 'it just felt wrong to believe in all of this'. For Farhad, it was the arbitrariness of the Quranic concept of predestination:

> The very first thing that got me thinking was, why do I get to go to heaven for simply being born a Muslim? Why does a mere accident of birth dictate one's destiny? Why do people not 'lucky' enough to have been born Muslim deserve to go to hell simply because they were not born Muslim? I always thought that was really unjust.

For Mustafa, it was the injustice and inhumanity of the Quranic punishment for unbelief:

> A god that provides no solid physical proof of his existence and then sends everybody to hell for eternity just for doubting him, and irrespective of whether they led a good life or were good people, is not, to me, a kind, benevolent or fair god.

And for Yasmin, as for all the female respondents, it was the unequal treatment of women in Islamic scripture and practices:

> These are some of the questions I was asking. Why do women have to cover up and not men? It's not fair. I also remember being very disturbed by the whole four wives thing. I wasn't necessarily disturbed that there was an allowance of four wives. I was disturbed that there was there no allowance for four husbands.

Other types of moral doubt centred on the elemental unfairness of specific Islamic commands, ranging from the injunction to punish apostasy to the prohibition against conducting a sexual relationship with a non-Muslim.

● Instrumental Doubt

A small number of respondents reported that they had experienced instrumental doubts: that is, reservations over the practical or rational utility of various Islamic commands. Wahid, for example, recalled his childhood obsession with artwork and how his mother would reprimand him for violating the prohibition on drawing eyes. This frustrated and perplexed him in equal measure: 'It made me give up drawing completely and then later I became angry that this silly rule had stopped me from doing something I loved and was really good at.'

Masood was similarly troubled when he came across a *hadith* prohibiting the game of chess: 'There's a *hadith* which says playing chess is the equivalent of dipping your hand in swine's blood. And it's apparently because it can distract you from being devout to God. But that's absurd. Chess actually builds up strategic thinking. Prohibiting it is just moronic.'

Often, respondents used the rhetoric of instrumental doubt to express and to amplify their moral doubts. Keisha, for example, remarked, in reference to the issue of predestination, that 'I couldn't understand how it could be that if you are a good person and you're not a Muslim you have no chance of going to heaven. It doesn't make any kind of logical sense.'

Pathways to Doubt

Most respondents were able to identify a trigger or cause of their doubts. Preeminent were the following: (1) significant personal experiences; (2) exposure to alternatives; (3) scriptural discoveries; (4) spiritual alienation; and (5) political events. One or a combination of the aforementioned sparked reflection on assumptions hitherto taken for granted and unexamined. And this brought to light reservations, uncertainties or ambivalences.

• Significant Personal Experiences

Certain events or situations occur in the course of life which prompt sustained personal reflection on fundamental existential questions. The death of a loved one; the souring or severing of a life-long friendship; the break-up of a marriage; the diagnosis of a terminal illness; the loss of a business or a home; the discovery of a sexual infidelity; the development of a new romantic attachment; the experience of terrible physical suffering or violent abuse; the cumulative build-up of familial obligations and pressures: all of these may provoke rumination on the meaning and point of life. And this may involve a re-examination of previously held assumptions or convictions.

For Tasnim, who I interviewed just a stone's throw away from the East London Mosque, the hinge-event was the death of a childhood friend who had been suffering from leukemia. She recalls how devastated and confused and angry this made her feel:

> He was just such a good person and he was so young, and I thought: how can God do this? I really wanted to believe in God. I really did. But then it was like, 'Fuck God, I can't be bothered. You can't exist, and even if you did, I don't want to believe in you.

For Alia, who is in her mid-twenties and from the north of England, it was Stephen: he was the ground-breaking event. She had met him at a music concert. They exchanged numbers and went out the following week. She liked him and stayed the night at his place. Alia knew this was wrong Islamically,[7] but:

> I kept thinking, well this is not actually penetration, therefore it's OK and that was my excuse for ages, but then we started getting a bit more sexual and eventually went all the way. And that's when the issue of Islam started coming up. I thought I can't be doing this. But the more I was with him the more I thought there's actually nothing wrong with what I'm doing. That's when the questions started coming. That's when I started questioning Islam and all those doubts I'd previously repressed came out into the open.

I shall return to Alia's story in the next chapter.

For Ahmed, a twenty-three-year-old political science student from Ontario, the decisive triggering event was his coming to consciousness of his gay identity. For a long time, he had denied it. Then he admitted it: that he was sexually attracted to men. And he wanted to explore that. But he knew that gay sexual relationships are off-limits in Islam:

> I was not doing anything wrong, so why should I be punished eternally for being myself? People were telling me to control it, saying that it's a test from God. That didn't make sense to me. Why should I be tested and not others? But sometimes I believed that and said to myself that being gay is wrong. For a time I convinced myself that I was not gay and started to be really anti-gay. Then it really hit me that that's just wrong and I can't be doing it. And then I realized that maybe I need to be questioning the bigger picture here—the whole religion and its fucked-up attitude to sexuality.

BECOMING AN APOSTATE

- Exposure to Alternatives

Islam for Abdullah was a central reference point. It defined what he did, how he saw the world and how he saw himself. He didn't question it. Then this happened:

> I got kicked out of school. And for about two years I basically spent the whole time in my room, surfing the internet. It became like an addiction. It's a very stimulating place and just having those comparisons raised a lot of questions. It expanded my world, my way of viewing things.

One incident in particular caused him to reconsider his own assumptions. He was in an internet chartroom, discussing the latest solecism of the former England soccer captain John Terry. Abdullah recalls:

> I'd read a story about John Terry having an affair. And I was speaking to someone online about that and they were saying how footballers are immoral and then it turned into a discussion about morality itself and I was saying, 'Of course you can't have morals without God,' and someone produced a quote from Einstein about morality. It said, 'morality is of the upmost importance—but for us, not for God'. And that was the first time in my life that caused me to give God a thought. I remember thinking, what is the point of doing good if there's no reward for it and abstaining from evil if there's no punishment? And then there was another Einstein quote about how he didn't believe in a personal God and that phrase was new to me. It had never occurred to me that God does not have to have a personality and it just became so obvious how human the Muslim God is and once I saw that there was just no going back.

Abdullah, who grew up in a strict Islamic household in Bradford—'I was basically spending six hours a day in the mosque'—says that before this incident he had 'never even come across an atheist before', much less questioned the existence of God. As he told me, he had grown up in an environment 'where there were a lot of nodding heads and where everyone just agrees that Islam is true and there's just no reason to question it'. 'Until I came into contact with differing beliefs,' Abdullah says, 'it just never occurred to me to analyse my own beliefs.'

Luqman, whose family is also strongly devout and whose father is an *imam* in the Midlands, traces the onset of doubt to a business dinner in Rome. He was with a small group of work colleagues. The topic of religion came up and the tone of the discussion was decidedly irreligious:

> That was the first time I actually had to defend Islam. It was strange, because we had never discussed religion at work before. We ended up talking about

evolution. I was arguing against it, but not doing a very good job. That triggered something for me, because when I returned from Rome I started going on Muslim websites. I wanted to find ammunition to argue against my atheist co-workers. But the more I looked at it the more it hit me that the Islamic arguments were not very strong.

For Nubia, who was born in Saudi Arabia and whose mother follows the strict Wahhabi version of Islam dominant there, the catalyst was moving to London to study. For the first time in her life she was forced to reexamine her religious beliefs and assumptions:

> Because most of the people I knew were non-Muslims. So they'd always ask me questions and I had no answer at the time or I'd make up something and then go home and check that it was right. I wanted to be ready when people asked me and to convince myself as well, because a lot of it didn't make sense to me.

But the more Nubia looked into Islam the more she began to doubt it. Living away from home undoubtedly facilitated this:

> I guess I always had doubts. But they really intensified when I moved on my own because I didn't have my mum to shout me down or laugh at my ideas. At home it was just, 'You're too young, you don't know what you're talking about'. Once I moved, I didn't have that. I didn't have anyone to belittle my ideas or belittle my thoughts.

- Scriptural Discoveries

For many respondents, Islam was a crucial part of their lives growing up. It shaped what they did and how they saw themselves. Moreover, it profoundly shaped how they felt about themselves. And how did they feel about themselves? They felt Muslim. Very deeply. This is who they were: they were Muslims. There was no denying that. In fact, a large number of respondents reported that not only did they feel Muslim; they had aspired to be *devoutly* Muslim. 'A good Muslim': this is the term they used and that was the ambition of their young lives. Not all of them had principled reasons for wanting to achieve this august status. Quite a few respondents told me that their reason for wanting to become a 'good Muslim' was to please their parents.[8] Motives aside, they had all struggled to become more devout. For some of the women I spoke with, it was at this point that they decided to wear the *hijab*. Not at the instigation of their parents,[9] but because they felt it was the right thing to do. It was also at this point that they embarked on a journey to better understand Islamic theology and history. As Wahid put it, 'I genuinely wanted to be a good Muslim, so I really looked into what would make me a good Muslim'. This journey of self-discovery had especial significance for South Asian respondents. As children, they had attended Quran lessons. They had learned to recite it. But they had not learned to understand it, since it was written in Arabic: a language they had not been taught and barely understood. In an effort to become better Muslims they took it on themselves to properly understand the meaning and history of Islam. And this is when they first ran into problems.

Yasmin's story is emblematic of many stories which have been relayed to me. Her family moved from Pakistan to Canada when she was twelve. By that point she had already learned to read the Quran in Arabic, although she 'had no idea what all of it meant'. Moving to a new country was 'hugely exciting' and truly 'eye-opening': 'It was a huge change. I'd never met somebody who wasn't a Muslim before I came to Canada.' And challenging, too: Yasmin's teenage years were unsettling. Her parents were having difficulties in their marriage. There was a lot of turmoil in the home and they were always moving from place to place. Her mother became increasingly religious and this was reflected in a new strictness toward the children. Make-up and short skirts were banned and there was now 'a lot more pressure on me to pray and to go to the mosque and get involved in various activities and help out and volunteer and for this and that'. Yasmin rebelled against this and by her mid-teens she had had sex, was smoking and drinking and had tried marijuana. But after her first year of university, 'where I felt freer than I have ever felt', it 'all kind of crashed and all of my guilt sort of caught up with me. I had lapsed just too much'.

In that first year of university she had been living in a dorm, but now she was back in the family home and for a two-year period she resolved to:

> really be everything that my mum would have wanted me to be. I stopped drinking, though I still smoked from time to time. I would pray regularly, fast. Before, if you'd asked me, I would have said, 'Yeah I'm Muslim, but I'm not living up to it'. Now I was trying to live up to it. I wanted to please my mum, I wanted to belong, I wanted to feel connected to my roots, I wanted to have a certain identity. And I really wanted to believe.

This involved revisiting the Quran, but this time in an English translation: 'so I could properly understand what I was supposed to believe in and say "this is why I believe, this is why it's true"'.

I remember looking up a few different translations. I read the verses that we were taught to memorize and to repeat by memory and I remember coming across a lot of crazy violent shit, like God peeling off your skin and putting it back on and peeling it off again. There was a lot of crazy stuff like that and I was like, this can't be right. I remember putting it down, because I didn't want to read it any more. I didn't want it to be what it was and I remember at the beginning stepping away from it, I didn't want to read it any more.

Reflecting on this experience, Yasmin says that 'the fastest way to turn a Muslim into an atheist is to have them actually read the Quran in a language they understand'.

Maryam relays a similar story. She recalls her mother buying her an English version of the Quran and a complete set of *hadiths*, also translated into English:

And ironically that's probably the worst thing she could have done because that's what set me on my apostasy...I remember one of the first issues I had was about the idea of the Abrahamic God throwing non-believers into hell. Why would you throw non-believers into hell, especially good ones? It didn't make sense to me...I didn't really want to believe what I was reading because it was going against what I thought I knew. And the more I read the Quran and the *hadiths* and into early Islamic history the less I believed it and gradually I just realized that I didn't believe in any of it.

Amir's story is also emblematic. His aspiration wasn't to discover Islam, but to defend it—against what he then saw as the basic misapprehensions of an Islamophobic western media. So he sought out the relevant classical scriptural sources:

Initially, my interest was in defence of Islam. I wanted to believe that Islam in reality was a peaceful religion and that those who said otherwise were simply misunderstood. But the more I looked into it the shadier it became. I was trying to reconcile Islam with my liberal views. However, after a while, it became clear to me that I could not.

Those who followed a similar trajectory were all too aware of the irony: that in trying to disabuse others of their misconceptions about Islam they had in fact disabused themselves of their own, as they had come to see them.

For some respondents, the first stab of doubt came after learning about various aspects of the Prophet's behaviour. Kareem, for example, says that he first started questioning Islam when he discovered the story of the slaughter of the Jewish Banu Qurayza tribe in seventh-century

Medina. As Kareem narrates the story, the Prophet Muhammad, having defeated the Meccans in the Battle of the Trench in 627, accused the Banu Qurayza of collusion with the Meccans and duly authorized the slaughter of all their male members, even though by that point they had surrendered. Kareem was troubled by this: he simply could not understand how someone as reputedly decent and moral as the Prophet Muhammad could countenance such an inhumane act. This prompted further reading and further questions arose from it.

- Spiritual Alienation

A small number of respondents reported that their doubts were sparked by feelings of spiritual alienation: they felt they had been abandoned by God and this made them question their faith. Aisha, for example, says: 'I think one of the reasons why my faith was weakening was because I didn't feel a direct connection with God. I really didn't. I just felt so empty when I prayed.'

Azhar speaks in similar terms about how his faith started to unravel: 'My faith just kind of went away. It flickered out. I just felt as if the presence that I felt in my teens wasn't there anymore. I stopped feeling the presence of God. And that's when I took seriously the possibility of Islam being wrong.'

For some respondents, feelings of spiritual emptiness only became salient after other doubts had emerged and gone unanswered. Kareem, for example, was for a long time tortured by the suspicion that God had deserted him and was utterly indifferent to his 'spiritual plight', as he called it: 'I just felt unanswered from God, and, yes, angry.' For Kareem, spiritual emptiness was a product, and not the cause, of first doubts, whereas for Aisha and Azhar, it was the other way around.

- Political Events

Mohsin, a formerly politically active ex-Muslim, doesn't know exactly when it ended, but he knows when it started: 11 September 2001. As Mohsin describes it, the catalyst for his doubts wasn't the 9/11 attack itself, but the reaction of certain Muslim friends and colleagues to it. They had been trying to defend what he took to be both morally indefensible and profoundly un-Islamic: the murder of innocents. What struck him in particular was the sheer force of their conviction. And this made him think about the foundations of his own worldview. Referring to a friend who had sought to argue that the Americans who had died that day could not be classified as innocent civilians, Mohsin remarks:

> I couldn't understand how such a devout and pious Muslim, who carried out every religious duty to a fault, could be so confident in beliefs that were so obviously immoral, so obviously wrong. This led me to an even more troubling thought: was I like him? Not in the sense of trying to justify killing innocent people—but what if I was also confident in beliefs that were wrong?...What if the Quran is not the word of God? What if Muhammad is not the Prophet of God? And what if Islam is not true?[10]

Mohsin, relating his own experiences with those of other ex-Muslims, says that 'something upset the natural order of our lives and forced us to reassess our worldview'. And for Mohsin that something, that fateful event, was 9/11.[11]

The Phenomenology of Doubt: Guilt, Fear and Loneliness

Karl Marx's famous injunction to 'doubt everything'[12]—*de omnibus disputandum*—is a salutary warning against epistemological arrogance and self-certitude, but it isn't an especially sound basis for living a serene and happy life.

Many ex-Muslims liken the onset of doubt to contracting a painful illness and describe the process as fundamentally unsettling. Omar, for example, recalls: 'The doubts just kept coming and I would say to myself, "stop that, I don't want those thoughts to come, that's the devil whispering in my ear".' For Farhad, harbouring doubts 'just felt wrong': 'Even from an early age I had doubts. I was always doubtful of Islam. But I would try to suppress them, because I knew they were wrong.'

Failure to bury or shake off doubts often results in guilt: 'good Muslims' do not doubt the word of God, still less deny his existence. Mohsin says that doubting Islam gave him a bad conscience: 'It made me feel like a traitor.' Wahid also feared this: 'I didn't want to feel like a sellout'. According to Kareem, 'I would feel arrogant and ashamed if I asked too many questions.'

Ex-Muslims do not believe in hell. But they *used* to believe in hell and thus a common source of anxiety in their doubting phase was fear of eternal damnation. For many respondents, paradise meant very little to them as believers. They couldn't readily imagine it. It seemed too abstract. But hell didn't: hell seemed all too real. Hell they *could* imagine. This, primarily, is because the Quran's rendering of hell is far more luminous and expansively detailed than its rendering of paradise. This is Salim:

> Hell was actually the main reason I was a Muslim in a way. As a kid I'd always been told about hell by my mum and dad. So every time I'd do something which I thought may be *haram*, I would think, oh no I'm going to hell now and that was a massive part of my upbringing. I remember one time I ate non-*halal* meat at McDonalds and thought, fuck, I'm going to hell now. But if as a kid you asked me about heaven I wouldn't have been able to tell you much. I mean, kids aren't really interested in going to a heaven which has rivers of wine and couches and so on. But hell terrified me.

Here is how the Quran evokes the fate of unbelievers:

> We shall send those who reject Our revelations to the Fire. When their skins have been burned away, We shall replace them with new ones so that they may continue to feel the pain: God is mighty and wise.[13]

Another verse describes how those 'deceived by the life of this world' and 'who take their religion for a mere game and distraction' will be 'damned' and 'have boiling water to drink'.[14] The following verse graphically enlarges on this:

> Garments of fire will be tailored for those who disbelieve; scalding water will be poured over their heads, melting their insides as well as their skins; there will be iron crooks to restrain them; whenever, in their anguish, they try to escape, they will be pushed back in and told, 'Taste the suffering of the Fire.'[15]

It is thus not surprising that for many respondents the process of doubting was deeply unnerving, raising fears of terrible suffering and torture in the hereafter. Nubia remembers that as a teenager she was beset with doubts, but would constantly fight them off: 'It was just out of fear I think. I didn't want to anger God.' One of Maryam's concerns growing up was that she had already aroused God's anger and that he was punishing her for her doubts in the here-and-now:

> I spent a lot of my teenage years unhappy because of the way things were at school. I didn't understand why I was being bullied. I hadn't done anything wrong. I wasn't a horrible person. And then I actually remember, I think I was about fourteen or fifteen, I got quite scared and thought that God was punishing me because I was questioning the religion.

An equally potent and no less common source of anxiety was fear of social ridicule and censure. This, says Omar, was at the forefront of his mind when he first began to experience doubts:

I was aware of another fellow, who was a few years older than me. He was having his own doubts. He actually became an atheist long before I became an atheist. And everybody would talk behind his back, 'Oh, he's completely gone off his rocker' and so on. That basically shut my questions up. I didn't want to seem like an idiot, so I just forgot about those questions and they didn't resurface until later.

Tasnim was similarly anxious about sharing her doubts:

Because I was scared that those doubts might be seen as negative and that they'd [her family] think I'm possessed. I remember my brother used to say that people who are possessed are put in a circle and beaten to get the ghost out of them. And I was scared of that and I was scared that they would think something has possessed me and that's why I'm having these doubts.

And so Tasnim kept her doubts a closely guarded secret.

Because many respondents felt that they could not openly share their doubts for fear of social ridicule and rebuke, the process of doubting was a punishingly lonely business. This is Tasnim again:

I was scared of questioning, because I was always taught, never question. But when I did and I had all these questions I knew that I couldn't talk to anyone. I couldn't ask my mum. I couldn't go to my Arabic teacher. I couldn't go to the mosque and ask somebody. I was scared of how they would react, so I just didn't really speak to anyone.

Returning to this theme in a second interview, Tasnim said:

You don't talk about atheism. You don't talk about not believing in God. For me, when you were confused you kept it to yourself. You didn't go and talk to people about it. Because they were going to set you alight—'she's a devil woman!'...My sisters obviously know about people who don't believe in God. But to have a sister who doesn't believe in God is unimaginable. Because even one of my closest friends, she was saying if her sister was to say she didn't believe in God, she'd beat the shit out of her. But I didn't confront her, saying, so you'd beat the shit out of me, then?

Farhad, who is in his mid-twenties and lives with his family in East London, also felt alone:

I kept it all in because there was no one I could talk to. I lived in a predominately Muslim area and everyone around me was Muslim. I didn't want it to get out that I was having doubts. So I just kept it to myself. Not having anyone to talk to was horrible.

For Hanif, too, doubting Islam was an exclusively solitary venture:

I don't think I actually confided in anyone about this. It was something that was entirely personal to me. I felt that if I said something I would get an overreaction or they'd get the wrong end of the stick or whatever so I couldn't really tell anyone.

Only one respondent—Samir—contradicted the above picture:

I can't remember anyone telling me not to ask questions or that something was true 'just because'. This includes my parents who were pretty openminded and discussed things with me in a mature way.

However, it is instructive to note that this respondent fiercely concealed his apostasy from his extended family and that when he announced it to his uncle, whom he esteemed for his 'liberal-mindedness', 'he was the one who took it the worst'.

Probing Doubts

All respondents probed their doubts. They wanted clarity and illumination. Above all, they wanted reassurance: they wanted their doubts to go away. They wanted the tranquility of secure belief. So they went in search of this.

For many respondents, this search began with the click of a mouse: they went online. For hours on end, they would trawl the internet for relevant material. The read, they watched and they listened.

In addition to this, they solicited the advice of others. They sought out confidants with whom to share their doubts: people they knew, trusted or respected for their knowledge and wisdom. This was challenging, because doubting in Islam is frowned on. They didn't want to raise suspicions about their commitment to the faith, still less incur condemnation. The challenge was to walk the tightrope between expressing a doubt and expressing disbelief. Respondents negotiated this task by querying: that is, they would voice their doubts indirectly in the form of a question and in a tone which indicated innocent naivety or pious concern. Nubia, for example, did it this way:

I wouldn't say, 'Why did God say that?' Because that is blasphemy. You can't question God. So instead, I'd say, 'What is the wisdom?' That's the way you're supposed to phrase it. 'What is the wisdom?' 'What's God's wisdom in doing this or that?' Like that. You have to pretend that you want to know what God meant by this, because God knows all.

Maryam, referring to her parents, similarly reported that 'I was always quite careful to not sound as if I was challenging them but just as if I was asking an innocent question'. Because of this Maryam 'was never able to speak freely with anyone about all the doubts and all the questions that [she] had'.

Some respondents said that they were so fearful of being outed as a 'bad Muslim'—or worse, as an atheist[16]—that they surreptitiously, if not altogether convincingly, expressed their own personal doubts through the voice of others, real or otherwise. This was Omar's strategy:

About my doubts. I will tell you how it worked. One of my uncles is an athe-ist. But he keeps it well-hidden. And so I'd use my uncle as a proxy to ask questions. I would put my words into his mouth and write to the scholars and say, 'I have this uncle, he is an atheist and he has these doubts and he is asking these questions'. But they were *my* questions. Because what I didn't want was for the scholar to pronounce apostasy on me because that's what they can do—to say, 'Right you are an apostate, you are going to have to remarry again' or, 'You are going to have to pronounce the *shahada* again'. I didn't want that. So I used to put my words into my uncle's mouth.

Yasmin's proxy wasn't a wayward uncle; it was her worried mother. About her doubts, Yasmin was cautioned to keep quiet:

My mum would say, 'Don't say things like that in public. I don't want to hear that again'. I was like, 'Can I ask that lady this question I have?' 'No, I'll ask her'. So she would word it in a better or more acceptable way. When I spoke with the *imams*, she would never let me ask the questions, because she was afraid of what I was going to say. She would always do it on my behalf.

For many others, the preferred proxy was a self-invented pseudonym, deployed in online discussion forums. Masood explained that the ano-nymity of a pseudonym gave him the courage to explicitly express his concerns to other Muslims. I asked him whether he had done that out-side of this 'virtual' context. His response: 'Only online. I never did that face-to-face. Because I was afraid of their reaction, you know, like the *imam* at the mosque and people who knew me back then.'

BECOMING AN APOSTATE

Dissatisfaction

All respondents probed their doubts. And all experienced dissatisfaction with the Islamic response to their doubts. Thus probing had the unintended consequence of intensifying, rather than clearing up, their original doubts.

A common experience was having doubts rebuffed. Masood, for example, had joined an Islamic website with the aim of discussing his doubts with Muslims equally or more knowledgeable about Islam than himself. He wrote a number of posts in which he expressed his key misgivings. The response, he said, was almost uniformly negative: 'pure derision.' He responded by writing more posts, expanding on his earlier misgivings and also adding some new ones. This attracted a different order of response: silence.

Hanif recalls writing an email to the Green Lane Mosque in Birmingham, hoping its luminaries would answer his doubts. But they didn't reply and he interpreted this as a snub.

Sometimes, doubting occasions not silence, but a plea for silence. Tasnim remembers that when she was a child she didn't understand why her uncle had three wives. She asked her mother about this. Her reply was that 'you don't ask questions like that'.

Yasmin relayed an almost identical story. She would talk to her mother about her doubts and every time the response was the same: '"You ask too many questions" or "don't ask questions!"'

Nabilah, too, was counselled to stop her questioning and to 'trust in Allah'. She would visit her local mosque and talk with the *imams* and *sheikhs* about her doubts: 'I remember one of them saying, "Oh, we just don't ask those questions, we're not capable of thinking that far, there are certain things we just leave to the will of Allah."' One memory is particularly vivid:

> So when I asked about the dinosaur the guy laughed at me. He goes, 'really?' 'Really?' I asked if there's anything about dinosaurs in Islam. He laughed at me. He said, 'Really, does it really matter?' Like, how silly is your question, does it really matter? Is it going to affect your faith whether it was mentioned or not? Is it going to make you a better Muslim if it was?'

Jaffar also refers to the derision he encountered in discussions about Islam with family and devout Muslims friends:

> I'd have these discussions and I'd have to be careful, because if you go too far then you start pissing people off and you get into blasphemy territory and that

was very frustrating for me. I had read all this stuff and yet I kind of felt like they were all treating me like a kid who doesn't know what he's talking about. They said, 'No, you have to go back, you have to study more'.

Despite repeated pleas to stop asking questions, Nabilah didn't stop: she carried on regardless. Indeed so naively dogged was she in her questioning that her mother began to worry about her. And then her mother began to worry about what others would think and how this might reflect badly on *her*:

> I guess I asked too many questions because then they [the authorities at the mosque] started getting upset with me. 'Why are doing this?' You see, my mum volunteers at the mosque every Friday and she does the dinners and she's really good friends with the *sheikhs* and she started getting embarrassed because I was asking so many questions. I was rocking the boat where I'm not supposed to.

Omar's questioning had so exasperated his friends that they implored him to stop.

> I would discuss my doubts with my friends and they are quite hardcore Muslims, these two friends of mine. And there came a point when they said, 'Omar, you know what, we can't do this, we've decided between us that we can't have these discussions with you anymore'. And at that point I just said, okay. I didn't discuss it any further with them.

Unlike Nabilah, Omar took the hint, but his doubts didn't go away; they just became larger, heavier, louder.

Even the closest and most trusted people can respond to doubts in the coldest and most dismissive way. When Omar first shared his doubts with his wife, she responded by saying, 'You'll get over it'. Omar's two closest friends, with whom he would raise his doubts, were similarly dismissive: 'I'd tell my friends that I had this discussion with my uncle last night and he said X, Y and Z. I'd say, "I think he's got a point" and they'd say, "Oh, tell him to fuck off. Why are you keeping his company? Your uncle is a *kāfir*."'

An even more common experience among respondents was dissatisfaction over answers they regarded as evasive, weak or even nonsensical. This is how Maryam describes the reaction to her doubts: 'They either danced around the question or just said "Allah knows best" or "God works in mysterious ways". These were the two responses I seemed to get.' As well as raising her doubts with both her parents and an *imam*, Maryam had also contacted a scholar via an Islamic website. Unlike Hanif, Maryam *did* receive an answer to her inquiries: but it didn't satisfy her. 'They would never give you a straight answer', she said in reference to this.

Nubia recollects asking her mother, 'If God is all knowledgeable then why doesn't he just send us to hell or to heaven right away?' In reply, 'she just basically said we're not supposed to question God. It's beyond our understanding. And she gave me this *hadith* where some person asked the Prophet something and the Prophet smiled and said, "some questions aren't to be answered."' Not satisfied with this:

> I ended up calling this Islamic TV channel, it's an Arabic one, Iqra TV. And I asked the scholar what I'd asked my mum, and he said, 'Well, God knows what you're going to do tomorrow but you don't know so you have to live through your life, blah, blah.' But that really didn't make sense because it didn't address my question.

Aisha was confused by 'the whole issue of destiny'—why would Allah intentionally lead some people astray and not others? So she consulted her *salafi* friends about it: 'But the only answers I was given were, "God knows best and don't think about this sort of thing, this is God's wisdom". I wasn't satisfied with those answers.'

Omar decided to consult the 'top guys, the real deal'. He corresponded with various eminent scholars. One in particular he visited and spoke to in person, this time fully opening up about his doubts:

> I told him that I was having doubts. I said, 'First of all, how do I know that God exists?' And building on from that, 'Even if he does exist, how can I know that Islam is true?' And he says, 'It's not about empirical proof, it's about a receptacle in the heart', okay? But that didn't answer my doubts. My doubts were intellectual doubts. I wanted an answer which would satisfy me epistemically, not emotionally. I didn't want emotional satisfaction. I wanted a reason to believe.

Manzoor's approach was more democratic. He made a short anonymous post on a popular Muslim website. In it, he posed a question that 'had been nagging me for a while': 'why do you believe?' The post provoked a number of different answers from Muslim believers, but 'none of them were any good'.

Reflecting on her life so far, Nubia says:

> When I started doubting it properly I never in a million years thought I was going to leave Islam. I thought I was going to have all my questions answered

and be proven wrong. Yes, I thought it was going to strengthen my faith actually, but it completely went the other way.

And one of the reasons it 'went the other way' is because Nubia didn't receive any satisfactory answers to her original doubts. At some point in the doubting process Nubia thought: well, then, maybe I was right all along; maybe my doubts do have some foundation.

Discord

As doubts intensify and amass, the mental strain of containing them becomes greater and creates the conditions for a crisis of the self.

- The Pains of Jihad

Jihad, as understood by many Muslims, is primarily a form of mental struggle against worldly desire and corruption. Ex-Muslims, more than anyone, know just how psychologically and emotionally demanding this struggle can be.

So what is like to be in the frontline of this most intimate of wars? This is from an email to a best friend:

> wa alaykum as salaam......remember when i said either i come back better or more astray...being here has had no effect on my heart i didn't even cry when i saw the ka'bah like most people do my Nafs has been attacking me soooo much since i got here and ive been having all kinds of thoughts about wearing abaya and stuff, taking photos, i don't know what i want anymore. one min i wannna do sin but i remember the hereafter only have 2 choices dnt think im strong enough as a person. im soo jealous of my stepmum she is always cryin!!!!!!!! 24/7 she has been taking advantage of this trip soo much she does have the upper hand of being a native arabic speaker tho ......dunno whats wrong with me i like dred the witr prayer because i know the imam is gonna cry and so is everyone else and im just left saying ameen thinkin....what the heck is he say-ing!! cant stop thinking, subhanAllah im my own worst enemy satan aint even here and im still evil, im literally counting the days till i get back which is sad and its very soon... now i feel like i wasted my time...this aint a proper letter im just writing my every thought right now its like 10 am and cant sleep not fasting today in jeddah gonna do shopping, staying with fam they have twins my age really cute and sweet lol....i really understand the concept of getting married for the sake of Allah......my iman needs it, wish i was married now!!!!! looool some nasty sudanese guy older than my dad wanted to marry me in medina ewwwwwwwwwwwww! i was wondering why he was giving me weird

looks, when am i gonna get a decent offer so i can turn him down and feel better about myself lol....hope i dont go astray, and if i do please dont abandon me, to be honest u guys give me *iman* lifters weekly and i need the reminders sooo much, right now i hate life, i really do its just not going well for me right now, im a characterless sad thing this isnt even a proper test and im already failing, although u didn't say much in the email u kinda reminded me of the hereafter and everything else, still look at those old txt reminders u sent... dunno how these last 2 weeks are gonna be but i regret not taking advantage, just remembered on my period gonna miss *taraweeh* when they do *surah yusuf*,...... also find out if its okay to read an english translation while praying it really helps...yeeah what else happened found out my dad is a *sufi*......EWWW, did my *umrah* 2 days ago *inshaAllah* gonna get my reward as *hajj* inshaAllah may Allah accept it *ameen*, yeah while in medina after *fajr* around 6.45 they opened the *rawda*....omg it was like a stampeeedd!!!! everyone was running like crazy. i feared for my life!!! in the midst of the crowds people were praying......they nearly got trampled over dunno what they were thinking never seen the worst of character in my life...but ppl in medina are much nicer than makkah.... makkah reminds me of new york nobody smiles, lol...internets crap and i cant sleep and im emotionally drained!!!!!!!!! better reply later with some wisdom or ELSE!!! think i have said enough for one day......got my life to sort out, i come back on the 4th and u better come over to my yard to visit me, may Allah keep you firm upon the religion and bless you and your family *ameen* xx

Aisha was eighteen when she wrote these words. 'I was just writing every thought that occurred in my head, like a stream of consciousness', she says, embarrassed now at the grammatical train-wreck of her writing. She had just performed one of the mandatory obligations of Islam: the *hajj*. Prior to this she had been experiencing serious doubts about Islam and her commitment was wavering. Her family had noticed this and were worried about her. Going on the *hajj* was suggested and she responded positively to the idea.

Muslims speak of the *hajj* in tones of reverence and it is supposed to be a profoundly moving experience. Aisha hoped it would reignite her faith. But it didn't: it weakened it even further. In the historic birthplace of Islam and amid florid displays of religious piety Aisha realized just how far she had drifted.

● The *Haram* and the *Halal* Voices

Aisha's case sharply illustrates just how fraught and tumultuous the doubting process can be. The overwhelming emotion is confusion. This is caused by the two warring voices inside the would-be-apostate's head: the *haram voice* and the *halal voice*. The *haram* voice is the voice of doubt, whereas the *halal* voice is the voice of Islamic rectitude.

In the initial stages of the doubting process, the *haram* voice resembles a kind of murmur: faint, but loud enough to merit examination. Later on, after probing exacerbates existing doubts or reveals new ones, the *haram* voice is emboldened and becomes more insistent and unruly: it is now radicalized. If the *haram* voice belongs to Satan, as many Muslims believe, then Satan evidently has Tourette's: with its register of blasphemous internal verbal tics, the *haram* voice randomly and uncontrollably prods, mocks and provokes. If the *haram* voice has a soundtrack, it is unquestionably punk: irreverent, profane and above all loud. At the same time, the *halal* voice fights back and competes for mental hegemony, remonstrating with the would-be-apostate to discount the *haram* voice and to return to the righteous path. The louder the *haram* voice, the more punitive and threatening the *halal* voice becomes, vigilantly warning against the shame and danger of disbelief. The confusion for the would-be-apostate lies in not knowing which voice to listen to and to credit.

Because of this fundamental uncertainty, the would-be-apostate goes schizoid: skeptic the one minute, believer the next. Thus begins a tortuous and self-perpetuating cycle of doubt and belief. Farhad describes this restless and anguished state as 'a sort of limbo'. Azhar captures it in these terms:

> There was a period where I thought to myself, 'Oh my God, I'm actually seriously considering the possibility of Islam not being true, what's wrong with me, do I really want to burn forever in hell?' But then you think, 'wait a second, I'm not exactly certain that there *is* a hell' and that level of certainty that I had has gone. And so you're kind of stuck between two doubts, not knowing whether to embrace the religion or just walk away from it.

For Azhar, there was no escape from doubt: doubt over Islam and doubt over disbelief. He wasn't certain that Islam was true. But, equally, he wasn't certain that it *wasn't* true.

Salim summarizes the feeling like this: 'One time I'm saying I was firmly a Muslim and one time I'm not, it was a very, very confusing time for me, you know, I wasn't sure what I was anymore.'

- Self-Denunciation

If, as many respondents testified, the spectre of doubt was a constant presence in their lives, so too was the sting of self-rebuke. For Omar, no sooner would he entertain a doubt than scold himself for having done so. This made him feel wretched and inadequate: 'I thought there's something wrong with me. That's what I thought. I was all the time having doubts, but I wanted to believe that God existed. I thought it was my fault, that there is something lacking in me.' Laxity in behaviour was also a powerful source of shame for Omar:

> It was starting to get sloppy towards the end of my twenties. Because the doubts were becoming more intense and I wasn't getting any answers...I stopped getting up for the morning prayers. I'd sleep through and make up for it later in the day. I was doing the bare minimum, but I wasn't doing the *sunnas*, the non-obligatory stuff. So I wasn't going to the *taraweeh* prayers during Ramadan. I wasn't integrating with my friends during *iftar*. I was becoming careless. Even washing for the prayer was becoming quite a chore. The devotion wasn't there. When I was praying I was thinking about, have I paid such and such a bill yet, that type of thing. I wasn't reading as much Quran as I should and it was all just going downhill.

Reading this, it is as though Omar's body, propelled by his subconscious, was telling his conscious mind what it didn't want to hear: that his faith was in serious crisis and on the verge of collapse. But his conscious mind wasn't yet prepared for that and would respond by castigating itself for its failure to discipline the body.

Aisha was entrapped in a similar cycle of belief and doubt. And this, too, left her feeling low in self-esteem, as though something was 'wrong' with her. This feeling would be especially heavy whenever she thought of the fierce piety of her *salafi* friends, whom she aspired to be like. But by comparison with them, she 'never felt good enough', despite all her efforts. And the more she tried the clearer that became:

> I was thinking compared to them I'm nothing and I'm clearly not doing enough. That would bother me, so if I'd commit one sin I'd feel really, really horrible about it and I'd feel like, okay, there's no point in you trying to create this façade that you're religious when you're clearly not and so maybe you should just give up the whole religious fiasco and just abandon it because you're clearly not good enough.

Aisha's story, like so many reported to me, is poignantly tragic: she so desperately wanted to be a good Muslim, but felt that it just wasn't in her and this made her deeply unhappy. Many other respondents confided the same: that they had a heartfelt desire to be a good Muslim, but their intellect or core self or whatever it was inside refused to go along with this, sabotaging their efforts to become their idealized Muslim self. And they hated themselves for this. 'Even when I became an atheist', Wahid said, 'I still wanted to be a good Muslim.'

The intensity and duration of the discord phase varied among respondents. It was especially tumultuous and prolonged for those who had previously been devout in belief and practice, whereas for those who had previously been moderate, it was appreciably less so, since their psychological investment in Islam was smaller. It was also intensely tumultuous for those from devout families, where the weight of expectations related to religious affairs was very heavy indeed.

For some, the discord phase was so tumultuous that it left them feeling mentally drained. Ahmed recalls that at one point his doubts became so insistent and obsessive that he couldn't think of anything else. The issue of God in particular troubled him: 'I remember it being in my head all the time, just nagging me and nagging me...always preoccupying me and I just had to get it out of my head and I swear I was going into depression for a while.'

Kareem was similarly bedevilled by doubts, so much so that at one point he thought he was going insane. A friend had died in a car accident and he was desperate to make sense of it. It was the fate of this friend in the hereafter: this is what he couldn't stop thinking about. Would he find salvation in heaven or would he forever burn in hell? This in turn questions about his own fate: how would God judge *him* in the end? He looked to Islam for answers. He also sought the advice of his parents and scholars, but was always left feeling 'perplexed' by the responses he received. He implored God to guide him, but guidance there came none. His doubts intensified ('does God exist or not?') and became 'suffocating'. He was 'confused, angry and so *tired*'. There was 'an ongoing war in my head' and he was desperate for it to end.

Deliberation

The point at which the discord phase ends and deliberation begins is the point at which the would-be-apostate comes to realize the untenability of their situation and resolves to make a firm decision on the core issue of belief (what is true?) and identity (who am I?). Amina puts it like this:

'I was tired of being stuck in between and not sure. I wanted to make a decision: be religious and believe or don't.' This initiates a new and even more intense phase in the probing process, where doubts are now faced frontally and in a spirit of open critical inquiry.

The deliberation phase is itself divided into two distinct, but closely connected, phases, each involving a question related to the 'truth' of Islam. In the first, the would-be-apostate addresses the following question: 'Is Islam true to the world?' This requires a mode of reflection which is outward-looking, engaging with empirical and moral propositions about how the world is and how it ought to be. I call this *macro deliberation*. In the second phase, the would-be-apostate asks: 'Is Islam true to me?' This requires a style of reflection which is inward-looking and retrospective, focusing on feelings relating to how the core private self is and how it ought to be. I call this *micro deliberation*.

• Focusing Events for Deliberation

What makes someone like Amina resolve to make a final decision about Islam and their fidelity to it as a form of belief and identification? Usually, it is an event or situation which vividly brings into focus the magnitude of the would-be-apostate's doubts—and the futility of indefinitely trying to contain them.

For Aisha, it was the trip Mecca which focused her mind and forced a reckoning. Before going, her purpose was clear: to reinvigorate her faith; to fully become the good Muslim woman her family and close friends could properly esteem, that *she* could properly esteem.

> My dad was like, 'Do you want to go to Mecca?' and I said, 'Sure'. But I remember asking my friends what they thought and they were all like, 'Why don't you go? This is a golden opportunity and most people don't even get it in their lifetime'. Dad gave me the chance to go to the holiest place on earth. I thought perhaps if I go it might restore my faith and I'd come back a completely different girl.

Aisha stayed in Saudi Arabia for a month. But it wasn't what she thought it'd be:

> I had this image of what would happen in my head. It was going to be magical. Everyone who goes there is like, 'Yeah, as soon as I saw it, I was crying my eyes out'. And so I'm walking towards the *ka'bah* and I'm feeling quite faint

because I'm really nervous and then I see it and I'm like, well, this is not the emotional experience I'd assumed. I didn't feel anything. My stepmum was right next to me crying and my dad's in deep thought and prayer and I'm just, like, okay, I guess I should say something or make a prayer and my prayer was God please keep me on the straight path. I was really surprised at myself that I didn't cry. And I felt really bad, like, how come I'm not crying? Why aren't you feeling any emotion?

And the longer Aisha stayed, the more her faith weakened: 'It got to a point where I didn't want to pray. I'd have to *drag* myself to pray.' Her thoughts would also frequently deviate:

It was quite weird. I was getting these thoughts about removing my *abaya* and *hijab*, dating, many things that I found extremely sinful. I don't know whether it was the environment of Saudi or what, but I was thinking of people that had their freedom and fun in their youth and I'd always have these ongoing debates in my head like I would before about taking my *abaya* off, but it got much more serious now. I just felt so complacent towards it.

Once back in London, Aisha felt immense relief. She also now felt ready to confront her doubts: 'I was spending a lot of time on the internet and I kept stumbling across atheist videos. There was no going back after that.'

About her trip to Mecca, Aisha reflects this it was a defining moment in her life: 'I think going there was the pushing force, like it pushed me off the edge. So if I didn't go there then it [her apostasy] would have never happened.'

For Luqman, the catalyst for deliberation was the prospect of an arranged marriage with a woman from a 'very religious family'. He says he was 'pushed into it a little bit', although he doesn't blame his parents for this, since 'I didn't make it clear to them that I didn't want it'. There was an engagement. And that proved to be the decisive moment:

Before the engagement, I was starting to think, okay, I have all these doubts, but, oh well, never mind, I'll just ignore them and get married and have a family. But after getting engaged, I couldn't shake off all these doubts.

Entering into a marriage with this woman, Luqman feared, would forever entrap him in a life-world from which he was becoming increasingly estranged:

I had this big dilemma. Either get married and carry on and remain a Muslim. Or break the engagement, leave Islam—or leave Islam and break the engagement, same thing. I knew that if I married and then left Islam I would basically have to live as a closet atheist for the rest of my life pretty much. And that would be crazy, having to support a religion whose values I don't support, believe in something I don't believe and raise kids to follow all that.

Hence: 'I knew then that I had to decide once and for all. I had to decide whether to get married to a Muslim and stay a Muslim or to reject Islam.'

Amina reports an analogous experience, but it wasn't an impending marriage which focused her deliberative energies: it was the possibility of an illicit relationship with a non-Muslim. She liked him and he liked her. But she knew that if she began a relationship with him she'd be crossing the line Islamically:

> There was this guy on my course who I liked and that made me think I have to make a decision. I can't just be in between. I knew he liked me and I sort of liked him but I was thinking I can't be half a Muslim and take anything forward. I had to make a decision, whether to believe or not to believe.

Manzoor said he'd *already* entered into an illicit relationship by the time he came to face his doubts. He had met and fallen in love with a non-Muslim British woman, who was also an atheist. They were planning to marry and he announced this to his parents, who responded by insisting that his wife-to-be convert to Islam. Manzoor's now wife refused and he supported her decision. But this changed something for him, because it compelled him to think in a sustained way about Islam and his own uneasy and fragile relationship with it. As he describes it: 'I was in love with someone who obviously didn't believe and who was quite happy not believing and I wasn't very far off myself, to be honest, so it made me think, oh, okay, why am I hanging on to this partly?'

• Macro Deliberation: The Moratorium on Islam

This phase is a fateful period in the apostasy process, because, prior to this, Islam had been probed with respectful restraint and from the perspective of exclusively pro-Islamic sources. But in this phase, Islam, for the first time, is subject to critical scrutiny and the would-be-apostates deliberately expose themselves to sources which previously they would have avoided or dismissed as Islamically unsound. As Hanif puts it, 'I reached a point where I started to read the Quran more critically rather than just accepting it as the truth'.

As Luqman characterizes it, macro deliberation is a carefully structured and rigorous process, whereby both sides of the argument are considered and critically interrogated. It is also an activity embarked on in a spirit of utmost seriousness. No one I spoke to took it lightly. They knew what was at stake. Leaving Islam would have a profound impact on their lives. Of this they were certain. Luqman says that for a long time he tried to repress his doubts, because 'I partly knew that if I did confront my doubts and conclude that it was all bullshit it would wreck my life.' And if that was to be the final outcome, he wanted to be positively certain that he had given Islam a proper hearing before renouncing it.

'I didn't want to be wrong. I was questioning myself, what if I was wrong? I wanted to be sure about these things.' This is Farhad. God and heaven and hell just seemed 'so unbelievable' to him. But he wasn't certain and he needed to be. And so it was with most respondents: they didn't want to be wrong. They wanted to be *sure* in their doubt.

Luqman explains that 'it was really about whether Islam is true or not. That is really what it's all about'. His conclusion in the end was that it wasn't true: that Islam, epistemologically, was false. But before he arrived at this position, he 'did a lot of research'. This was done mostly online. He read extensively and watched many videos, both for and against Islam: 'I was trying to decide for myself, looking at both arguments, which is true?' And what he found was that 'the scientific and philosophical arguments supporting Islam were very weak'. A video recording of a Ken Miller lecture on the fallacies of creationism was especially impactful on his thinking and persuaded him that evolution was true. And from this, he drew the conclusion that Islam must be false.

Amina recounts a similar deliberative experience. For a long time, she was in a state of 'constant uncertainty' about Islam. She didn't know what to believe and that frustrated her: 'So I did the research.' This involved assessing the claims of both Islam and its detractors, because 'I couldn't really defend either side'. Amina also researched Christianity, but could neither fully understand nor accept the concept of the Holy Trinity. Nearly all of this probing was done online over a period of two months. By the end of it, Amina 'was convinced that all religion, not just Islam, is manmade'.

In exposing themselves to critiques of Islam respondents were able to revisit classical Islamic sources with a new attitude of hermeneutic scepticism. For Nabilah, it was reading Hirsi Ali's writings which provoked her to think more critically about Islam, returning to the classical texts with her 'eyes wide open', as she phrased it:

> How blind was I? Seriously, how blind was I? Let me see this for what it really is. Open it and just read it. And so I read the Quran again, in a way like, okay, come on, what do you understand from this? Each *sura*, what did I understand? What did it really say? Don't try to make it pink and fluffy, just read it and what does it say? And that was another moment. Read it and what does it say? What do you think about Aisha's marriage? Not what the *sheikh* told you, not what you're supposed to say or think, but, really, what do *you* think?

Mustafa similarly revisited the Quran, but now with an open mind, having been shaken by his exposure to various atheist writings online:

> I took everything in the Quran for granted and believed in everything. Because when you read the Quran as a Muslim even if something doesn't make sense to you, you'll just say, you know, I'm not knowledgeable enough or I haven't studied theology in enough depth to understand what this is but I'm sure God has a plan and, you know, God works in mysterious ways. But when I read the Quran from a non-Muslim, atheist perspective nothing made sense to me.

For some, adopting this newly critical interpretive approach helped them to finally see the futility of their prior efforts to reconcile the Quran with their own innate liberalism. For Samir, the *hadiths* were the first to go: 'I realized that some *hadiths* were just morally abhorrent, no matter how you interpret them (like the ones mandating the killing of Jews just because they're Jews).' Samir could justify this because 'unlike the Quran, the *hadiths* may be fabricated'; they were not composed by God, but by his fallible subjects. This left the Quran: which, after fully probing it, he was compelled to conclude that, it, too, contained many passages in direct and unmistakable conflict with his own deeply felt liberal values.

Similarly, Aisha had tried to 'interpret the Quran freely according to how I view the world', but the closer she scrutinized it, the more she realized how futile an exercise it was: 'Because you just can't ignore verses that are blatantly violent and misogynistic, so what am I supposed to do about that? And I really acknowledged my true place in Islam as a woman. It's like I didn't see it all along.' And now, viewing the Quran through different eyes, she could.

In all of the above cases, and in fact in much of the testimony reported to me, the decisive moment in the deliberation phase came with the discovery of anti-theist source-material. Many respondents specifically cited the works of Richard Dawkins and the late Christopher Hitchens and indicated that these two writers had a momentous impact on their thinking. In them, and in the work of other atheist writers, they discovered a voice with which they could readily identify. Azhar, for example, says that reading the work of Schopenhauer and Nietzsche[17] enabled him to think about Islam and religion with 'a greater clarity and sophistication' and out of his engagement with their work he came to realize what he had suspected for a long time but up to that point was unable to fully articulate and develop: that 'there really isn't a defense for any of it.'

For Omar, the 'turning-point', as he refers to it, came when he walked past the display window of a book store. The book which caught his eye was Dawkins's *The God Delusion*:

> I was looking at it, it was in hardback. I walked past and then I walked back and I looked at it again and it just disturbed me. Just the title of the book, I found it disturbing and then when I got in the car I switched on the Radio and Richard Dawkins was on. I didn't catch the beginning, it was towards the end, and then I thought, do you know what, I've got to nail this down...So all those things I'd avoided reading before I started to read. The first thing I read was a book called *Atheist Universe* by David Mills. I was reading that and in the bibliography section at the end I came across a list of websites. One of them was called Secular Web and I went on there and I was just bombarded with all these articles. I was overwhelmed by it. I just thought, you know what, I'm already thinking this stuff.

Omar's reading continued and he voraciously absorbed the writings of Dawkins, Hitchens, Daniel Dennett and Sam Harris, among others. And what all this reading did was to 'confirm what was already in my mind'. Omar was now ready to acknowledge what he had long been denying: that, as he finally told his wife, 'I don't believe in God anymore, I've just been chasing a mirage, I've lost the jihad, and I can't do this anymore'.

Mustafa also felt it: the spark of connection, the thrill of vindication. He came across videos of Dawkins and Hitchens on YouTube and he was mesmerized, hooked, and for nearly a month, 'that's all I did. I just watched these videos':

> And I completely understood what they were talking about. I've always questioned the omnipotence of God, this doesn't make any sense: if he's omnipotent why is there famine in Africa and why are there wars and why are there natural disasters and why are there children born with horrible congenital

defects? Why, if there is an omnipotent God, would he allow these children to be born this way? So I had always questioned that from the time I was sixteen/ seventeen but I couldn't actually put my thoughts into words or organize them in a clear way. I didn't have any arguments. If I was going to argue with some-one at sixteen I would lose that argument because I hadn't given it enough thought, but when I started watching these videos it kind of all made sense.

After consulting more atheist source-material (including one of Dawkins's books), Mustafa reached a point where he 'stopped believing in God'. And if God wasn't true, he reasoned, neither was Islam.

Reading the work of atheists and agnostics was thus a fundamentally validating experience for respondents. Their own intuitions were correct. They were sound. Their doubts had substance: the *haram* voice was right all along. And this recognition empowered them to move forward and to finally renounce Islam. It gave them the self-confidence to disavow: because it legitimized their doubts. And with that legitimation and newly found self-confidence, their sense of guilt and anxiety began to fade. They were surely right in doubting Islam, so there was no reason to feel guilty or anxious anymore: this is what they thought, although their feel-ings were not always in tune with this.

In a few cases, the crucial moment in the deliberation phase came with the discovery of ex-Muslim anti-theist source-material. Khadija, for example, credits Ali Sina[18] as playing an important role in helping her to clarify her thoughts. Wanting to learn more about the history of Islam, she remembers typing into Google, 'The truth about the Quran'. And there, in the extensive list of first results, was a link to Sina's FFI (Faith Freedom International) website. She followed it and this is what happened:

> I spent about three solid days reading, going from FFI to my Quran and *hadith* books and checking if what he was saying was really there and it really was. I was so stunned. I didn't know that the Prophet Muhammad let his men rape women. I didn't know that they sold them as sex slaves. I thought that Islam came to free slaves, not that it made more slaves. I didn't know all of that. I had actually been quite ignorant up until that point and I think I made one post on FFI saying, 'You're all lying, this can't be right, this isn't true'. Although you had a lot of haters, there were a lot of nice people there, too—in the forum, I mean—and they spoke to me and the very next day I woke up and I was like, 'I'm not a Muslim anymore. I'm not, I don't believe in it anymore'.

FFI, says Khadija, back when she joined it, was for the most part 'a nice place to be' and from its forum members she received warm support and encouragement. And this, she adds, was 'all really helpful in my apostasy journey'.

Salim, who is in his mid-twenties and lives in the south-east of England, also singles out Ali Sina as a seminal influence on his thinking. He recalls coming across him at FFI. When he first visited the site, his reaction was one of vigorous disagreement: he thought Ali Sina was wrong about Islam. He even wrote an impassioned riposte to Sina's criticisms, pointing out that they were reductive and misleading. This he posted on the site. And then he read a debate, published in the form of an eBook, between Sina and two Pakistani scholars, and that's when he changed his mind: Ali Sina was not wrong about Islam. Ali Sina was right about Islam. As Salim says, by the time he finished the book he was convinced, in 'a kind of light bulb moment', that the Quran 'can't be true and that I've been lied to'. He then immersed himself in other critical material, all archived at FFI. And when he revisited the Quran, it was like reading a different book from the one he had grown up with and his reaction was, 'this doesn't make any bloody sense'. Sina, he reflects, 'opened a door for me'.

- Micro Deliberation: The Moratorium on the True Self

Islam of course is not only an epistemological and moral account of the world—that is, a theory of how the world is and how it ought to be—it is also a way of life: a set of ritual practices and commands which comprehensively and intimately govern how its followers live. And so this, too, was a key subject for deliberation.

For many respondents, Islam had become alien to them. They couldn't identify with it anymore. It wasn't who they 'really' were. Indeed some respondents said that they had *always* felt ill at ease with it. But it wasn't until they properly deliberated on it that this became clear to them: that Islam wasn't true to their core sense of self. It wasn't an authentic reflection of how they now saw themselves and how they wanted to live their lives.

For Keisha, there was a dawning awareness that Islam, as she had experienced it, didn't fit in with her own personal moral ethos: it was 'just too rigid' and 'too dogmatic'. She felt 'confined' by it and did not want to restrict herself to 'any one box'.

Nubia similarly experienced Islam as confining. Although she had vigorously defended the *hijab* in her early teens, when it came to actually wearing it, she found herself stifled by it: 'I just felt completely awful having to do it. It just wasn't me.' Nor was 'having to treat your atheist or Christian or Jewish friends differently from how you treat your Muslim friends. That didn't sit well with me at all.'

Wahid recalls feeling profoundly uneasy about the mechanics of the Islamic prayer: to him, it all felt spectacularly demeaning, like he was 'a slave bowing to a master'. And his conscience couldn't bear that. This is not how he wanted to live his life: in a constant state of submission. So this is what he decided: that he alone was, or would be, the master of his life. If this made him arrogant then so be it, he thought. Leaving Islam, as Wahid describes it, was a necessary step in being 'true' to himself and his conception of how he should live his life—as a fully autonomous person. And this recognition was at the forefront of his mind in the period just prior to making his resolution to leave: 'As I grew out of my teens, I actively decided that I couldn't be part of something that I felt was not me.'

Azhar similarly concluded that his greatest ambition was to live fully, richly and, above all, autonomously. Reflecting on the ultimate values and ends in life, it occurred to him that what he most prized was 'the idea of grasping hold of your own life by yourself and doing what you will with it'. Islam, he thought, was radically incompatible with this, since 'as a Muslim you're basically just a cog in a machine, a servant of God all your life'.

Aisha also came to feel very strongly that Islam was alien to her fundamental approach to life and how she wanted hers to be:

> I was just thinking that Islam prevents me from doing all the things that I love and want to do—going to a Shisha café, feeling the wind in my hair, being able to say whatever I want, being able to think whatever I want, being able to choose what career I want, being able to think for myself.

In the same way that the writings of anti-theists gave respondents the self-confidence to trust in their doubts, so, too, did the kind of self-knowledge displayed here. Intellectually, they had decided that they couldn't go along with Islam. But they had also decided emotionally, at the level of the core self, that Islam didn't speak for them or reflect how they truly felt about themselves and how they wanted to live.

• Lonely Deliberation: The Silent Moratorium

For most respondents, the deliberation process was a largely solitary affair: it was done alone and in secret. Farhad said that just prior to leaving Islam he 'became more withdrawn than usual' and this was common among many respondents. They retreated into themselves. Seldom did they allow others into their inner world. Before, in the first phase of probing, they had sought Muslim confidants, where possible. But not now: indeed they had pointedly decided that there was to be no confiding in Muslims and no engagement with them on religious issues. This in part was because they didn't want to raise further suspicions about their commitment to the faith. But it was also because of their disillusionment with the standard Muslim apologetics: they had received little illumination before, so why should things be any different this time? As Aisha remarked, there came a point—it was not long after returning to London from Mecca—at which she deliberately gave up confiding her doubts to other Muslims: 'I knew they'd give me the same old answers that I had heard before, it wouldn't be anything new.'

Accordingly, the deliberation process is largely absent of the drama associated with the probing activity described earlier, where the doubter communicates, however obliquely, his or her doubts with chosen confidants. For nearly all respondents, this was emotionally taxing, since they were anxious that by sharing their doubts or by just raising questions they would be singled out for censure. If this is a hot kind of activity, then probing in the deliberation stage is a cold kind of activity. There are no words to carefully craft and obsess over, there are no lines to mess up and there are no rebukes to suffer. There is only contemplation and self-reflection. 'Just a lot of cold, clinical reading', as Farhad describes it. There is intense argument, certainly, but it is conducted primarily with the self.

The Apostasy Phase

Disavowal to Self

The apostasy phase is the period in which the apostate, after many months or even years of self-examination and rumination, comes to the realization that their doubts about Islam, whether epistemological (does God exist? is the Quran the word of God? was Muhammad God's messenger?), moral (is Islam just?) or instrumental (is Islam rational?), are warranted and concludes that Islam is neither true to the world nor to their core sense of self. This takes the form of a personal memo and comes in two instalments. The first reads: 'I do not believe in Islam.' The second builds on this and takes it to its logical conclusion: 'I am not a Muslim.' All of the ex-Muslims I interviewed made these two memos, often in close succession.

Because the moment of disavowal was such a colossal event in their lives, many respondents remembered exactly when it occurred and where they were at the time. This is Abdullah:

> I knew this was an important time in my life. My whole outlook had shifted. I made a note of the time, the exact time. It was late. I just started pacing around the kitchen for a while and then from that moment I knew things were going to change. So I made a mental note. 2.35am on February 19th— that was when my life changed.

Alia doesn't remember the when, but she remembers the where: it was a nightclub and she was lost in thought, oblivious to all the noise and human traffic around her:

> I'd been thinking about it all day. I'd been thinking about it solidly for the last few weeks and so at that moment it just finally hit me that there's no point in arguing about this: there's clearly no evidence for God.

Amir, also using the metaphor of being 'hit', remembers it this way:

> I was sitting on a couch at night at home. I had turned off the TV and was thinking about religion. I'd watched many YouTube lectures by various atheists and mixed with my learning of Islam's origins I just came to the conclusion that Islam itself was false. It hit me like ton of bricks, honestly.

Salim's 'light bulb moment', as he called it, came on the day of Eid [the Islamic festival marking the end of Ramadan]: 'That's when I said to myself, well this is a load of crap isn't it? What am I dedicating my life to? It's stupid. It doesn't make sense.'

Masood similarly crossed over on a day of great religious symbolic importance: 'It sort of all came to a head on the first of Muharram [the Islamic New Year]. That's when I realized I was no longer a Muslim and I had abandoned Islam.'

And so did Maryam: she recalls disavowing at some point in the month of Ramadan: 'It was when I was pretending to fast and I realized that I didn't feel guilty about eating in secret. I think that was the point when I officially acknowledged that I wasn't a part of it because I didn't think what I was doing was wrong anymore.'

A few respondents, however, were unable to locate the exact point at which they finally disavowed Islam. Indeed far from being 'hit' with the self-knowledge that they no longer believed in Islam, they had in fact acquired this gradually and could not therefore pinpoint the moment it fully materialized. Fatima, for example, says 'there was no light-bulb moment where I thought this is bullshit'. Rather, 'it was this long transition'. Nabilah similarly reflects that 'it wasn't just one moment; it was a bunch of moments.'

The Phenomenology of Disavowal

What did it feel like in the aftermath of renouncing Islam? A range of conflicting emotions was reported:

- Relief

Many respondents testified to feeling a strong sense of relief at the moment of disavowal. For many months or even years they had been living in a state of anxiety, uncertainty and conflict. They had been at war with themselves. But that was now over. They had made a decision: they were now one thing and not the other, whereas before they had been neither one thing nor the other.[19] Although they still had far to go in working out who they were or what they believed, they were now clear on who they were not: they were not Muslims; and they now knew what they did not believe: they did not believe in Islam. And just knowing that was a good feeling, because it was massively clarifying.

As a Muslim, Ahmed had always erred: 'I was lax even before I started questioning.' And he had always punished himself for this. Ahmed's relief came from the knowledge that he didn't have to do this anymore: he could now 'transgress' freely, with a clear conscience: 'Initially it was just a matter of God doesn't exist, so now I can live my life like I already did without feeling guilty about it.'

Kareem's relief, by contrast, was relief not from self-rebuke but from self-doubt. For a long time he was tormented by doubts over the existence of God and the question of his own spiritual fate had become an obsessive preoccupation. But after he renounced Islam he didn't have to think about this anymore: 'I feel relief. I don't have to make excuses related to God's existence. I don't have to burden myself about hell or heaven. I'm fine now. And I don't feel like dying anymore.'

- Excitement

Connectedly, many respondents felt a sense of excitement. Because they were no longer handcuffed to what they saw as a false system of belief and identity, they were now free to reinvent themselves and their view of the world. Azhar describes the feeling as one of 'exuberance':

> I became more and more carefree I guess, less worried about the feelings of guilt and, yeah, just more and more as if, I'm the man, I'm in charge, I can do what I want with my life right now. I was on wave of exuberance, thinking, I'm young, I can start a new life.

For Aisha, the excitement came not from exercising her newly discovered freedom, but from anticipating it: from the knowledge that she could now do what before she felt she couldn't.

> I felt extremely liberated at first. I was really, really happy. I was like, well, although I can't exercise my freedom right now, theoretically I could do just about anything I want, within reason. So it felt amazing...I could drink if I wanted to. I could listen to songs that I had been avoiding which were quite blasphemous. I could watch South Park[20] again happily. I could eat a bacon sandwich. I could enter a club. I can wear whatever I want. I could date, although I didn't date.

Abdullah's excitement was similarly theoretical, but in a different way: it had to do with cosmology and the Himalayan expansion of his own imaginative universe.

> Until that point everything to me was certain. But now it wasn't. And just having that uncertainty about life and what the purpose of the universe is or how things work, that was very exciting to me. Just not knowing, just having something to find out rather than having it all dictated to me from a book— that was quite a magical feeling. Even just reading something that before I wouldn't have been allowed to read because it was philosophy and it was anti-God. It was very liberating in those first few months.

• Guilt

Some respondents reported feeling guilty about renouncing Islam: not because they thought they had done anything wrong, but because they felt that they had violated their family's wishes. They constantly replayed the same scene in their minds, imagining the shame and disappointment their apostasy would cause their parents if it became public. And this made them feel wretched, even though they knew they were doing the right thing:

> Because leaving your faith is the worst thing that you could do and I knew they would never understand it. So there was a lot of guilt and shame and self-hate, there was a lot of that. (Tasnim)

> I feel like I've let my mum down. A lot. But at the same time I know that I'm in the right. I feel right but at the same time I feel guilty. I know I've done nothing wrong but I feel as though I've hurt my mum even though I know I'm in the right. It's difficult. (Farhad)

• Anger

Many respondents said they felt angry just after they had disavowed Islam. And some said they felt very angry indeed. What was the source of this anger? Primarily, it was this: a crushing awareness of lost time and missed chances. And at what or whom was this anger directed? It was partly at Islam, but also at the self: for naively or complacently accepting Islamic belief in the first place and for not disavowing it sooner. This is Khadija:

> I had dedicated so much of my life to trying to be a good Muslim, not always for the right reasons, but always trying to do this thing and then I find out that there's more to the religion, that I've been doing all of this in the wrong name. I just felt so deluded and I felt like a real idiot and I was so angry.

Omar similarly recalls feeling 'angry at all the time I had wasted'. 'Why didn't I do this earlier, why didn't I do this in my twenties or why didn't I do this in my early teens?' Nabilah also felt angry, but above all sorrowful:

> There was a lot of sadness and regret. Why didn't I think of this earlier, what was I thinking? So for a long time I felt really bad for all the time that I've lost. I wish I would have seen it earlier.

Some respondents were very specific about their regrets. Ali, for example, confided that, 'I thought I had lost a lot of time and in fact I had declined quite a few partners because I thought that this was wrong.' One ex-Muslim, in an ex-Muslim online forum discussion, also touches on this, using humor to contain what is obviously a source of hurt:

> Heck, I don't even blame Islam. I blame myself...I was a sincere believer and practicer of Islam. That means I actually lowered my gaze and shyly stayed away from female company. Now, I'm no player, but I can recall a dozen obvious moments on campus when I could have *easily* pulled a number and perhaps gotten laid...but Noooooooooooo I was too fucking busy doing *dhikr* and trying to avoid private places with my fucking hot lab partner.[21]

Some respondents were so angry at the moment of disavowal that they felt moved to publicly denounce Islam in the form of a short personal memoir. Khadija, for example, wrote a bracing and excruciatingly candid account of her life, detailing the many horrors to which she had been subjected and for which she blames Islam. It is 8,000 words long and she posted it on the website of FFI. About this, Khadija says: 'I was so angry when I wrote that. I was one of those angry, hostile, militant atheists, you know, and I would argue with everybody about religion'. Especially her father:

> I was hostile towards my father. I would phone him up and I would just accuse him. 'Did you know? Did you know the Prophet Muhammad could rape women? Did you know that? Did you know that they did this? Did you know that they made slaves? Did you know?' I was so angry on the phone. Every new thing I found out on FFI I would scream at him. My dad, you know, led the prayers in the mosque for a while. He was very knowledgeable. He used to read loads of books. He had all of the Arabic books of the *hadiths*, he read them, he knew all of this stuff. He knew it and he never told me and he still believes. He still believes in spite of all of that. I was disgusted.

Eventually, though, Khadija's anger 'began to fade' and she became less militant and more and more uneasy about the tone of her co-thinkers at FFI, deciding in the end that she was 'in the wrong place'.

Salim followed a similar trajectory. After 'lurking' on the FFI website, he contacted Ali Sina and sent him an unsolicited memoir recounting his journey out of Islam. He also donated some money to FFI and 'even volunteered to go on some radio shows with Ali Sina, where we would talk about how terrible Islam is, blah, blah, blah'. Recalling this period, Salim says, 'I was self-hating, I was resentful, I was angry, I hated Muslims'. Salim is not exaggerating—not a bit. This is the penultimate sentence of his online testimony: 'Ali Sina is right, there is no such thing as a moderate Muslim, only an ignorant Muslim and a terrorist one.' Salim now cringes at the thought of his former hateful self:

> Ali Sina had been a sort of mentor and in a way he was the reason I left Islam so I was into his way of thinking and my views were really extreme to the point that they embarrass me now. It was just internet extremism coming out of my mouth and this was weird because my mum is a Muslim and my brother is a Muslim.

Although he firmly remains (and identifies as) an ex-Muslim, Salim no longer stands by that 'hateful, crying, drivelling testimony' he first wrote for FFI.

Masood's anger found a more nuanced expression, but it was no less pungent for all that:

> There was a lot of anger. I wanted to criticize the Islamic God, to say that the whole idea was worthy of derision. I remember I started posting on certain Muslim forums with the name Pazuzu bin Hanbi, Pazuzu being a Mesopotamian storm demon and Hanbi being his father who was a deity of wind. Both predated Islam and one of the big things in Islam is you do not take the names of false idols and so that's what I did. So I've taken the name of two Gods and I'm being anti-Islamic. It was like that for a bit, but that's kind of calmed down now.

- Residual Anxiety

Some respondents said that in the later stages of the deliberation phase, just prior to disavowing Islam, they had experienced a recrudescence of doubt and uneasiness. The *halal* voice had returned with a vengeance and this is what it was saying: 'What if you're actually wrong, *kāfir?*' This prompted a kind of testing behaviour. Intellectually, they knew it was absurd, but they did it nonetheless. Aisha, for example, gave God an ultimatum: 'I thought, okay, I'm going to give God a week to convince me that he exists. I knew deep down that nothing was going to happen but I still gave him an ultimatum.' Aisha was right: nothing happened and she apostatized soon after. Wahid was slightly more brazen. In the months leading up to his apostasy, he resolved to be a badass:

> I thought, you know what, now I'm actually going to disrespect God, because up until that point I'd never disrespected God. So let's see what happens then. If my logic is right, then things should get even worse. But my life didn't change and in fact I kind of started feeling better about things because I'd taken God out of the picture.

Masood did something similar: but after, and not before, his disavowal.

> I desecrated the Quran, you know, the Arabic Quran. I was at home and I remember stamping on it and tearing it and ripping out some of the pages and flushing them down the toilet. And nothing happened to me. Except a year later when I developed colitis.

No one else among the respondents went this far, but many felt a lingering sense of 'what if: what if I'm wrong?' Aisha's 'what if' went like this: 'what if Islam is true in the end? What if Satan really did mislead me and I end up in hell forever?' The same 'what if' had tormented Farhad: 'What if you're wrong, what if you've got it wrong and you have to pay the ultimate price? You're tortured forever. So yes, it does weigh heavily. It did, it used to. What if I'm wrong?'

And it wasn't just a fleeting emotion, this 'what if'. On the contrary, it had real staying power. It was resilient. It had stamina. Aisha, for example, felt its presence 'for a long time.' So did Farhad: 'Even after I'd become an atheist I was thinking, what if I'm wrong?' And so did Ahmed:

> It does, it did scare me for a very long time. I had this fear of being eternally punished, even after I'd stopped believing for years. I always had this issue that maybe, what if I was wrong and what if the Quran is right. I would always be scared whenever I think about the question of hellfire, but eventually I just forced myself to realize that it can't be true and is just a threat to scare people into believing.

So Farhad said it and Ahmed said it: they both said *does* ('it does weigh heavily' and 'It does...scare me' respectively), before correcting themselves to the past tense. One need not be a Freudian to intuit in these slips an ongoing latent anxiety about hell and correctitude. They could see the irrationality of it. They knew it was a hangover from their past—from their socialization, or as Ahmed put it, 'indoctrination', into Islam. But periodically they felt—and feel—it: fear of error, fear of damnation.

- Confusion

Many respondents testified to a period of feeling lost and confused. Leaving Islam had created a void and they weren't sure what to put in its place. They had rejected Islam as a source of belief and personal identity. Hence this much was certain: they knew what they didn't believe in and they knew who they were not. But that still left open and unanswered a multitude of other large and pressing questions. If they didn't any longer believe in Islam, then what now did they believe in? And if they didn't any longer identify as Muslims, then with what did they now identify? They weren't Muslims, so who were they?

In the weeks and months after disavowing many simply didn't know. And that left them feeling uneasy and uncertain. Tasnim, for example, said she felt lost. She expanded on this:

> Why do I do the things I do? Why do I even exist? Why do I exist—what does this mean? I used to think you live your life to please God and get into heaven, but I don't have that anymore. So where do I go from here? How do I live the rest of my life without a purpose?

Khadija had similarly struggled with this very question—and soon:

> At the beginning it felt exciting. Very exciting. I felt so free. That didn't last forever. I became quite depressed. Very depressed. I didn't leave my house for a long time. I just debated online because the only time I was feeling okay was when I was online talking. As soon as I would switch off the computer I would just be depressed again. Everything just seemed pointless. It all seemed empty after the initial buzz of being free wore off.

For Aisha, the dominant feeling wasn't one of pointlessness, but of uncertainty. Before she had a script; now she didn't. And this confused and scared her:

> I was just in the biggest state of confusion afterwards. My conception of the world is going to be completely different now. What am I supposed to do? Everything I said and everything I did was in accordance to Islam. What am I supposed to do now? That's my whole life shattered, I don't know what to do, even about the little things. What music do I like now? Because I avoided music for quite a while. It was all so confusing.

For Abdullah, the dominant emotion was dread:

> I became depressed for the first time in my life. The only thing I was thinking about was death, basically. I had spent my whole life thinking this life is meaningless and that I will live forever in eternal bliss and then it just hit me that I was mortal and I've wasted most of my life and I've only got a relatively short period left and the thought of death, which never bothered me in the slightest before, was really disturbing me all of a sudden, having to think about dying and growing old and everything. So for two months all I could think about was death. Sometimes I would go for a walk to distract myself and I would literally just burst into tears in the middle of the road.

Abdullah says that it wasn't until he came into contact with other ex-Muslims via the CEMB website and shared his anxieties with them that his depression began to lift.

Disavowal Rituals: Disclosure and Pigging Out

'There are some things', writes Mary Douglas, that 'we cannot experience without ritual'.[22] Leaving Islam may be one of them.

Rituals are the symbolic resources through which life is lived and made meaningful. Rituals, more concretely, are created and performed by people to mark specific passages or events in their lives.[23] Rituals are defining. Solidifying, too.

How did respondents ritualize their exits? With trepidation and uncertainty, which came from knowing that what they were doing was deeply transgressive from an Islamic perspective. Two rituals in particular warrant attention: disclosure and the violation of the dietary prohibition against pig meat.

- Disclosure

They had all *un*said the *shahada*: privately. To themselves. That was a line crossed. But saying it out loud, to others: that would be yet another line. Yet another act of transgression. And a test, too. Of sincerity, belief, resolve. A sign that they meant it. That they were serious. This is how Masood explained it:

> I declared it online in this Islamic forum I used to post at. I made a thread saying how I'd realized I was no longer a Muslim and had abandoned Islam and didn't believe in God. I needed to sort of make it official, but I didn't want to tell my parents because it would kill them, basically. I suppose in some ways I wanted to have a cut-off point, a kind of boundary for this is where I was Islamic and this is where I've grown out of that. I just wanted to make it official, so it's not just bandying ideas about in your head; you're actually saying, 'this is the stance I've taken'.

Yasmin also reported that it wasn't until she verbalized her apostasy that it became fully real to her. Before she had done this, it was abstract, inchoate. But saying it gave it solidity:

> Eventually I realized that I couldn't believe in it on a logical level and I also couldn't be part of that community. I didn't want to pretend to believe in it

anymore and my mum and I started having fights again, like we used to before I went to university, and at one point I said, 'I'm not going to pray', and she said, 'What do you mean you're not going to pray?', like 'What are you saying, you're not a Muslim?' And I said, 'I'm not a Muslim' and I was nineteen and that was the very first time I said those words. And it felt like they echoed in my own head a lot and then I realized what I had just done, like I realized that it was possible. Until then I don't think I had realized that it was possible to stop being a Muslim. I was a lapsed Muslim. I was going to come back to it someday. I was trying to be a good Muslim but I hadn't thought it was possible not to be a Muslim.

Azhar says something very similar about the first time he declared his apostasy:

The first person I confided to was my then best friend. He's a Muslim and we were talking online and I told him my argument against Islam, my thoughts about what Islam is and means to me. And then I finished the whole diatribe with, 'I'm not a Muslim anymore'. Yeah, and I said that, 'I'm no longer a Muslim' and it was quite a liberating feeling because I remember saying it to him and saying it out loud and realizing that that was the first time I'd properly admitted that to myself, that I know right now that I'm not a Muslim. And I probably won't be ever again.

For Masood, Yasmin and Azhar, as indeed for many respondents, coming out to others is the ultimate end-point, serving to finalize the journey out of Islam. It was, indeed, the focal point of their apostasy, the event which truly cemented it in their minds and the event they all remembered, however difficult and upsetting the memory. This is because, as Masood suggests, coming out to others is the ultimate test of sincerity. It is proof-positive of apostasy. But it is not the only kind of proof.

• Pigging out

Some respondents tried alcohol for the first time. Omar recalls marching into a pub and ordering a pint of the strongest lager available: 'I thought, sod it, I've got to go for the proper taboo stuff here.' He hated the taste of it: 'it was like treacle, you could eat that stuff.' But he emptied his glass nonetheless.

Aisha says of her first drink that 'it was an official rite of passage to go through, like, it's finally over'.

One respondent decided to go out and get laid: 'The moment that I decided to have sex [outside of marriage] is the day I counted as officially leaving Islam.'

For some female respondents, the decisive ritual act was the removal of their *hijabs*. Amina says that wearing it had 'sent out the message that I'm a Muslim and there are certain values I live by'. Removing it, she reasoned, would send the opposite message. So she removed it: 'It was not who I was anymore...there was now a different me.' Nubia similarly says of her decision to discard the *hijab*: 'I wanted everyone to know that I'm not that person anymore. I just wanted them to know that I left Islam.' Tasnim also said this: 'the main transition was when I stopped wearing the scarf...this isn't me anymore.'

But by far the most common disavowal ritual reported by respondents was the consumption of pig meat. This is forbidden in Islam.[24] Most respondents said that before their apostasy they hadn't (knowingly) eaten it. Many indeed said that they had a deep aversion to it: pig-meat, especially bacon and pork, disgusted them. Just the very thought of it made them want to wretch. Breaking the taboo against eating pig-meat is thus, alongside disclosure, the acme of disavowal rituals among ex-Muslims.

Salim remembers well the day he lost his 'pork virginity'.[25] It happened just after his 'bullshit' epiphany on Eid day:

> It sounds so stupid to me now, but that was like my jumping over or something. I'd already tried alcohol before, but I'd never eaten pork. It's just a massive taboo. Muslims will drink but they'll never, never eat pork so that was to me like a renunciation and I was like, I don't believe in this stuff anymore. It was a Cumberland sausage. It wasn't very good, to be honest. I remember I was kind of paranoid that someone was going to catch me buying it and even when I was eating it I was thinking, this is weird, this is uncomfortable, but you have to do this. That sausage, it was the exit for me, there was no going back after that.

For Farhad, the process was somewhat more protracted. It began with a non-*halal* cheeseburger: that was the first act of transgression, the first outward expression of his disbelief. As he puts it: 'I think the cheeseburger is sort of just me realizing that I don't believe in Islam anymore. Even though it was just a crappy cheeseburger it was more symbolic than anything.' But Farhad was not content with this: his apostasy required a more dramatic means of substantiation. It required...bacon:

That didn't happen overnight. It was really difficult. It was one of the most difficult things I've ever done, as ridiculous as it sounds. So I went to Tesco and finally bought a bacon sandwich. Because so many times before I'd go in and I'd pick one up, I'd look at it, I'd want to buy it but I just wouldn't. I'd put it down and buy a tuna sandwich or something else instead. It's so ingrained into you that eating bacon is wrong, a totally different level of wrong. A lot of Muslims have sex, drink alcohol and eat non-*halal* meat, but the ultimate thing for them is the bacon, is the pork. So for me it was symbolic. It was the last bit of Islam.

Omar tells a similar story:

So just to put the final nail in the coffin, I went out and I bought a ham sandwich. This was a couple of weeks after my apostasy and it was really an odd feeling. But it was gradual, because initially I went for non-*halal*. I went out for a KFC and a McDonald's, that type of thing. But I had this revulsion to ham and you'll get a lot of Muslims who'll drink but they'll never eat pork. I don't know how they decide between the two because they are both prohibited, so I don't know how they say well we'll drink but we won't have pork. So I decided, you know what, I'm going to go and have myself a ham sandwich and I went out and I bought a ham sandwich...It didn't really taste of anything. I just thought it needs a bit of mustard or something.

Abdullah's first time, he remembers, was suffused with guilt and anxiety:

In the week after I apostatized I had some bacon. I felt a little guilty and it felt pretty weird. I think it's just a sort of a mental block and it's almost like feeding yourself poison because you've been taught that it's dirty. I went into town and I was pretty nervous and anxious and looking over my shoulder all the time. I went into Greggs and bought a bacon roll and then hid it. I made sure I had a black bag to hide it in. I went into the nearest park to an area where there weren't really any people and I tried some of it and I was surprised at how normal it tasted. That was a pretty big moment for me. It's just sort of breaking free, breaking some shackles and just being able to eat what you want.

For the ungodly the consumption of pig meat can be a source of pleasure. But for ex-Muslims it is something more enduringly meaningful. 'I felt truly apostatized' is how one respondent revealingly described her first experience of eating non-*halal* meat, also echoing the idea that what we eat is also what we emphatically are.[26]

Disinvolvement

Disinvolvement, to paraphrase Bromley, refers to a 'pulling back from the group'[27] and occurs both emotionally and physically. For all respondents, disinvolvement, in both these aspects, was a gradual process and began before the point of disavowal. Omar, for example, had cut his beard in the year prior to leaving Islam. His beard was an outward expression of his piety: cutting it assuredly meant something. Khadija had ceremoniously removed her head-scarf six months before she renounced Islam: that, too, meant something. And so did Hanif's drinking and partying in the year before his apostasy.

It all meant something. And what it meant was an increasing estrangement from Islam. All respondents, regardless of the strength of their initial belief, had gone through this: estrangement from Islam. And by the time they came to renounce Islam, they had reached a point of complete estrangement from it. Islam, as a source of belief, moral guidance and personal identity was once very important to them. Now it wasn't. If, to use the language of the Quran, their hearts were once open to Islam, now their hearts were sealed to it. And this was reflected outwardly in their behaviour, as far as this was possible, because many respondents were 'in the closet', keeping their apostasy hidden from their families and other Muslims. Even those who had told their families and close friends about their apostasy had to rein it in now and then, not wanting to cause undue pain or upset to their loved ones. And so they 'involved' themselves when they had to: when it would have been unreasonable not to. The level of involvement differed from person to person; some were more involved than others. But involvement there was.

For Yasmin, as indeed for nearly all respondents, the process played out like this:

> I slowly just started shedding these sort of persona or whatever and so I stopped praying, I stopped going to the mosque, I stopped fasting...my mum didn't like it. At every step of the way I remember having lots of fights with her, lots of arguments, lots of yelling and I felt very trapped but I just kind of stood my ground. But I didn't want to make things worse for her so I didn't want to be drinking in front of her or anything like that so I would be, 'Just leave me alone' and do what I needed to do but there was still constant tension. There were a few times when she just guilt tripped me or somehow made me go to the mosque or I'd drive her to the mosque and then she'd pressure me into going inside and just things like that. So I would do the minimum just to get through. And that minimum became less and less.

Two things are striking here. The first is that Yasmin disinvolved gradually, step by step. And the second is that at every point in the process she encountered resistance. Which, paradoxically, made her even *more* dogged in asserting her right to become the person she was becoming. If Islam had seemed reactionary and unreasonable before, this was now made all the more apparent to her in the form of her mother's heavy-handedness, which, far from bringing her back into the fold, served instead to further estrange her from it. The issue of disinvolvement and how ex-Muslims manage it recurs throughout the remaining chapters of this book. I shall now focus more squarely on the issue of disclosure.

4

COMING OUT

DISCLOSING APOSTASY

I was dying to tell them, to shout out I don't believe all this.

Luqman

There is no compulsion in religion. Tell that to my parents.

Farhad

If you're going to come out to others, do not be under any illusions: it *won't* be easy. People can be assholes.

Samir

I guess it's almost like telling your parents you're gay.

Nabilah

Who, When and How?

'The death of the contemporary forms of social order ought to gladden rather than trouble the soul. Yet what is frightening is that the departing world leaves behind it not an heir, but a pregnant widow. Between the death of the one and the birth of the other, much water will flow by, a long night of chaos and desolation will pass.'[1] So writes Alexander Herzen, the Russian exile, in rumination on the turmoil of revolutionary political change. It is not too dramatic to say that becoming an apostate, for many ex-Muslims, is a bit like this: a long and tumultuous process of

79

change and metamorphosis, involving many difficult challenges and problems, both existential and practical. Between the first throb of doubt and the clarifying moment of disavowal, 'much water will flow by' and 'a long night of chaos and desolation will pass'. Perhaps it is overstating matters to put it like this. But not by much.

This chapter is about more dark nights: not of the soul, but primarily of the heart. For the apostate, the decision to renounce Islam is a daunting one and is taken after a prolonged and often agonizing period of sustained reflection and self-questioning and self-doubt. But no less daunting and agonizing is the decision to 'come out' as an apostate or disbeliever, since it involves the feelings, sensitivities and reactions of others. Once taken, more difficult decisions follow, concerning, variously, who to tell, when and how. This chapter is mainly about how ex-Muslims handle these decisions and what happens in their aftermath.

The Catch-22 of Disclosure: Outed and Ostracized or Closeted and Crazy

The American comedian Chris Rock is a master of acerbic observation. One of his best jokes is about marriage and singledom. Both, he says, incur severe costs and one must choose between two evils: 'Married and bored or single and lonely. Ain't no happiness nowhere.'[2] Married life supplies security and love, but also, over time, monotony and sexual boredom.[3] Single life, by contrast, offers great opportunities for spontaneous adventure and sexual excitement. But it can also be profoundly lonely. This, then, is the tragedy of adult life: 'married and bored or single and lonely'.

Rock's skit is a good example of what philosophers call the 'incommensurability of values': some ends in life are simply incompatible. And hence we must choose between them. There must be a trade-off. We gain one thing, but we lose another. We cannot have everything and we must accept loss. Our lives consist of myriad opportunities and choices, but also of countless missed opportunities and jettisoned choices. Michael Ignatieff calls this the 'tragic view' of social and political life,[4] citing Isaiah Berlin as its most articulate exponent.[5] Here is Berlin:

> We are doomed to choose and every choice may entail an irreparable loss. The world we encounter in ordinary experience is one in which we are faced with choices between ends equally ultimate and claims equally absolute, the realization of some of which must inevitably involve the sacrifice of others... If, as I believe, the ends of men are many, and not all of them are in principle

compatible with each other, then the possibility of conflict—and of tragedy—can never wholly be eliminated from human life, either personal or social. The necessity of choosing between absolute claims is then an inescapable characteristic of the human condition.[6]

And so it is with ex-Muslims: they 'are doomed to choose' between two competing evils. If they disclose their apostasy to loved ones, they risk hurting them and incurring their rejection. Yet if they conceal it from them, they must endure the psychological misery of living a lie. This is the catch-22 of disclosure: outed and ostracized or closeted and crazy.

All respondents had struggled or are struggling with this dilemma. Here is how one ex-Muslim characterizes it: 'I felt I would never be truly happy. If I broke free and lived my life, I'd hurt and dishonour my family. If I gave into my family's wishes I'd be sacrificing my happiness and living a lie...I was stuck living a lie or facing rejection.'[7] Wahid similarly said: 'For me to be fully satisfied is an impossibility because for me to be fully who I want to be I would have to deny the rights of my mother. Therefore no matter what I do I won't be happy.' Farhad summarized the dilemma in this way: 'I had to make a decision: be open about my apostasy and hurt my parents or lie to them and be trapped in a life I don't want. It's really, really difficult just being in that position.'

Recipients of Disclosure

Who are the recipients of disclosure? Among respondents, it was mainly Muslim friends. And then siblings: they were next in the audience hierarchy. For those who had disclosed to their parents, it was commonly friends first, then siblings and then parents. Disclosure, clearly, requires considerable practice and refinement. And even then it can go very badly wrong.

All respondents felt a profound urge to disclose their apostasy. 'I wanted everyone to know that I'm not that person anymore,' said Nubia, expressing a sentiment which could stand as a manifesto for all ex-Muslims. They all felt it, this urge, but most didn't act on it, not straight away and almost always not fully, exercising caution on the matter of whom to trust with their disclosure.

Nubia told her mother about her apostasy. But not before telling a close friend—an Afghan girl who was also, as it turned out, an apostate. And not before telling a 'handful' of non-Muslim friends. But this is the extent of her disclosure, because even now, four years after apostatizing, she still makes a point of avoiding the issue with Muslims she doesn't know or fully trust: 'I'm really scared of telling Muslims that I've left the religion. It's completely terrifying to me, I can't do it. Only online.'

Masood, who is single and lives with his parents in Yorkshire, hasn't told his mother and father. But he has told his two sisters. Just over half of respondents are like Masood: one or more of their siblings knows about their apostasy. But their parents don't know. And this is how they want it, for now at least. Only a small number of respondents have kept their apostasy hidden from *all* members of their immediate and extended family.

Ramesh, who lives in Canada and converted to Islam in his early twenties, has told his wife, a life-long Muslim, but not his wife's parents. That's the deal they've struck. He isn't happy about this, but he accepts it and is willing to compromise. He has also reluctantly agreed not to tell their two young children. Hanif's wife, by contrast, doesn't know: he hasn't told her about his apostasy and isn't planning to. Hanif's parents are similarly in the dark about it, but his non-Muslim friends aren't: they all know.

Even among respondents who have disclosed their apostasy to their parents, most operate like Nubia: they are selective. They choose carefully who to tell, weighing up the respective advantages and disadvantages of disclosure. They tell some people, but keep it from others, either out of fear of condemnation or out of sensitivity to their feelings. Or to prevent the circulation of rumour. Or because disclosure is simply unnecessary. Hence they are simultaneously *in* and *out* of the closet, constantly switching between two worlds and two different personae. And this was true of most respondents. They inhabit the closet and they don't inhabit the closet: it all depends on who is around and what is at stake. For Tasnim, who is in her early twenties and from a Bengali family in East London, the vital issue is this: are they Bengali or not? 'I'm okay with telling non-Bengali people about it because I know they won't judge me. But I'm wary of telling people who are Bengali in case they know somebody who knows me'. For Mustafa, the crucial factor is religion—or what he calls 'the religious mindset': 'When I first started telling people I only told friends whom I trusted and who were not religious'. And for Omar, who lives in a city with a relatively large Muslim population and whose friends 'are all hardcore Muslims', it is devoutness: he won't disclose his apostasy to pious Muslims. Not, at any rate, now, after having made the mistake of telling his two close friends, who both responded negatively to his disclo-sure. Luqman is even more selective, having learned the hard way from some bruising experiences with his own family: he won't disclose to Muslims *tout court*. Commenting on the issue of disclosure in an ex-Mus-lim online forum discussion, he writes: 'I don't trust Muslims at all...Once the information leaks out, there's no telling where it will get to. I do what-ever I can to avoid getting into conversations with Muslims I know.'

For most respondents, this is what it comes down to: what is their ethnic and religious background? Are they devout? And can they be trusted? These are the considerations which figure in their decisions to disclose their apostasy to others. Only a small number of respondents disdain to engage in these considerations: that is, only a few are fully 'out', in the sense that they're accountably open about their apostasy in all private and public contexts.

Motives for Disclosure

What reasons did respondents give for disclosing their apostasy? Why, according to their own lights, did they tell friends, family, community members or strangers about their disbelief?

Two contrasting types of motives were reported: personal motives and political motives. Of these, the former was the most commonly cited.

Personal Motives

For many respondents, disclosure didn't feel like a choice. On the con-trary, it felt like a compulsion. Telling others about their apostasy was something they had to do. It was necessary. Not telling not only felt wrong, but psychologically impossible. Alia, for example, says she couldn't lie to her family and 'pretend to be a Muslim'. Not just because that would have made her feel horribly guilty, but also because she knew for a certainty that living a lie would make her life an intolerable misery: 'There was no option. I had to tell them.'

Many other respondents felt the same way: that they had to tell some-one, or risk losing their minds. This is what Kareem says: that concealing his apostasy from his family was 'driving me insane'. He had tried for a period, keeping it secret. But he reached a point where he felt that 'I just couldn't keep it inside anymore—I had to tell them'. Luqman, who came out to his parents and siblings, similarly remarks: 'I needed to get it off my chest.'

For some respondents, telling was motivated by a desire to preempt entrapment—or at least to halt its intensification. This, Maryam explains, is why she had to come out to her mother: to signal to her to back off, especially on the issue of marriage:

> I thought if I don't tell her now, when I finish university she'll be pestering me, saying, 'Oh, so and so's friend is an engineer, do you want to meet him?' And things like that. And so I thought just to put her off being like that and so she knows from the off that I don't want an arranged marriage and I'm not going to marry a Muslim. I thought it's better to tell her as early as possible. And now by telling my mum that I no longer consider myself a Muslim I'm not obliged to have an arranged marriage anymore. It's taken that control away from her. At least I hope so.

Wahid, too, reasoned that if he didn't tell his mother about his apostasy he would be pressured into a marriage with a Muslim woman. And this, he feared, would make his life even more miserably confining.[8]

Political Motives

For some respondents, the reason for disclosing their apostasy to others was overtly political: they did it, they said, to advance the 'ex-Muslim cause'.

Azhar, for example, disclosed his apostasy online. This isn't unusual: there are thousands of ex-Muslim online testimonies. But attaching his name and picture to his testimony was, because most testimonies are anonymous. It was also risky, because at the time he hadn't yet disclosed his apostasy to his extended family, although he had told his parents and a few friends. Reflecting on his motives, Azhar says:

> Because there is such a taboo surrounding apostasy in Islam I wanted to make sure that people who wanted to do it would realize that there's actual real living people who can do this and if I put my picture there I can make it seem as if it's a normal thing to do and you don't need to be afraid and you can do this. I wanted to do my part for the apostate community, I guess. To normalize the process of apostatizing. To put my picture there so that people can know that I'm a genuine person. To say, 'I'm an ex-Muslim, you are not alone, you are not the only apostate in the world'. That was the major motive for me to do it.

When Azhar's extended family eventually discovered his testimony, they shamed his parents and this deeply upset Azhar, because, as he told me, it wasn't their fault and it was his decision. But, he adds, 'it will have all been worth it if only just one person finds encouragement from it and feels less alone after reading it'.

Yasmin strikes a similar note: it is 'important to inspire others', she says, and to let other Muslims know what she had *not* known when she first started to experience doubts: namely, that leaving Islam *is* possible and that ex-Muslims exist.

Salim's political ambitions were somewhat grander: 'Just after I apostatized, I thought, you know what, I'm going to write a testimony and I'm going to post it so that people can be inspired and I can be a hero or something.' Abdullah had similarly been thinking on the grand scale: indeed he wanted to 'change the world' by disclosing his apostasy and to 'save' Muslims from the errors of their thinking. Abdullah, like Salim, is now slightly mortified by the fervency and grandeur of his former ambitions.

Methods of Disclosure

Hinting

Coming out is a cumulative process. Nearly always, it is initiated by hinting. Respondents did this in a variety of ways and with varying degrees of tact. Luqman, for example, would turn up late for prayers. This wasn't out of indolence. This was out of vigorous intent. He also began to dress differently, 'in western clothes as much as I could', and remembers discarding his prayer hat which he was expected to wear during prayers. This, too, was deliberate: 'I wanted them to know that I was not enthusiastic about religion,' he told me, referring to his immediate family.

Aisha's hinting also involved disrobing. On her return to London from her fateful trip to Mecca she decided to stop wearing the *abaya*. She also decided to remove her *hijab*. In addition to this, and at the same time, she began voicing her increasingly liberal views on all manner of issues: 'I really should have kept my mouth shut, but I couldn't help it.' Nor did she try to conceal her new interest in atheism, openly watching atheist videos in front of her older sister. This all drew notice, as Aisha must have known it would: 'My sisters were like, you've changed, you've changed, you've changed.' And, more ominously for Aisha, her parents had noticed the change too.

As well as removing her *hijab*, Amina had also discarded the carapace of pious affectation from her vocabulary. The Arabic word for 'goodbye' was the first to go: 'My mum uses it all the time and the appropriate response would be to say it back to her but I don't. I just say 'bye' and that's only a recent thing. I know I could just say it, but it's like I feel I'm trying to find myself more and this is who I am rather than someone in between.'

Mustafa's hinting took the form of bloody-mindedness. He didn't have a pious beard to cut off. He had never worn religious clothing, so there could be no ceremonious removing of all that get-up. And he was already extravagantly lax in his approach to prayer, so not praying wasn't even an option: just more of the same. So he would do this instead: 'I would bring up discussions and start criticizing Islam. It happened once, it happened twice, it happened three times and my dad and my mum were like, "where is this coming from?"'

Hinting of the kind described above has two key purposes. The first is to 'test the waters': to roughly gauge how others will respond to full disclosure of disbelief. Some respondents said that hostile responses to hints made them rethink or even abandon their decision to disclose, whereas positive responses had given them the confidence to go through with it. Alia, for example, prior to coming out to her parents, had deliberately raised the question of religion with her father, confiding to him what she thought he already knew or suspected: 'that I wasn't religious'. To her surprise and relief, she found him to be extremely progressive on the fundamentals. He even told her that he would support her if she were to abandon her Islamic faith: 'He said I don't mind if you don't want to be a Muslim, I still love my family.' This greatly encouraged her: 'It gave me hope that when I was ready to come out he wouldn't go mad.' Ahmed, by contrast, found his father to be fiercely intransigent on the issue of faith. He wanted to tell his parents about his apostasy, and was about to, but the reaction of his father cautioned him against the idea:

> I didn't want to come straight out to my parents because I didn't know how they'd react. I wanted to set a stepping stone towards it, to test the waters, I guess. We were talking about religion and I told my dad that I could understand where atheists are coming from because atheists believe in reason and Muslims believe in faith. And that really aggravated him because he said that Islam is based on science and evidence. He reacted really badly because he saw that I was disconnecting myself from the Islamic version of science and

that I was going to the other version of science and he really started calling me names, like, 'Oh you're a bastard' and 'you're going to go to hell, you should find a proper way'. And so by then I just knew that saying that I'd stopped believing was a bad idea and nothing good would come from it.

The second purpose of hinting is to recalibrate expectations, so that when the full confession of apostasy is announced the relevant recipients will be prepared for it. Maryam, for example, said that well before announcing her apostasy to her mother she had significantly paved the way toward it:

> I can't remember exactly how the conversation started but we got onto the topic of Muhammad. I think it was something to do with men having four wives. I said that even though that's a law in Islam Muhammad had about fourteen wives, one of them he married when she was only six years old. I said I had a problem with this. And I also told her that I had a problem with throwing non-believers in hell and the ban on homosexuality. I think it was obvious to her that I was questioning what was written in the Quran and so when I told her over Christmas I felt like she might have been expecting it.

Maryam has yet to disclose her apostasy to her father, but intends to adopt the same approach: 'The best thing to do is to do it slowly by planting the seeds of doubt. And go from there and see how he responds.'

Hinting is an activity fraught with risk. First, there is the risk that a hint will be missed. Second, and more seriously, there is the risk that a hint will be taken as evidence of outright apostasy and so, far from cushioning the final blow of disclosure, the hint ends up delivering it prematurely and with full force. This can result in not a recalibration of expectations on the part of recipients, but a reinforcement of them.

This is exactly how it was for Amina. She had removed her *hijab*, at first slowly by loosening it and then later discarding it completely, hoping that her parents would eventually get used to the 'new' Amina. But they didn't get used to the new Amina. They just got very worried, wondering what had happened to the old Amina and what this change meant. First, with the shunning: for about a week Amina's mother ignored her. Then with the drama: Amina's mother wrote her a letter. 'The letter said "can you please put your scarf back on, you're my daughter" and it was about how much she loves me and she doesn't want to see me go to hell and things like that'. Amina ignored it: 'I didn't know how to react to it.' Then her mother wrote a second letter, which she left outside Amina's room: 'That one said that I'm no longer her daughter and I'm dead to her and I should never talk to her again.' Amina ignored that letter too. And then, after a while, they spoke to each other. But it was awkward and tense.

Luqman's hinting had the same effect on his immediate family. It didn't warn them; it worried them. And then it angered them: they punished his laxity and 'growing rebelliousness', as he calls it, by shunning him. For three days his parents refused to speak with him or even to acknowledge his presence in their house. This didn't bring him back into the fold, as they'd hoped it would, but served to estrange him even further from it, because it made him even more angry and frustrated.

Another area of risk relates to misjudging the reactions of others: positive responses to hints of disbelief are not always a guarantee of a positive response to confessions of actual apostasy. Some respondents, on hinting to others, had encountered displays of tolerance and understanding. They took this to mean that news of their own apostasy would be met with equal tolerance and understanding. So they took a chance and disclosed. And they were met not with tolerance and understanding, but with shock and disapproval.

Alia's father, for example, had lied when he said he wouldn't mind if Alia apostatized, because when she did finally come out to him, he minded—a great deal. Indeed, he responded with hostility and verbal aggression. Omar misread the signals, too: when he confessed his apostasy to his two close friends, they responded by condemning him; he had thought, wrongly, that they might have been more understanding, given how long they had known him and how deep their friendship was. Abdullah similarly got it wrong: he thought his close friend from college would be sympathetic. But he wasn't: he was contemptuously judgmental—'he just freaked out and started calling me names'. Abdullah took this as a salutary lesson: from now on, he would be more careful in deciding in whom to confide.

Delivery Systems: The Spoken Word and the Written Word

By what means did respondents disclose their apostasy? In the main, there were two: the spoken word and the written word.

• The Spoken Word

The dominant method was verbal speech: most respondents said the unsaying of the *shahada*, either in face-to-face conversation or via telephone. Azhar, for example, confessed to his lifelong confidant, a local *imam*, in person. But he wasn't able to do that with his parents, whom he told from distance over the phone: 'I just wasn't able to say it to them in person.' This, he told me, made him feel cowardly and is why he later came out openly online: to inspire others to do what he himself had lacked the courage to do. Similarly, when Omar told his two lifelong friends about his apostasy he did it over the phone.

● The Written Word

Masood, when he first came out to one of his sisters, used the written, albeit heavily abbreviated, word: he told her via text message.[9] But by far the most common delivery system for written disclosure was the personal computer: respondents went online and wrote a testimony, ranging from the abbreviated to the expansive and the elevated. Here in the virtual world and under the cover of a pseudonym, they could freely declare their apostasy, so they did—either casually in the form of private online chat with others or, more formally, in the form of an anonymous post introducing themselves.

Amina, Alia and Nubia, although they had all anonymously disclosed their apostasy in an online ex-Muslim forum, decided on a more antiquated method when it came to disclosing to their parents: they all wrote letters. Nubia, because her mother, after first learning of her apostasy, was shunning her and there was no other way of reaching her; Amina, because 'we were raised not to talk about our feelings' and because her mother, whose grasp of English is poor, would better understand a letter;[10] and Alia, because she could better explain herself with written words.

Sound Systems: Telling Them Softly and Telling Them Loudly

In disclosing their apostasy, what words did respondents use? This primarily depended on to whom they were disclosing. To friends, they were direct, sometimes even resounding. But not always: to the devout among them they treaded more carefully. To family, they treaded more carefully still, not wanting to exacerbate or inflame an already difficult situation. Indeed to family, their tone was often apologetic and defensive and their pain evident. To fellow ex-Muslims, they were far more forthright and their tone, far from being apologetic, was sometimes abrasive and triumphant and not a little self-righteous.

- Telling Them Softly

What does the more cautious voice of disclosure sound like? To Muslim friends and family, it sounded like this: 'I just don't believe'. Wahid, for example, in conversation with a Muslim friend, said precisely that: 'I just don't believe.' And that served as a template for other future acts of disclosure. Reflecting on his choice of words, he said: 'Like I can't say Allah is not real. That would hurt their feelings and it would shock them. So I would simply go, "I just don't believe" and that leaves ambiguity, *what* doesn't he believe? But they know deep down what it means.' Salim was similarly ambiguous and yet clear on the issue: when he first disclosed his apostasy to his brother he said, 'I don't believe in this stuff'. He didn't say he didn't believe in God or Islam, but in the context in which he uttered these words—his violation of the fast in Ramadan—it was obvious what he meant. Nabilah was more specific: she told her mother that she didn't believe in the existence of God. But she didn't say that she had renounced Islam; nor did she say that she was no longer a Muslim.

Some respondents had prefaced their declaration of unbelief with the words 'I feel' or 'I think', as if this would somehow take the sting out of what they were about to say. Nubia, addressing her best friend, recalls saying, '*I think* I don't believe in God anymore'. Azhar, also addressing a best friend, told him that 'for the first time in my life *I feel* as if I just don't believe', adding that, 'it's not that I think it's wrong, it's just that I don't have that sense of certainty in my heart any more about Islam'.

Few respondents who'd become atheists made reference to the word 'atheist' in coming out to their families. For Maryam, it was a matter of comprehension:

I haven't told her I'm an atheist. She definitely wouldn't be able to understand the idea of not believing in a God at all—her head might explode. She just would not understand how I could possibly have come to that conclusion because she doesn't think like that.

For Mustafa, too, it was a matter of comprehension, because he knew that were he to describe himself as an atheist to his parents they would understand all too well:

I didn't say that I was an atheist because the word atheist in Arabic has a very negative connotation. So that's why I said, 'I don't believe in God. I don't believe there is a God. I don't believe there is a God who created us or who cares for us or who oversees us or that there is a God who would hold us accountable for our deeds in the afterlife'.

Kareem similarly erred on the side of caution: 'I just told them that I don't believe that God exists. I would never have said to them that I'm an atheist.'

With the exception of just four respondents, no one came out to their friends or family by declaring that they had 'apostatized' or that they were 'apostates' and no longer saw themselves as Muslims. Fatima, for example, says, 'I don't think I've ever come out like that and said I'm not a Muslim anymore. I may have said things around it, but not those exact words.' Nor did she need to: 'They know I'm not a believer.'

Salim recalls the following conversation with an acquaintance from Brunei:

> He said, 'Salim right?' And his name was Salim as well. And I was like, 'Yeah' and he says, 'Are you a Muslim?' and I said, well I didn't really want to say I'd left Islam, so I said, 'My parents were Muslims, but they never brought me up to be a Muslim'. And there were a few Muslims who I was willing to say that to.

It is revealing that even to those whom Salim knew and trusted he would pointedly avoid saying he had left Islam or was no longer a Muslim.

• Telling Them Loudly

To their friends and family, most respondents affected a cautious and apologetic tone, carefully moderating their words so as to minimize their wounding impact. They said what needed to be said, but in a muted way, simultaneously revealing and concealing how they truly felt. But to fellow ex-Muslims and to countless distant others online, under the protection of anonymity, they were able to strike a very different tone: abrasive, unapologetic, celebratory, defiant even. This, for example, is how Ahmed opened his introductory post on an ex-Muslim forum: 'Hello, people! New member here. Ex-Muslim and devout enemy of God. May Islam rest in pieces.' Needless to say Ahmed doesn't talk like this in earshot of his family, who remain uninformed about his apostasy.

Respondents who wrote about their experiences online clearly revelled in the freedom of the anonymity of the internet, admitting to thoughts, feelings, anxieties, habits and desires which would doubtless shame them in face-to-face interactions. Some had taken particular delight in relaying their acts of defiance against Islamic prohibitions, using humour and irony to animate their accounts. Masood, for example, happily reported:

> I left Islam in 2008 and blame my apostasy for my growing fatness: as a reaction to Islam (surely all of us who believed devoutly went through a testing, anti-Islamic phase shortly after turning away from our erstwhile religions?) I started eating richly during Ramadan. Oh dear.

Farhad had this to share: 'LOL I deliberately whacked off while fasting for EXTRA sin. FEELS GOOD MAN.' And another respondent confessed: 'I left Islam under the threat of eternal punishment because I wanted to eat bacon and have copious amounts of degenerate sex. Ah well one out of two isn't too bad.'

This abrasive and defiant tone was certainly not the only register respondents adopted online, for they could also be serious, balanced, nuanced, receptive, tender. But behind the shield of anonymity they were able say things they would never have dared say to their family and Muslim friends. And for some, clearly, that was precisely the point: to rant, to vent, to let-off steam.

Themes in Disclosure Narratives

When respondents came out, they didn't just announce their apostasy; they also offered an explanation for why they had left Islam—or rather, why, as they saw it, it was right they had left Islam. This, primarily, was because they knew that from the perspective of other Muslims their leaving would be viewed with scepticism, if not outright disdain, and that correspondingly an explanation would be demanded from them. And so they all had prepared for this. They would be called to account.[11] And account they would. This is Maryam:

> I had a set of arguments pretty much memorized. Because I think in these instances you have to. I would revise them. If you really do need to tell your parents you have got to have something to say to them because otherwise they will accuse you of trying to act like a western person or that you're this or you're that. You can't just say I want a freer lifestyle. You have to have a set of well-thought-out statements as to why you have left the religion. So I had some things pretty much scripted for that.

Nubia had also carefully prepared an exit account, because, like Maryam, she knew full-well that when she told her mother about her apostasy she would need one:

I made a comprehensive list of everything, every argument she could come up with and everything else I'd say back to her...And I wanted her to know that I didn't hate her. I wasn't doing this so I could make her life harder. There was a lot of, 'I really appreciate you and I don't want you to feel that I want to leave this family or anything like that'. And I didn't want her to constantly worry about me and pray for me. I didn't want her to feel like she did something wrong. 'You didn't do anything, it's just me'. Because your child leaving religion is just a complete failure in terms of Islam.

And that indeed, in the event, is exactly how Nubia's mother saw it.

Omar's account of his disbelief, which he delivered to his two close friends, was somewhat less circumscribed, something he now regrets. They hadn't seen him in a while and wanted to know if he was okay: 'Omar, is everything all right? How is Ramadan coming along?' 'I'm not fasting', Omar replied, which invited further questioning: 'Why not, is it because of your diabetes?' Omar: 'No'. 'What is it, then?' Omar: 'I have apostatized.' They demanded an explanation and wanted to know where this was coming from. So Omar duly gave them one, but not then over the phone. Instead, he responded later and in writing:

I sent them my reasons for my atheism and I also sent them stuff that I thought was wrong with the religion. I sent it through to them in an email. So the first one was my argument for rejecting God. The second one was the problem I had with Islam. I remember I went all out. I absolutely criticized Muhammad's character and his flaws. I think they were genuinely more upset about that than my rejection of God. They emailed me back and said, 'You know what, we can't believe this is coming from you, especially after your Islamic background'.

In crafting their exit accounts, respondents not only sought to explain—or rather to justify—their apostasy, but also to preempt any possible counter-ripostes. As Nubia testifies above, her chief concern was to forestall the accusation of desertion. She was renouncing *Islam*, not her family: this is what she wanted to communicate to her mother. Maryam, too, was acutely aware of how her apostasy might look from her mother's perspective. And so she needed to neutralize any possible objections or misconceptions straight off the bat. In particular, she didn't want her mother to think she'd done it for 'a freer lifestyle', because she intuitively knew that this is how her mother would read it.

All ex-Muslim personal testimony, both public and private, takes this form. It is explanatory and it is anticipatory. This is especially evident in

Alia's coming out letter to her parents, where she explains that 'the more I read, the less I became convinced that Islam is the "right" religion (if such a thing even exists)'; that 'I cannot follow/worship the god proposed by Islam, or indeed any other religion, as none provide enough evidence for me'; and that 'certain ideas proposed by Islam can never be justified'. Where she also makes it explicit that 'This is the hardest decision I have ever had to make...It wasn't a decision I made overnight, it took me years to make it. I have done my research'; that 'I wish there was an alternative, but there simply isn't...nobody chooses to believe or disbelieve in god/ Islam. I didn't choose to leave, it was an automatic process'; that 'When I was a Muslim I was never happy with it. I spent most of the time pushing all questions to the back of my head and ignoring them. I was so afraid of facing them and accepted any justification available without thinking about it'; and, finally, that 'I still love you all so much and that will never change...I still want to maintain good relations with all of you and continue to see you all...I am still your daughter who will always love you.'

Hence Alia's account reflects a deep sensitivity not just about how her parents and other Muslims would judge her apostasy (in terms of right and wrong), but also about how they would account for it. And how would they account for it? They'd think she had left Islam hastily and without giving it proper consideration; that she had done it deliberately, for any number of degraded worldly motives; that it was a phase; and that it was a personal slight. Or rather, this is how Alia anticipated they would respond.

Alia's sensitivities were universal among respondents. They were all sensitive to how their apostasy would be constructed from within a Muslim perspective. Two legitimizing themes in particular stood out from the interviews: 'leaving Islam wasn't a choice'; and 'I always had doubts':

> If you have a belief in Islam and you were a hardcore, devout Muslim and somebody comes up to you with a list of points that proves Jesus is the son of God and therefore Christianity is correct you're not going to go, 'Oh right, that all makes sense, now I'm a Christian'. You're still going to say, 'Well I don't feel that in my heart and I don't believe it', and in the same way I can't help having come to these beliefs. In the same way a person can't help believing, being a Muslim, I can't help believing now that there isn't a God. (Masood)

> I think I'd always been uncomfortable about the harsher aspects of Islam. (Farhad)

It never occurs to them [Muslims] that disbelief is not really a choice, it just happens, and you can't just decide to believe in God again. So they usually just assume it's for selfish reasons. (Abdullah)

I was always slightly sceptical about the whole idea of heaven and hell anyway. (Manzoor)

I did not want to leave Islam. It's not something I set out to do. I was trying really hard to hold onto it. (Nabilah)

When I was younger I never really gave the question of belief too much deep thought. I partly knew that if I did confront my doubts and conclude that it was all bullshit it would wreck my life. So subconsciously I probably had that in the back of my mind so I went along with it. (Luqman)

I wanted to believe but I just couldn't. It just wasn't in me. I couldn't get my head around a lot of the stuff so I just had to leave. (Farhad)

I've always had doubts that I've always repressed...I lived a lot of years in the dark about Islam on purpose probably subconsciously...I always knew deep down that Islam was probably not quite as pretty as I tried to make it out to be. (Alia)

These two legitimizing motifs also recur with striking frequency in a great deal of online ex-Muslim testimony. And it may well be true, true to their feelings, that ex-Muslims sincerely feel that their apostasy wasn't a choice but an evolution of selfhood over which they had little control and that at some level they'd always felt uncertain in their faith. But it may also reflect their deep and enduring sensitivities to how other Muslims see them or would regard their apostasy.

The persistence with which ex-Muslims insist, in particular, that their apostasy wasn't intentional is, I think, especially revealing: if ex-Muslims are truly convinced that leaving Islam is not wrong and that, indeed, they are morally in the right, then why is it so important to explain so often and so insistently that it wasn't a choice? I address this issue in Chapter 6.

The Context of Disclosure

What were the circumstances in which respondents came out?

In a few instances, respondents came out under pressure. They had said or done something to raise suspicions. And when questioned about this, they ended up admitting to their apostasy, feeling that they had no choice but to do so.

For Ramesh, it was his persistent drinking: this is what first raised the suspicions of his wife. Worried, she confronted him about it and other aspects of his un-Islamic lifestyle: 'She suspected I wasn't Muslim anyway and she asked me one night and I just admitted it. I said, "Yes I don't believe it anymore."'

For Tasnim, it was the loose talk of a confidant: 'I told someone I thought I could trust at college and she was having a discussion about me in a chip shop. My sister's friend heard it and then went and told my sister. My sister asked me, "Do you believe in God?" It's so strange, because I could have said yes, but I said no.'

For Aisha, it was the underhand behaviour of a friend who, on breaking into her Facebook account, saw a record of a text-conversation in which Aisha had spoken about her disbelief. 'She asked me if I was an atheist. I tried to wriggle my way out of it and make a joke, but she's like, "No, I read your Facebook messages". So I told her the truth.'

And for Ahzhar, it was his secret marriage to a non-Muslim woman, for whom he'd left home and his country of birth:

> I told my mum that we'd got married. And she said, 'Oh, did you get a Muslim marriage?' And I don't know why I lied, I said, yes. But my mum knew I was lying. She said, 'You're lying, I can tell you're lying, you didn't do that.' And so I said, 'Actually, you're right, I am lying, I didn't do that, I'm sorry I just don't feel like I need a Muslim marriage because I don't feel like I'm Muslim.

In some cases, respondents had deliberately said or done something so as to create the circumstances under which they could feel they had no choice but to disclose. Mustafa, for example, recalls:

> I remember we were having dinner and I think they [his parents] might have suspected something from all of the questions I had been asking. And, I don't know, something came up and I think the news was on and there was a report about a terrorist bombing or something and my dad was like, 'What are these guys thinking? This is not Islam'. I said something like, 'But dad, if there was no religion then these bombings wouldn't be happening'. And that's when I started telling them about all the stuff that I didn't feel comfortable with. You know, stuff about Islam, various passages in the Quran, certain *hadith*, and my dad said, 'Mustafa, what are you trying to say?' And I just told them I stopped believing. I was like, to be honest, I don't believe in God anymore and in Islam.

Nubia's coming out occurred under similar circumstances, in the context of an argument with her mother: an argument which Nubia herself had orchestrated, in spite of her plan to come out at a later point:

COMING OUT: DISCLOSING APOSTASY

A month before my exams in May I went back home. I had a whole plan about how to tell her...This was supposed to happen midway through my holiday but, I don't know why, the first day I was there I got into a huge argument with her. It just escalated very quickly and it got to a point where she said to me, 'do you believe in God?'

Nubia didn't say a word: 'She had never asked me that before and I just kept quiet, I didn't say anything.' And she didn't have to, because her deliberate and heavy silence said it all.

Luqman had also contrived the circumstances in which he could, as he puts it, 'snap' and announce his apostasy to his immediate family. In the months preceding this, he'd put a lot of effort, a lot of hard work, into being Islamically lax, making sure he was late for prayers and not dressing appropriately. And this all drew heat from his family, as he knew it would, giving him the impetus he needed. He recalls his brother warning him,

'Do you want to wait until you can see hell for yourself before you start doing things?' I argued back and said, 'Where's the evidence?' That is what I said. Where is the evidence that God exists? Where's the evidence that the Quran is the word of God? That was the first time I'd told them in clear terms that I didn't believe it. Not only was I not very religious, but I didn't believe it.

For other respondents, however, the circumstances in which they came out were not of their own choosing, but imposed on them from above. Invariably, it was event or situation which crystallized in their minds not only the abjectness of their lives but also the impossibility of carrying on as they were.

For Salim, that event was Ramadan. In the days preceding it he had renounced Islam. But not with equanimity: indeed all his emotions were running the other way. He felt angry and resentful. Ramadan—and specifically the obligation to fast—served to dramatically focus and intensify those feelings. And so he needed a release: he told his brother.

I said to him, 'Why are we still bloody fasting? It's stupid. It doesn't even make sense'. And my brother was confused. He couldn't comprehend this sort of thing, but I kept on and he was like, 'Stop complaining please', and obviously I was wrong to keep banging on but it was basically my frustration, my, you know, wanting to come out.

Alia similarly disclosed her apostasy to her parents in the month of Ramadan. For Muslims, Ramadan is a month of piety, a chance to reaffirm the bonds of faith and community and to redeem previous acts of impiety. It is a period saturated in religious meaning and symbolism. And so when it came Alia felt an overwhelming feeling of personal encroachment, as though some unbearable weight was pressing down on her. Like Salim, she, too, had reached her limit:

> It was during Ramadan I told them. I had to keep getting up and praying and after a few days I was just so sick to death of it because I don't believe in God and I just can't deal with all this bullshit anymore. I thought I'm going to have to tell them.

And so she did.

Ramadan was also the immediate context of Wahid's disclosure to his mother. He had refused to fast and was refusing even to conceal this. When his mother confronted him, they began to argue and on the back of this:

> I said to my mum, 'My friend, apparently he's going to get married off to this girl and the thing is he doesn't believe in God and she is Muslim. What do you think he should do?' And my mum knew straight away that I was talking about myself. She said, 'That friend of yours should just accept Islam and do it'. And I was like, 'But he can't. He just doesn't believe in it'. And then my mum turned around and was like, 'I know you're speaking from your point of view'.

The Impact of Disclosure

There is a hierarchy of difficulty as regards disclosing apostasy. For ex-Muslims, disclosing to non-Muslim friends is relatively easy, if often mildly frustrating, because they neither fully understand nor particularly care. Disclosing to trusted Muslim friends is more difficult. But the most challenging task is that of telling the immediate family, especially parents. Which is why only less than half of respondents have come out in this context.

Telling the Family and their Reactions

'I was absolutely shitting it', Alia said, remembering the first time—there would be a second and final time later down the line—she came out to her father.

> It took a lot of guts to come out to him. I was hanging around outside his bedroom for ages, thinking, right, I'm going to tell him, I'm going to tell him.

And he walked out and started going down the stairs and I stopped him. I was absolutely terrified and I said, 'Dad, I'm not a Muslim anymore'.

Maryam, describing how she felt when she came out to her mother, was 'adrenalined up'. Which is also an apt description of Luqman's state of mind in the period between telling his brother about his disbelief and having it out with his parents. He didn't think they'd do anything crazy. 'My family are not gangsters or anything, they're religious but they're not violent.' But neither could he quite repress this thought: that they might.

> I was anxious that they would do something. Because, obviously, when someone is extremely upset or angry they do irrational things, that's why honour killings happen. I was conscious of that. So I knew I had to keep the temperature down.

It is indeed indicative of his agitated state that when both his two brothers confronted him about his apostasy the day after he came out Luqman surreptitiously recorded it on his mobile:

> My family is religious enough to support the death penalty for apostates, but obviously in this country [Britain] they can't do anything. I remember talking to my brother about this and I challenged him to go on record and say what he thinks and he did. It's weird, I know. I guess I did that partly because I knew something profound was happening in my life. And I didn't tell anyone what was going on. So I thought, maybe I should record some of this. Because if they do anything to me—you know, if it heats up and they do anything to me—at least there will be a recording.

And Luqman wasn't taking any chances: 'I did upload the recording on the internet—on a hosting site for big files. But I didn't do anything with it and I didn't tell anyone I'd uploaded it.'

Most respondents who came out to their parents and siblings would be able to identify with this. There was anxiety, rooted in an uncertainty over how the family would respond: would they understand? would they be accepting? And there was an element of fear: would they do something rash?

So how *did* they respond in actuality?

● Shock and Hurt

Many respondents said their parents and siblings had reacted with surprise and even shock, as though a terrible catastrophe had befallen the family.

One ex-Muslim, in an online ex-Muslim forum, said that 'I had quite a soft landing, as I had expressed my doubts from the beginning as a kid. So when I finally told them it was not as much as a surprise to them as I thought it would be.' But for the formerly pious, who hadn't fully expressed their doubts, the landing is undoubtedly harder. Omar reported that when he announced his apostasy to his aunts, 'it was a huge shock for them because I was known for my piety.' Masood, who was also esteemed in his family for his piety, similarly said that when he told his sister: 'Her response was, "That's a bit sudden". From her point of view, it must have seemed I was a Muslim one day and then the next day I'm an atheist.' Masood, whose parents remain unaware of his apostasy, says that he had been very effective at concealing his doubts from his sister, as indeed from everyone else.

Even among respondents who had voiced their doubts and left a trail of hints, many said that when it came to fully disclosing their apostasy they had encountered surprise and bafflement. Evidently, it is one thing to be a 'bad Muslim' and quite another to renounce Islam altogether. Aisha, for example, referring to her sister, recalls:

> She kept asking, 'Are you an atheist, are you an atheist, are you an atheist?' I said, 'No, no, no, no', and then I told her that I was and she was like, 'What?' And it came across as a shock. And I'm like, 'Why, you're the one who's been asking me, I thought you already knew, don't be in denial right now'.

In addition to shock, hurt, too, was widely reported among respondents as a common emotional response to their disclosure. About her mother, Nubia had this to say:

> She asked me, 'Do you believe in God?' I didn't say anything. And she was really hurt and it was horrible. It just ended in tears. It was really, really bad. I'd never seen my mum cry in my entire life. She's the strongest woman I know, so to see her cry over that was heart-breaking.

Nubia, not knowing what to say, decided to write a letter, 'describing how I felt'. She left it on her mother's bedside table. But: 'She didn't touch it. For three weeks she didn't touch it. And she wouldn't talk to me.' This went on until Nubia summoned the courage to confront her mother, marching into her bedroom and pleading with her to read the letter:

> And she said, 'Okay, I will read it on my own'. And she read it and then she called me back in. She said, 'What do you want to say to me?' And then I just

poured my heart out and said everything. I don't believe in God, explaining my reasons. And I told her that I didn't want to wear the *hijab*. I don't want to do any of this stuff. I just want to completely disassociate myself from Islam. And to her that was insane. Again with the crying. And there was just this look of complete disbelief on her face, because it must have seemed so sudden to her. I know I asked her a lot of questions and everything but she never in a million years would have thought that it would lead to anything like that. So I can imagine for her the shock. But I really didn't care at that point, I was so suffocated by it, I just wanted to get away from it, by any means. So I knew it would shock her, but I thought she'd get over it. But she didn't.

Wahid says that his mother was similarly distraught when he came out to her. Not, though, at first, because at first 'she had seemed cool with it'. That was in the afternoon. But later in the evening it became clear that she was not cool with it. Indeed, she was very far from being cool with it: 'I'm guessing it must have sunk in, because she was really upset. She was crying, she was angry, she was saying stuff that didn't really make much sense.' Indeed so distraught was she that Wahid was anxious that she might do something stupid: not to him, but to herself: 'I was so worried about my mother that I feared she may develop suicidal thoughts.'

Alia's memory of what happened when she first disclosed her apostasy to her family is 'foggy, because I've tried to block it all out'. But this she can't forget: 'the look of hurt on my mum's face'.

• Anger and Vilification

According to the Prophetic tradition in Islam, there are three modes of forbidding wrong: with the hand, with the tongue and in the heart.[12] Among respondents who had announced their apostasy to family members, no one reported that they had been admonished with the hand. But they all said that they had been admonished with the tongue. And this ranged from gentle admonition to vehement castigation. More often than not, though, admonition from family members took the latter form.

Wahid says that his mother was harshly condemning: 'She attacked my character, she attacked my personality and she attacked my living habits.' Tasnim says that her sister, when she found out, directed her fire not at Tasnim's character but her motives: she accused her of trying to 'ruin' the family. To which Tasnim replied: 'I'd rather die than do that.' Khadija, who is now completely estranged from her family, similarly says of her stepmother: 'She basically accused me of destroying the family. She said

I set out to do it and that I did it on purpose.' Khadija can't and won't forget this: 'This was the day I stopped talking to my stepmum officially and I haven't spoken to her for two years now.' Aisha says that her sister responded to the news of her apostasy by saying, 'You're as bad as a pedophile'. To which Aisha replied: 'Well, wasn't it your Prophet who married a six-year-old?'

Some respondents reported that they had been threatened with social death. Nubia, referring to her mother, remembers:

> She said at some point, 'Well, you can leave the religion, but it would mean losing us'. And she said we'd only do family duties towards you (because in Islam the parent has to look after the children until they are independent). So she's like, I will only do that because Islam says so. I don't want anything to do with you, you're not my daughter.

According to Nubia, her mother also issued a warning:

> She said if you decide to come out and tell everyone about it then I had better face the consequences, because the ruling on apostasy in *shariah* is death. If anyone decides to carry that out I won't stop them. So it really hurt. I didn't imagine my mum would say that. I know she's really religious but she's my mother too.

Abdullah's brother was similarly forthright: 'he told me that he can't be my brother if I'm not a Muslim'. As was Ali's father: 'he said, "well you have 3 years and if you don't adopt the religion of the book in that time then you're not my son anymore."' Kareem says his father had put it this way: 'If God doesn't exist, then neither do you.'

Alia recalls that when she first came out to her father, his initial reaction was to brush her off. He mumbled a few words and left the house to go to the mosque. It wasn't until later in the evening that he confronted her.

> Later that night when he came back from the mosque he called us all downstairs. Then he made me tell mum. He told me to say to her that I'm a *kāfir*. 'Say you're a *kāfir*.' So, I went to my mum, 'I'm a *kāfir*'. And she burst out crying and went ballistic and then tried to beat me and my dad stopped her. My sisters just sat there, crying their eyes out. And my dad was crying and very angry. Then he sent us up to bed.

Alia was not the victim of an honour killing, but it's not overly dramatic to say that something in Alia died that day—the day of her ritual humiliation at the hands of the two people with whom she is most intimately connected, the two people she can't help but love and care about, despite their differences.

- Despair and Self-vilification

Parents, said respondents, were liable to blame themselves for their son's or daughter's apostasy, worrying that they may have permitted them to stray by not being sufficiently strict.

All respondents had anticipated this. And it was a major source of anxiety prior to coming out. Nubia, for example, said of her mother:

> She's going to trace it back to her. She would then say, what did I do wrong? And, the thing is, when we were younger my dad didn't want me and my brothers to go into the English system, to British or American schools. He said that's dangerous and they will grow up and leave us and move to the west. But my mum fought against that and said, no they need to get a good education. And I felt like she would blame herself for having made that decision, for going against my dad. She thought that I had just surrounded myself with non-Muslims and that's why I ended up disobeying her.

Luqman similarly reported that his mother had berated herself for his apostasy: 'She felt she had failed in her duty to bring up a good son.' A good Muslim son. Wahid said exactly the same thing about his own mother: 'She certainly blames herself about my lack of belief.' 'And that's why,' he added, 'I felt really bad and thought she might do something silly. Because she's failed. That's the big thing that hurt me and her.'

Siblings, too, may blame themselves. Referring to her sister, Aisha remarks: 'She said that she had cried herself to sleep many times because she felt like she was actually responsible for my apostasy, that she should have tried to stop it from happening and if I had doubts I should have spoken to her about it first instead of wandering off on my own.'

- Shame, Fear and Denial

Leaving Islam leaves a mark, a stain. It is shameful.[13] And not just for the person who leaves. It is shameful also for the leaver's family, because the stain of apostasy risks marking and contaminating it, too.[14]

Wahid is convinced that this is why his mother responded so hysterically to his apostasy, because were it to go public her failure would be exposed and her reputation in the local community shattered. 'Saving face', says Wahid: 'that's what really matters to her'.

Shame, Yasmin similarly contends, was preeminent among her mother's concerns: 'She said don't ever mention this to anyone.' Judging by the experience of Azhar's immediate family, Yasmin's mother's schedule of concerns was by no means misplaced:

> When my extended family found out that I'm not Muslim they collectively embarrassed my parents for being bad parents. They shamed them and ruined their reputation. They refused to socialize with them and thought that my brothers could be bad influences on their kids. And so my parents had to suffer all of that from their relatives. They, the relatives, don't really understand that it was my choice. I mean I know I'm a blot on my parents, but in the end I did make my own choice to leave Islam, it wasn't them failing as parents. But unfortunately I don't think I will be able to ever make that point loud enough to have them stop.

Luqman, whose family, he says, has concealed his apostasy from the wider Muslim community in which they live, also offers a revealing commentary on the matter of shame. 'It would be extremely shameful for them', he says of his family, 'were other people to find out that their son had left Islam.' So much so that: 'If I went online and said my name is this, my dad is this person, and I've left Islam. If I did that and it became public in the community, that would upset them and they would probably do something crazy.' It is perhaps necessary and instructive to reiterate here that most respondents have not done what Azhar has done and gone fully public about their apostasy.

Some respondents reported that their families had responded to their apostasy as though it were a contagious disease and had sought to warn them about 'infecting' other family members. This, Nubia says, was one of her mother's abiding concerns: 'She said never talk to your brothers because I don't them to get any of this stuff planted in their brain.'

Aisha, paraphrasing her sister, commented: 'She said that I shouldn't be allowed near her children in case I indoctrinate them and turn them into atheists.' Hence it was no accident that Aisha's sister had called her a 'pedophile'. For the pedophile is not only morally depraved, but also the moral and mortal enemy of children: a corrupter of innocence and purity.

Khadija similarly testified that her parents had expressed worry that her apostasy might unhinge other members in the family.

Some respondents said that their apostasy had provoked bewilderment and even disbelief. Maryam says her mother refused or was unable to credit that it is theoretically possible to leave Islam:

I think she seemed quite confused when I told her. For her and of lot of Muslims, Islam isn't just a religion; they think it's like some sort of genetic trait. Because she kept to saying to me, 'I know, but my mum was a Muslim and I'm one so you are too'. But I was like, 'But I don't believe that Muhammad is the prophet of God and so just by that I can't be a Muslim'. She seemed to think it was like being Asian or something.

Manzoor similarly says of his father: 'It's fairly obvious that I don't do anything even remotely Muslim and dad sort of accepts that now. But whether he will ever bring himself to think that I'm not actually one I couldn't tell you.' Yasmin is more certain on the matter of her own father: 'He would still think that I am a Muslim,' despite all the overwhelming evidence to the contrary.

Nabilah says of her mother that she is adamant that no decent right-thinking Muslim can truly leave Islam and that it's only a matter of time before her daughter recovers her senses and returns to the fold:

> She knows that I don't identify as a Muslim anymore. She's not happy about it, but I think the only reason she's okay with it is because in her mind I'm going to go back one day. I personally think she's in denial. When I say God doesn't exist she goes, 'Argh!', like I'm talking nonsense and I'll come to my senses. I don't know, I guess it's almost like telling your parents you're gay. I think maybe it's, oh they'll get over it. She's taking it like that from what I understand, that's her response, as if I told her I'm lesbian and she's like, oh yeah, you'll get over that.

Mustafa says his parents responded in the same way: 'I think for the first year after I told them they thought I was going through a phase. They didn't think that it was going to be something permanent.' Ali also said this: 'My dad said that I'm going through a phase, and he still thinks I'm going through a phase.'

• Repudiation and Resistance

A common order of response, according to respondents, was the accusation of ignorance. The charge, approximately, is that the apostate hasn't adequately thought it through, that they lack a proper understanding of Islam or are devoid of the necessary intellectual resources to make such a momentous decision. This, Wahid recalled, is exactly how his brother responded to his apostasy: 'I was completely honest with him and told him that I don't believe in God. He didn't really care. He was just fine.

He was just, "You know what, you haven't really studied Islam, that's why you're saying all of these things, so it doesn't matter".'

Nubia says her mother wasn't nearly so nonchalant. To her mother, Nubia's disbelief plainly did matter. Very much. But, just like Wahid's brother, she wasn't remotely having it:

> She just kept telling me that I don't know anything about Islam and that I can't make a decision like that unless I've extensively studied Islam. She wanted me literally to be a scholar before I could make a decision. And even then she's like, it's a learning process and you can never really find an answer. That was what she said to me. You can never make a decision.

Luqman's brothers, the day after he had disclosed his apostasy, sought to make the same point: that he was insufficiently knowledgeable about Islam; that he had simply not read enough; and that his decision to apostatize was therefore ill-thought-out. Luqman neglected to mention this in the interview I conducted with him. But it is loudly present in the audio recording he sent me of his brothers' aggressive *dawah* efforts to bring him back to Islam.

Judging from what respondents said, some parents, on first hearing the news of their son's or daughter's apostasy, wonder how such a calamity could have happened. 'They thought I had been hanging around with the wrong group of friends,' Mustafa says. 'And my dad said that many of his friends, back in the 70s and 80s, had similar experiences and many of them were communists and socialists but now none of them are.'

Tasnim's sister, apparently, was similarly unable to countenance the idea that Tasnim's apostasy was predicated on reasons: 'She kept asking me if I was a lesbian and that's why I didn't believe in God.'

Some respondents told me that their parents had refused to acknowledge that their apostasy was actually a decision, linking it instead to demonic possession or mental illness. Abdullah, for example, says that when he told his brother about his apostasy he was met with the following response: 'He tried to tell me how stupid I was and how I was listening to the devil.'

Khadija says: 'My family thinks that I'm crazy. My stepmum told the *imam* everything that had happened. And the *imam* said it sounded like I'd gone crazy. So I was declared like insane.'

Kareem's family drew a similar conclusion: 'They think I'm a nutcase, as if that alone would be enough to sweep aside my confession.'

The implication here, as Abdullah, Khadija and Kareem are fully aware, is obvious: if there is no decision, there can be no reasons. Or, to put it another way, where there is pathology, there is unreason, stupidity, irrationality. If Abdullah, Khadija and Kareem are crazy or demonic, then so, too, is their apostasy.

Respondents also reported that even when their apostasy was taken seriously as a deliberate choice family members were liable to assume that it was necessarily predicated on bad reasons. 'They think that you just want to live a life of sin, that you want to sleep around and get drunk and go hedonist', says Abdullah, referring to his brother and the other Muslims he has come out to. Ali, reflecting on how his family sees his apostasy, says that 'they think you've turned white, that you're trying to be white as in you're trying to drink and do all these sorts of things'. Here, too, the implication is obvious: there can never be any good reasons for renouncing Islam.

Often, the family responds by exerting emotional pressure on the apostate to repent and come back to Islam. Typically, parents or siblings remind them of the essential truth and beauty of Islam, hoping that this will bring them to their senses and make them recant their apostasy. Khadija's recalled that her stepmother:

> would phone me up with advice from the *imam*. I had to read the *sura* of The Cow. I had to read that every night for thirty nights, all of it, every night for thirty nights and then I would believe in Islam again. And I had to read it in Arabic. And then she said, 'Don't just read it, you have to listen to it being recited'. And it has to be in Arabic and I said, 'Why does it have to be in Arabic?' She said, 'It just has to be in Arabic, you know, otherwise it won't work'.

Not uncommonly, the family will shun the apostate, believing that this will shame them into reconsidering their position. And when shunning doesn't work, doesn't bring them back, the family will often redouble its efforts by launching an all-out *dawah* campaign. Which is what happened to Nubia: first the silence, then the interference: 'you must see the *imam*. He will clear up your doubts'. More intrusively still: 'You must go on *umrah*'. Nubia reluctantly agreed to this, making numerous visits to various *imams* and going on *umrah* 'twice in a month'.

Alia's parents, as she relays the story, were especially dogged in their efforts to bring her back. The day after her bruising humiliation at the hands of her father—'say you're a *kāfir*'—her grandparents came round.

Alia's father had told them what happened the day before and they insisted Alia pray, closely watching her perform the ritual cleansing before the prayer. They also insisted that they read the Quran together and for the rest of Ramadan Alia was made to observe the daily ritual prayers. 'They were trying to bring me back to Islam, basically.' Alia went along with this and for nearly a year she managed to convince her parents that she had returned to Islam.

Then, just after graduating, Alia decided to come out again, because she couldn't take the prospect of moving back home and living the lie. But she couldn't do it face-to-face. So she wrote her parents a letter instead, explaining why she couldn't be a Muslim anymore. It was a long letter and in it she told them that leaving Islam had been the hardest decision she'd ever had to make, that she'd carefully thought it through and that she was sorry for the pain she would cause. But there was no other way. 'I can't live a lie for the rest of my life.' And then she patiently set out her position. Her tone was apologetic and regretful. But she was also firm, insisting that 'I have a right to believe what I want' and that she would not be returning home after graduating from university. 'I want my independence,' she told them. Alia ended by clarifying that none of this meant that she was turning her back on her family and that she still loved them and hoped that they could see past their differences and remain close. 'You are all still my lovely family who mean the world to me,' she told them as she signed off. What Alia omitted to say in the letter was that she had a boyfriend and that they were very much in love.

It was a difficult letter to write. Alia spent over a week drafting and rewriting it, all the while crying and fretting over how her parents would take it. She thought about sending it through the post, but what if it didn't arrive? And what if her father somehow contrived not to open it? She decided to send it via email instead. That would be safer, more certain. She remembers calling her father just after she sent it, saying, 'Dad, I've sent you an email, it's really important, can you please read it'. He called her back later that evening. There was a lot of shouting and crying. Alia's father implored her to come home, saying that the family would accept her no matter what she believed. She countered by inquiring, 'What if I want to do things that aren't Islamic?' Then she came clean about Stephen, the man she'd been living with for the past year. 'He was very angry and started saying you're shit, you're shit, you're shit over and over again.' She couldn't listen to this, so she terminated the call and switched off her phone. It was a tense evening: 'I was so scared he might come up to the house and try and take me and whenever the phone rang or when someone knocked at the door I was just petrified.' In the event, he didn't come and the next day he called to apologize and encouraged Alia to come home so that they could talk properly. Alia said, 'Ok, let's talk, but I'm not moving back home'.

So they talked and Alia cracked. She returned home. Her aunt had been very persuasive. 'What you are doing,' she warned Alia, 'will destroy the chances of your sisters ever getting married, you're going to wreck their lives, you should come back home so people don't start thinking that we are a bad family.'

Not long after this, Alia received an ultimatum. 'Alia,' her father said, 'if you don't want to come back to Islam, we can't have you here.' 'He said, "You've got a year to decide, and if you're not back within a year we don't know what's going to happen". And then a year suddenly changed into the weekend, the weekend on Eid, and he goes to me, "If you're not a Muslim by that weekend we're going to kick you out".' Alia felt that she had no choice and so the day before Eid she left. And this time it would be for good.

I asked Alia if she had any regrets. She said no, but that she deeply misses her brother and sisters: 'They're so important to me and they've always accepted me for who I am and losing them was the hardest thing about it all.'

- Protective Concern

Some respondents reported that their apostasy, as well as provoking shock and condemnation, had also aroused feelings of protective concern in family members.

Omar remembers his wife insisting that he not go public with his apostasy. Not primarily because of the shame of it, but because of how it would impact on their marriage:

She panicked initially. And then she had her own internal struggle because in Islam if one partner leaves the religion the marriage is over. She knew that, she was aware of that, and she said to me, 'Don't tell anyone. Please don't broadcast this'.

Maryam says her mother had made the same plea:

After telling my mum she said don't tell your dad and don't tell anyone else in the community. Not because she wants me to lie, but she said I just don't want them thinking that you're a bad person from it. Or having the wrong idea and thinking that you wanted to leave the religion just so you could go and sleep around or something.

Luqman also suspects that his family's denial about his apostasy is related in part to residual paternalistic feelings toward him: 'They probably, either subconsciously or consciously, want to protect me from the mob, if there ever was one.'

- Acceptance

Some family members actually surprise the apostate: by accepting their apostasy. Alia's siblings, for example and in marked contrast to her parents, were sympathetic, telling her shortly after she had left, via text message, 'It's okay, you're still our big sister and we understand and we still love you'.

Wahid was similarly surprised and gladdened by how his sisters reacted to his coming out: 'They were like really okay with it. In fact it's changed nothing between us. I thought they would have made a fuss, but they were just, "Oh, okay"'. Referring to his eldest sister, who is married with children, Wahid says 'she calls me, we still do the same things, like she still wants me to be close to her children'.

Masood reports that his two sisters, despite their initial surprise, were also accepting. As was Amir's father, who 'is very liberal and shares my views fortunately'.

Omar's uncle, exceptionally, was not just accepting but positively approving:

He's known in my family for being a rabble rouser. And he's an atheist. He pulled the Carlsberg out of the fridge and we sat down and had a good old laugh. We talked for hours and he said, 'You know what, I knew you would come out of that stupid Islamic phase'. And he said, 'You know what, I'm so glad it's happened'.

As an atheist himself, Omar's uncle clearly saw Omar's apostasy as in some way vindicating.

Telling Muslim Friends and Their Reactions

Disclosing apostasy to Muslim friends is an altogether different proposition from disclosing it to family members. For a start, it is easier to do, or at least certainly easier to contemplate, because losing a friend isn't the same as losing a family member. Which in part explains why most respondents did it: because they were able to. Because they could.

Friends, unlike family members, are apt to be calmer on hearing the news. But not necessarily accommodating. Indeed more often than not they were condemning, often using measured but firm language to express their concern and disapproval.

Just as parents are liable to think that their daughter's or son's apostasy is fundamentally misconceived, friends too are prone to mount the same accusation. Mustafa, referring to a confidant, recalls: 'He said something like, you know, I hadn't given it enough thought and if I'd read the Quran properly I would know that I was wrong. He basically thought that I was stupid not to believe in God.'

Masood, too, had come up against this accusation. He had just announced his apostasy for the first time—in an online Muslim forum. Of those who responded to his coming out post, Masood says, 'they didn't accept that I had any knowledge of Islam... they think you must not have understood it or that you should have prayed more'. This annoyed him. But not as much as this:

> They didn't even accept that I used to be a Muslim or that I was even devout. I felt really angry that in a sense they were denying what was such a major part of my life and the person that shaped me as the person I now am. Yeah, it's like, well how dare you, you don't fucking know me, how dare you say I wasn't a Muslim.

As hurtful as it was, it wasn't entirely unexpected. But the pity was:

> There was a lot of anger in response, but there was also much sadness, mostly from the female members of the site, along the line of 'I will pray for you' or 'I hope you come back to the right path' and so on. I knew that they would turn against me. But I wasn't ready for them to feel sorry for me. I didn't expect that.

And it irritated the hell out of him, because of what it implied. It wasn't pitiful what he had done and neither was he. Or so Masood felt.

Aisha was similarly wounded by the reaction of her two best friends to her apostasy, one of whom responded by saying 'you are ignorant, you are ignorant, you are ignorant', while the other insisted that Aisha rethink and return to the path of righteousness:

She wanted an explanation behind why I left, so I gave her my reasons, but, and I could tell from her face that she wasn't really listening, she didn't exactly get it because she thought that it was going to be some petty reason and that it was just a passing phase that I'm going through. And later on we were talking on Blackberry Messenger and just out of the blue she's like, 'Come back to Islam'. And then she said, 'I know you still believe deep down, because when you die you know what's going to happen. Turn back to Islam, you know it's the truth.'

'It was the most stupid thing anybody's ever written to me in my whole life,' Aisha says of that last remark. Which is probably an exaggeration, but it is nonetheless indicative of the intensity of her exasperation at her friend's lack of understanding. Aisha's had clearly expected more from her: not approval, she wasn't expecting that; but at least a spark of empathy.

When it became obvious that Aisha was firmly set on the unrighteous path, most of her friends abandoned her. As did Abdullah's:

Most people initially were just like okay it's weird but you're going to come back to the faith so I don't care. I'm still going to be friends with you for a while and that's always with the assumption that I'd made a mistake and they could talk me out of it and once they realized they can't talk me out of it then that's when it starts bothering them more and when they start making threats and that's when I got pretty much estranged from my social circle.

Omar has also become estranged from his friends, 99 per cent of whom—this is Omar's calculation—'are all hardcore Muslims'. This has been a difficult transition, especially for someone as outgoing and charismatic as Omar. Most difficult of all has been adjusting to the loss of his two life-long friends. This happened a few years ago now, but the wound is still raw. Their first reaction to Omar's apostasy was to implore him to reconsider. Having failed on that front, they then resorted to making veiled threats, bringing up the issue of his marriage:

They said you owe us an explanation...And then they dropped one on me. 'Oh, what about your wife, what about your kids, do you know that technically you are not married?' I said, 'Yeah, I know, so what?' 'What difference does that make to me', I said, 'that doctrine, that stipulation means nothing to me'. As far as I am concerned I'm married secularly under common law.

Once again they implored him to reconsider and once again Omar refused: 'I said, "There is nothing to discuss. What is it that you can possibly say to me that will convince me otherwise?'" And once again they raised the subject of marriage:

> They kept honing in on it—that you are not married and what they were trying to do was shift the burden now to my wife, that she is now living in sin. They were trying to guilt-trip me, but the thing is, I don't believe in sin, that doesn't register with me anymore so this is a pointless argument. It's pointless saying to me your wife's living in sin. Who cares? I said, 'Why don't you ring my wife and you tell her that? And let's see what she has to say to you'. She would just basically tell them to fuck off. 'It's none of your business, it's between me and my husband.'

Not long after this Omar's two friends sent him an email. It said, 'As of today, as of this moment, we are no longer friends.' It was their response to Omar's letter, the one in which he 'went all out', defending his reasons for leaving Islam.

Nubia, relaying an almost identical story, says:

> I told my best friend who's also Sudanese and who I've known since I was three. I've known her for a long time and I trust her. So I told her straight up I don't believe in all of this. And she decided not to talk to me, as if I'm some horrible influence apparently. When I started having doubts I always talked to her. And every time I'd tell her something she would be like, 'Oh, you'll find the answer'. At that point it was mild, it wasn't anything as dangerous as leaving the religion. It was just little questions. And then when I just finally told her that I don't believe in God anymore at first she tried to convince me, just look more into it, blah, blah, blah. Every time she said that I was like, 'This is not going to work, I've made up my mind.' And that's when she said I don't want to be friends. She wasn't really mean about it, she was just like, 'I can't have someone like that in my life'. Because we were quite close, so she was like, 'I'm sorry'. She said we're too different now, the way we think and everything.

Only a small number of respondents said their Muslim friends had responded positively to their apostasy and most reported that far from deepening friendships and putting them on a more sincere footing, disclosure in fact weakened, if not destroyed, them.

Taking It Back: Regret and Recantation

Alia did it, Nubia did it and so did Wahid: they all took it back or tried taking it back. No sooner had they voiced their apostasy than they had *unvoiced* it. It wasn't principled: they didn't take it back for moral or intellectual reasons. They didn't take it back because they had had second thoughts about their decision to leave Islam. Nor was it pragmatic: they didn't take it back out of self-interest or to improve their situation. Rather, they took it back because they felt guilty. It was that straightforward. It was an emotional decision; a decision of the heart. They took it back because they saw just how distraught and wounded their family was on hearing the news of their apostasy and because they urgently wanted to undo the wound they had inflicted on them. They took it back out of love for and loyalty to their families.

Alia, Nubia and Wahid all said the same thing: that they couldn't bear the look of hurt on their mothers' face when they made their disclosure.

Alia, referring to the first time she came out to her parents, says that she was 'emotionally blackmailed' into 'taking back everything I said'. 'I just couldn't take the look of hurt on my mum's face,' she recalls, 'so I took it all back and told her I will be a Muslim again'. The day before Alia was a lowly *kāfir*. But now that was to be forgotten. Now she was a Muslim again. If it had been humiliating for Alia to say that she was a *kāfir*, it was doubly humiliating now to go back on that and say what she knew to be a manifest falsehood: that she was a Muslim.

Wahid didn't care about the humiliation of taking it back: he just cared about the emotional well-being of his mother. She had not responded well to the news of his apostasy. Indeed, she responded altogether badly. So Wahid contrived to take it back, insisting to his mother that the 'friend' who was due to marry but had fallen into disbelief really did exist. She didn't buy it, though. 'I know you're lying', she told her son. Looking back on his decision to come out to his mother Wahid says, 'I felt extremely regretful,' adding 'it is the one part of my story I still regret'.

Nubia's mother, by contrast, did buy it:

> I felt really guilty just seeing my mum in so much pain. And I'm affecting my whole family. My mum said that because of this she'd made a mistake by sending me to London to live alone and she said that she'd keep my brothers in Sudan instead of sending them abroad for their education. I felt like I was sabotaging their future. I just felt like a complete idiot and I thought, I haven't thought this through and I should have known this was going to happen. And I saw it through for three days and after that I sat her down again and said, 'You know what, you actually have a point, I don't know enough about Islam. I think I should look more into it'. And she said she'd

take me to scholars and *imams* to try to convince me because she didn't know enough about Islam herself so she couldn't argue with me. And that's what we did when we went to *umrah*. We did *umrah* and I would speak to like *sheikhs* and stuff. I just pretended I was convinced but really it didn't make any difference to me. I just thought I'll keep pretending until I'm independent and then I don't know what the fuck I'm gonna do.

Nubia says that after completing her second *umrah* she had done enough to convince her mother that 'I'd completely gone back to being a Muslim'.

The Paradoxes of Disclosure

For many respondents, coming out is freeing. It is as though a great weight has been lifted from their shoulders. For months, and in some cases even for years, they had thought about doing it, ruminating back and forth on how they would do it and how it would be received. When it came to the eve of their coming out they could think of little else, focusing all their energies on psyching themselves up for it and preparing for the fallout. And so when they did it, it came as an immense relief. This was true even when it went badly, because it was now out there, because it was *happening* and they didn't have to second-guess anymore. As Luqman said of the day of his coming out, 'it was kind of a relief actually, I felt finally that the moment has arrived'. And there was relief, too, in knowing that from now on there would be no vast secret to protect and to fret over. Indeed, from now on they could finally be true to themselves—and what a joy that felt.

But respondents had also at the same time felt something else, equally intensely. They had felt pain and sorrow. They had let down and hurt their loved ones. And they wished they hadn't. But they couldn't unsay what they had said, even though some tried.

Coming out is paradoxical in another sense. It is meant to be liberating. It says 'I am not this person anymore' and 'this is not how I want to live my life' and 'please accept me for who I am'. And it is liberating, because it releases the weight of living a lie. But it is only a temporary liberation, since all too often disclosure is met not with understanding or equanimity, but impassioned resistance and far from altering familial and communal expectations in favour of the apostate it serves only to reawaken and inflame them to their detriment. So instead of paving the way for leaving Islam, disclosure can presage an ever greater entanglement in its life-world. Or even a return to the closet, which is the subject of the next chapter.

5

STAYING IN

CONCEALING APOSTASY

Some people say, 'We believe in God and the Last Day,' when really they do not believe. They seek to deceive God and the believers but they only deceive themselves, though they do not realize it. There is a disease in their hearts, to which God has added more: agonizing torment awaits them for their persistent lying... When it is said to them, 'Believe, as the others believe,' they say, 'Should we believe as the fools do?' but they are the fools, though they do not know it. When they meet the believers, they say, 'We believe,' but when they are alone with their evil ones, they say, 'We're really with you; we were only mocking'.... they are not rightly guided.

The Quran, 2: 8–10, 13–14, 16 (2004, p. 5)

There is hardly a legitimate everyday vocation or relationship whose performers do not engage in concealed practices which are incompatible with fostered impressions.

Erving Goffman,
The Presentation of Self in Everyday Life (London: Penguin, 1959), p. 71.

'Where's the intimacy?' That's what gets her crying every time. 'Where is the intimacy,' she says, 'when there is such a secret?'

Philip Roth,
The Human Stain (London: Jonathan Cape, 2000), p. 178.

THE APOSTATES

The Deceivers and the Deceived

In his brilliantly acute study of stigma, Erving Goffman says of those in possession of 'an attribute that is deeply discrediting'[1] that if their 'differentness is not immediately apparent' the issue is 'not that of managing tension generated during social contacts, but rather that of managing information about [their] failing'.[2] For the 'discreditable' person, whose stigma is hidden but always at risk of being discovered, the issue is: 'To display or not to display; to tell or not to tell; to let on or not to let on; to lie or not to lie; and in each case, to whom, how, when, and where.'[3] Whereas the last chapter addressed the dynamics of the disclosure of apostasy, this chapter looks at its concealment, focusing in particular on the avowed motives behind it, how it is performed and with what consequences. To not display, to not tell, to not let on: this is the theme in what follows.[4]

At the time at which I interviewed respondents, just over half were living in the closet. Outwardly they profess belief in Islam and identify as Muslims, but inwardly, and to a small group of select confidants, they are apostates: they do not believe in Islam nor identify as Muslims. They are engaged in 'persistent lying', in deception and dissimulation. And not just any kind of lying. They are not lying about small things. On the contrary, they are lying about a very large thing, a thing of fundamental importance: namely, their core self. They are lying about their 'true' identity, as they see and feel it. Or, to put in more neutral language, they are engaged in 'passing': the act of concealing a stigmatized identity.[5] And their stigma is their disbelief. Not by their own lights. By their own lights, their disbelief, far from being a stigma, is a sign of intellectual discernment or even sanity—a sound response to how the world is: namely, godless. But, by the lights of most Muslims, disbelief is an unqualified stigma: an 'attribute', in Goffman's phrasing, which is indeed 'deeply discrediting'. So discrediting and shameful in fact that they feel compelled to conceal it and pass as believers.

And to whom are they lying or passing? Not, *pace* the Quran, to God, for they do not believe in his existence. Not now. Not anymore. Rather, they are lying to those who matter most to them: to their kin. And, pre-eminently, to their parents or a parent: to the two people or person whose censure and rejection they most fear and whose loss to them or suffering would cause them unparalleled grief and torment. And, also, to the wider *ummah* of Muslim believers, whose negative judgment and skeptical curiosity they would rather escape. Closeted apostates are thus not only engaged in what William Ian Miller describes as 'big faking'—that is, lying or faking about 'essential aspects of identity';[6] they are also *Faking It*, to annex the title of Miller's study, in front of the people with whom they are most intimate, in whom they most trust and on whom they most depend: namely, their family.

The Great Mistake

In his memoir *Joseph Anton*, Salman Rushdie recalls that one of the lowest moments during 'the *fatwa* years'—on 14 February 1989 Ayatollah Khomeini, the then Supreme Leader of Iran, issued a religious edict declaring *The Satanic Verses*, Rushdie's fourth novel, blasphemous and calling for Rushdie's murder—was when he publicly declared himself to be a Muslim. He had been in hiding for over two years and his life was in turmoil. He was depressed and desperate. So when the offer came he took it. A group of 'heavyweight' Muslim intellectuals—Rushdie's inverted commas—had convened in London to discuss his plight. They would launch a worldwide campaign to lay the *fatwa* issue to rest, but in return Rushdie would have to publicly proclaim his fidelity to Islam. Otherwise, all bets would be off. And so, 'trembling with misery', he signed the document which had been prepared for him. A week later, Rushdie wrote an article, published in both the *New York Times* and the *Times* of London, in which he announced:

> I should like, however, to say something about my decision to affirm the two central tenets of Islam—the oneness of God and the genuineness of the prophecy of the Prophet Muhammad—and thus to enter into the body of Islam after a lifetime spent outside it...I have been finding my own way towards an intellectual understanding of religion, and religion for me has always meant Islam. That journey is by no means over. I am certainly not a good Muslim. But I am able now to say that I am a Muslim; it is a source of happiness to say that I am now inside, and a part of, the community whose values have always been closest to my heart. In the past I described the furore over *The Satanic Verses* as a family quarrel. Well, I'm now inside the family, and now Muslims can talk to Muslims and continue the process of reconciliation that began with my Christmas Eve meeting with six Muslim scholars.[7]

It was all lies. As Rushdie wrote in *Joseph Anton*, he was 'a man without religion pretending to be a religious man'. And this made him feel deeply ashamed, because it was a betrayal of who he was and all that he believed in.

Rushdie's case was unique: a foreign head of state had offered a bounty in his own name as a reward for the murder of a British national. That had never happened before.[8] But in lying about his faith in order to save his own skin, Rushdie was joining a long line of persecuted men and women throughout history, who, under threat of death, had to lie about their religious confederation. In the late Ottoman Empire, for example, it was common for Christians to publicly proclaim their conversion to Islam, all the while practising their true religion in the privacy of their homes.[9]

Among the closeted apostates I interviewed, no one is living in fear for their lives. This isn't why they're in the closet. It isn't the sword of Islam they're afraid of. They did not write *The Satanic Verses*. They are not living in the late Ottoman Empire. Nor are they living in present-day Saudi Arabia, Sudan or Yemen (not to mention a number of other Muslim-majority countries), where the punishment for apostasy is death and where religious vigilantes police blasphemy and religious deviation with impunity.[10] Rather, it is the sting of stigma. And rejection and disownment: having to say goodbye to their loved ones and having to go it alone without their support. And hurting their families, too. This is what scares them.

Motives for Concealment

All closeted respondents confronted the catch-22 of disclosure: to display or not to display? That was the question they needed to decide. They felt the weight of this. They knew what was at stake and that how they answered it would shape their lives forever. To come out and face the miserable prospect of censure and even ostracism. Or to not come out and face the no less miserable prospect of entrapment. Closeted respondents chose the latter. Their reasons, as they understood and relayed them, can be categorized under the following three broad concerns.

Protective Concern

Many closeted respondents said they did it out of protective concern for their families: they didn't want to hurt them. Most of all, they didn't want to hurt their parents. Coming out, they were convinced, would inflict not just hurt, but terrible pain and torment. And shock and even despair. So they resolved to keep their apostasy hidden: for the greater good of their parents and families. And that, indeed, was the language in which they expressed it: the language of loyalty—loyalty to blood, to family, to the people they were inescapably bound to. This is certainly how Masood frames it:

> I have considered it, but I keep remembering my mum's reaction to a guy she really liked on some TV programme she watches. He speaks a lot of sense and then it turned out that he wasn't a Muslim, although he has an Arabic name. And for her it was almost like a personal betrayal and she was heartbroken over it. I was like, this is a stranger that you happen to like on the television, fucking hell, what are you going to do when I tell you that?

And Masood's father? How would he react to Masood's apostasy? 'With a heart attack probably'.

Farhad invokes the same anatomical imagery. Were he to come out to his mother, he is certain that it would 'break her heart'. Elaborating on this, he comments:

> It would completely destroy her. I know she would just break down if I told her. Because if I don't believe she sincerely believes that I will burn in hell forever and obviously that would upset her a lot.

Amir, too, is convinced that his mother would respond badly if she were to discover his apostasy. He has told his father and he was accepting. Indeed, he was supportive: 'He is very liberal and shares my views fortunately.' But his mother isn't like his father. His mother is pious. She would never ask him to leave because of his apostasy. He is sure of that: 'she nor anyone in my family will ever disown me'. But Amir is certain that she would be greatly wounded by it and that is reason enough for him not to tell her.

Salim, referring to his mother, echoes this:

> I've never told her that I don't believe, not because she would kick me out, not because I face danger, none of that. It's just because she wouldn't be able to handle it. She would be thinking my kid isn't going to heaven.

Hanif, who lives with his family in an area where the 'the majority of people are Pakistani or Bangladeshi Muslims' and where 'there's a lot of pressure from the community to be religious and to know about your religion', is also wary of hurting his parents, but for a different reason: he doesn't want to shame them or have them berate themselves for failing to raise a 'good Muslim' son. So he lies to them. And he lies to others, too: not necessarily or always to spare their feelings, but because that way his parents won't possibly find out:

> I think the only thing that stops me from coming out to everyone is my parents. If my parents weren't around and if it was just my sisters I think I would just tell them, whereas I really don't in myself want to disappoint my parents.

So dedicated is Hanif to not disappointing his parents that when they propositioned him to marry a Muslim woman of their choosing he willingly went along with this. 'I kind of let myself get pressured into getting married,' he told me. He knew exactly what this would mean: that it would entrap him yet further in a life-world from which he was already deeply estranged. But he did it anyway, because he didn't want to upset his parents.

Like Hanif, Omar is also living the lie, but not to his family, who all know about his disbelief. He wishes that his mother *didn't* know, but she does and nothing can erase that or the regret he now feels about telling her. His two former best friends also know. But no one else does:

> I have to acknowledge that, look, I live in Bradford, okay. I live in the heart of a Muslim community. I can't go around blaspheming and swearing at Muhammad or openly declaring my apostasy to people I don't know or shouting from the rooftop I'm an apostate. It's not going to happen. If I want to live as an open apostate then I have to move, I have to accept that, I have to move from this community, I can't live here.

For Omar, concealing his apostasy from this wider community isn't about protecting the sensitivities of other Muslims; it is about protecting his own family and especially his children from the censure that would inevitably be targeted at them were his apostasy to be exposed. 'Have my kids ridiculed at school, my wife ridiculed by the community? No. So it's to safeguard them really.'

For some closeted respondents, staying closeted is about not wanting to inflict even more pain and suffering on the family. Masood mentioned this, recalling that as a teenager he'd put his parents through much worry and turmoil. He would go out drinking and return home messed up. And he did a lot of that. Weed, too. So he didn't want to inflict any additional pain on them: 'It just feels like I've already put them through too much to sort of unload this on them now.'

Hanif said something similar: not about himself messing up, although he had done plenty of that away from home at university, but about his sister messing up. And what was her offence? It wasn't getting wasted or getting high. It was marrying a white dude. It didn't even matter that he was a convert to Islam. He was white. And Hanif's family didn't approve, found it shameful. So Hanif didn't—and doesn't—want to be a cause of yet more disappointment for his much bedevilled and long-suffering parents. He put it like this: 'I had an arranged marriage according to my parents because I felt a bit guilty about my sister and what she had done'.

Sensitivity to existing pain thresholds was also a consideration in Alia's coming out and very nearly derailed it:

> There was no choice, either I tell them or I have to pretend to be a Muslim and I know that's not going to happen because I can't do that. But towards the end of university something happed that nearly destroyed everything. My cousin fell out of a second-storey window when she was about two years old and fell straight onto a concrete floor and she had to go to hospital. And I was thinking if she doesn't get better, if something happens to her, I can't tell my parents because they can't go through both those things at the time same time. I couldn't do that to them.

Alia's cousin miraculously survived with minor injuries. But had she not, it would have undoubtedly prolonged Alia's coming out. Or rather, prolonged it even further.

Self-Protective Concern

Adrienne Rich declares, with characteristic bluntness, that 'the liar is afraid'.[11] This is certainly true of many closeted respondents. They are fearful: fearful that their secret may hurt those closest to them. But they are also fearful that those closest to them, on discovering their secret, may in turn hurt them: that they themselves will be made to suffer. They anticipate that they will be censured or, worse, rejected.

This was one of Farhad's concerns: that not only would disclosure irreparably scar his mother, but that it would also 'make my life a lot more difficult because my family probably wouldn't accept me'. For Tasnim it is the primary concern:

> I'm willing to live in silence and let them think I'm a certain person and that I believe in God. I was watching this episode of Grey's Anatomy and it was weird. Because there's this character who's a lesbian and she's marrying this other

woman and her mother is very Catholic and Christian. There was a scene between her and her mum and the mother was saying she wouldn't go to her wedding. She was saying to her daughter that it's devastating to know that I brought up a child who'd go to hell. I think that really hit home because I realized that's how my own family would feel about me. I wasn't willing to go through that. Because I know I wouldn't be able to keep in touch with them.

Amir, too, expressed concern that if he announced his apostasy to his friends they would reject him:

I have many close friendships that have existed before my apostasy. That is why I don't want to come out. Muslims really look down on people that leave the faith. I am afraid I will lose many friends if I come out.

For Nubia, whose friends are mainly non-Muslims, the issue isn't about losing friends; it's about attracting the wrong kind of attention. Recalling a conversation with a girl who had removed her *hijab* at the same time as she had, Nubia says the question of motives came up and that after some probing on Nubia's part the girl told her that 'her family wasn't that strict' and that 'she felt that she didn't need to wear it anymore'. But, the girl added, 'she was still a Muslim'. 'I'm still a Muslim'. On hearing this Nubia's internal voice roared into life and told her not to do it: 'don't tell her'. And so she didn't: 'I just lied and said, yeah, same thing.' 'I just felt,' Nubia remembers, 'like I'd be judged.' That she'd be judged if she didn't lie, that the truth would condemn her.

Maryam is similarly sensitive to this possibility. So she tries to preempt it. Referring to her Muslim friends, she says: 'I try not to talk about religion with them for the main reason that I just don't want them thinking that I'm a bad person for it. I don't want to be judged solely on the fact that I left Islam.'

Some respondents said that not only did they not want to be negatively judged; they also did not want to be questioned, probed, pressed. They knew that if other Muslims learned of their apostasy it would provoke curiosity and inquiry. They knew that they would be called to account. And sometimes they just didn't want to give one. Not just because their account would in all likelihood be rejected and subject to critical challenge, but because accounting, with all its elaborate throat-clearings, scene-setting and contextualization, is a truly effortful activity. And on some occasions they didn't have the requisite strength or patience to engage in it. So they opted for the tranquility of not accounting. Masood explains it in these terms:

I realize that if I do happen across someone who knows me as a Muslim then I would have to go into that and I don't want to do that because it's just so mentally exhausting to keep justifying yourself. Instead of saying accept me as I am, the same way I accept you as a Muslim, you are wanting me to justify why I've given up that previous position. I just don't want to get into all those arguments.

Abdullah similarly confessed to feeling burned out by all the accounting. Burned out and bored by it, given how many times he has had to explain and justify himself to his friends.

Necessity

Some closeted respondents said that disclosing their apostasy was simply unnecessary. Their lives in the closet were eminently livable. They did not feel overly constricted. Family life was okay. It wasn't suffocating. They had a degree of freedom. So they had no reason to disclose. Indeed it would only bring unnecessary pain, with little compensatory advantage. Altogether, it would be a bad thing.

Salim says that because his mother is liberal and relatively lax 'the question of Islam doesn't really come up'. He does as he likes within reason and she rarely, if ever, asks him to pray. 'I don't see the need of telling her,' he said, adding, 'I don't need to shake her world.'

Mustafa speaks in virtually identical terms about the two years he spent in the closet before coming out to his parents:

I didn't feel the need to. I didn't think that there was any point in telling my parents because it never affected my lifestyle. My parents never told me to pray, they never told me that I should fast or go to the mosque or not listen to certain types of music.

Indeed, as Mustafa remarks, 'it was easy *not* to tell them'. But had it gone the other way, and had it not been easy not to tell them—had his parents, that is, been strict and demanded he become more observant— he thinks for certain that remaining closeted would have been impossible for him: 'I wouldn't have been able to take it for more than a month.' And when, after his two years in the closet, Mustafa did decide to come out to his parents it was because he wanted to, and not because he needed to: 'there was nothing that *made* me tell them'.

Among respondents who reported that it wasn't necessary to come out to their parents, most issued an important qualification: namely, that it wasn't necessary right now. But at some point further into the future, they acknowledged, it might well be. But not now; now they had breathing space. They didn't feel overly cramped; they could be themselves, more or less, most of the time. Among those who said this, there were two reasons why they were able to say it: they were either living away from home at the time or their family hadn't yet embarked on finding them a marriage partner. Nubia, for example, doesn't live with her mother. Nubia, indeed, isn't even living on the same continent as her mother. She is living, instead, in a house with secular non-Muslims. So Nubia is free to live a life beyond Islam, not all of the time, but most of it. For now, that is. And Nubia is aware of the temporality of it and that the issue of disclosure will not go away, that there will be a reckoning with it—again—at some point in her future:

> I think unless I absolutely have to tell her, where it is just impossible for me to go on with my life without telling her or I can't hide it anymore for whatever reason, then yes, I'll tell her. But I'll keep it a secret for as long as I can, or unless she finds out one way or another. But until then I think I should just keep pretending.

Abdullah, who is also living away from home at university, feels the same way:

> Right now, they [his parents] know I don't practise and they leave me be, probably thinking that I will become 'straight' on my own. So I see no reason to tell them I'm not a Muslim any more. But if push comes to shove and they try to force Islam on me, as much as I care for them, I'm going to have to tell them. I'm not going to give up my freedom.

When Wahid and Maryam came out to their mothers, the catalyst for it was the prospect of marriage. Farhad thinks that this may well be the catalyst for him, too: 'If I get married to a Muslim I'm in it for real.' So Farhad, like Nubia and Abdullah, is also playing a waiting game.

Another way in which respondents conveyed the senselessness of disclosure was by insisting that potential confidants just wouldn't get it: that they wouldn't be able or willing to understand what was being disclosed to them. Abdullah says:

> For me I knew I could never tell my parents because it was basically my parents' whole life and they would never even contemplate anyone leaving Islam. It's a totally alien concept to them. They would never understand and I would never be able to explain to them. And I can barely speak my mother

tongue [Pashto] so I wouldn't be able to explain it properly and express my emotions.

Farhad, echoing this, says of his mother:

I don't think she would understand because she's been brought up in Islam from an early age. That's all she's ever known, that's all she's ever believed and for me to tell her that I don't believe, that I don't believe in Islam, that I don't believe in God, I don't think she would even understand what all that is. When I was younger, she was always telling me that everybody needs a religion, that everybody has a religion. I don't think she even knows what atheism is. I don't think she'd understand where I'm coming from or that I could even explain it to her since my Bengali isn't good enough to explain those sorts of things to her.

Methods of Concealment

How do closeted respondents manage their 'discreditable' identity as apostates and present a suitable non-disbelieving front? How, that is, do they conceal or play down the *haram* self and pass as believers? In a variety of ways: by camouflaging, covering, and retreating.

Camouflaging

One way in which closeted respondents conceal their apostasy is by developing a public persona which they can plausibly claim as their own and behind which they can hide. The important thing to notice about this persona is where it morally positions the person who adopts it: that is, squarely within the bounds of Islam. It is a claim of membership of and belonging to the *ummah* of Muslim believers. More precisely, it is a counter-claim and this is what it asserts: 'your doubts about me are wrong, I am still a Muslim'.

In trying either to preempt suspicion about their faith commitment or to rationalize any impious behaviour for which they could be held accountable, closeted respondents adopt one or more of the following personae: the lazy Muslim; the liberal Muslim; the irreverent Muslim; the confused Muslim; and the pious Muslim.

• The Lazy Muslim

This, for a long time, was the persona Wahid was content to adopt. It wasn't a difficult task: he had always been lax. And when in his mid- to late teens he became even more lax—'I didn't pray and do the Islamic stuff'—he was able to explain it away in terms of his congenital indolence: it wasn't that he had apostatized, it wasn't that praying made him feel pathetic and slavish and that in any case there was no God to pray to, it was just that he was supremely lazy, that he didn't have the necessary fortitude and strength of character to properly commit to it. Because, Wahid says, there is a night and day difference between being a 'bad Muslim' and a disbelieving 'former Muslim'.

Amir is similarly alive to the distinction between indolence and insurgence. He is no longer observant. And it is a source of great tension between himself and his mother. 'I am pretty sure my mum thinks I am a bad Muslim,' he says. But he is resigned to go along with this, because the alternative would be to tell her that he is an apostate. And, 'If I told her that full out then she could get hurt or mentally very stressed'.

Farhad, who will 'never speak out openly against Islam' but whose mother 'knows that I'm not especially religious', puts it like this:

> I think to my mum, it's better to be a bad Muslim than it is to be a good non-Muslim because at least you have the faith, at least you have Islam in you. So I think she's okay to a certain extent with me being a bad Muslim, a sort of non-practising Muslim, because at the very least I am still a Muslim so she's okay with that. Not okay, but she's mildly tolerant of that. But if I was to tell her that I wasn't a Muslim at all it would completely break her.

- The Liberal Muslim

For most of her mid-teens Aisha was what Wahid emphatically was not: she was pious. Very pious: she was a *salafi*. And she had put a lot of work into that: into being a *salafi*. It had not been easy. She had had doubts and she had fought hard to erase those doubts—fought doggedly in fact because she so desperately wanted to be like her *salafi* friends and to earn their respect. But it ultimately proved futile: her doubts wouldn't relent and she began to waver. To seriously deviate. And this was noticed. How could it not have been? She had never concealed her *salafi* commitments. Indeed she had been brazenly *salafi*. And now she was brazenly liberal, loudly vocalizing her reservations about the role of women in Islam—'I realized that I did have a subordinate role within the Muslim community'—and other aspects of the religion which she saw as incompatible with her liberalism. In addition to this, she had removed her *abaya* and *hijab*. And she was going out now, drinking and partying and coming home late. This all drew attention, 'because one minute I'm fully covered and then the next minute I'm drinking'. Aisha recalls an episode in which her sister confronted her about her behaviour. She wanted to know what was going on and why. Aisha's response was that she was 'a liberal Muslim': 'I was just like, I'm a liberal girl.' Her sister didn't buy it and suspected the worst, questioning her about her commitment to Islam. And as the questioning became more insistent Aisha caved and confirmed her sister's darkest suspicions, telling her that she was indeed an atheist. But for a time it worked, for a time her sister bought it, right up until Aisha became so permissively liberal in her behaviour and views that her sister could buy it no longer.

- The Confused Muslim

This, for a short period, was how Nubia played it: confused, unsure, naive. She had come out to her mother and her mother had taken it badly. So badly in fact that Nubia felt compelled to take it back—to apologetically recant her confession. And she did this by insisting that she had been confused, that she did not know enough about Islam, and that she would endeavour to find out more and clear up her confusions. 'I am not an apostate, I am confused'. It was a lie. But it worked. It pacified Nubia's mother. And it brought Nubia some much needed relief from the perfect 'shit storm' her disclosure of apostasy had provoked.

- The Pious Muslim

Nubia knew it wouldn't work forever: that the 'confused card' had a limited life-span; that her mother wouldn't tolerate her being confused indefinitely. So she played another card: the pious Muslim. It was risky because of the effort required. She wasn't a pious Muslim, even though she looked like one. She would have to work at it. But she knew there wasn't any other way: that her mother wouldn't accept anything else from her—only piety. So that is what Nubia would show her: piety. Her mother demanded piety. She would get piety:

> After the last one [Nubia's second *umrah*] I think by then my mum kind of believed that I'd completely gone back to being a Muslim. And I was really playing the part now. Whenever something would come up I'd always defend

Islam. I'd come up with all the ridiculous ideas that I knew Muslims would say. And I'd just quote a lot of what the Prophet used to say, a lot of the verses, things like that. And I also did a lot of the *sunna* which you don't have to do. You only do it if you're a really good Muslim. So I did a lot of that as well. I think she's bought it now. She might have little doubts but there's nothing she can point to and say, 'Oh, but you're doing this'. She doesn't have any concrete evidence. And I make sure that every time I go to see my cousins here I have the *hijab* on, everything. My university ID card has a photo of me with my *hijab* on and my Oyster card, too—in case my mum checks. I just make sure that there are no holes in my story.

The Quranic invocations, the *hijab*, and most conspicuously, the *abaya*: these are all examples of what Goffman would classify as 'disidentifiers': symbols which serve to distance the discreditable person from their discreditable identity.[12]

- The Irreverent Muslim

Many respondents pride themselves on their irreverence: on their contrariness, on being contrarians, on their non-conformity. Hence among closeted respondents it is a source of great frustration that, having detected a lie or an untruth, as they see it, they can't thereby call it to account and expose it to open ridicule. Some respondents, however, can't help themselves. They ridicule what they don't like about Islam. And this feels good, because for a fleeting moment they're not living the lie. They're being true to themselves, to their contrarian spirit. Almost: because, from the perspective of those who witness it, their irreverence is so exaggerated, so outrageously controversial, that they cannot be taken seriously, that they must be joking. And, not wanting to 'out' themselves as an apostate, they collude in maintaining this impression. These closeted respondents are the 'irreverent Muslims': the contrarians, the nonconformists, the mavericks who, for all their irreverence and quirkiness, are still regarded as Muslims, as operating within the bounds of Islam. Amir, for example, likes to cultivate this persona in the presence of his friends, both Muslim and non-Muslim: 'I regularly use humor to hide what I feel.' And for Amir, the appeal is obvious: he can camouflage what he truly thinks and feels under the cover of an irreverent joke. He can maintain the lie by temporarily not lying, by telling the truth.[13]

STAYING IN: CONCEALING APOSTASY

Covering

For closeted apostates, the key challenge is to disinvolve from Islam without drawing undue notice from family members, especially parents, and the wider *ummah* of Islamic believers. This, as already seen, requires the adoption of various personae or masks; but it also involves a lot of straight-up lying or covering, because disinvolvement must be accounted for, must be excused or explained away. Its true meaning must be covered.

Wahid didn't need an excuse for failing to observe Islamic rituals: his general laziness covered it. When he didn't pray, which was most of the time, there were no alarm bells. Not praying for him was the norm. It was not out of character. It didn't symbolize anything more significant than his intrinsic laziness. Omar doesn't have this excuse. Because Omar was nearly always rigorously observant as a Muslim:

> I was praying five times a day. I used to pray at school. I'd pray at college. I prayed at university—they had prayer rooms, so I prayed there. I was a member of the Islamic Society at university. I was very devout. Even when the doubts were creeping in I was always devout.

Omar doesn't need to cover for his disinvolvement to his immediate family, because he has come out to them. But on occasion he still has to cover for it to those in the wider community in which he lives, because he has yet to come out in this context. One of the cover stories Omar currently uses is provided by his diabetes. He doesn't fast. And so when he is questioned about this by outsiders—when, say, it's Ramadan and he's out at a gathering with Muslims—he can safeguard himself and say: 'I am a diabetic, so I don't fast.'

Maryam doesn't have diabetes. But she menstruates. And that, right now, is her cover for not fasting. Cover designed specifically for her father, who, unlike her mother, doesn't know about her apostasy:

> Last year I'd just started a new job so I got out of it by saying that I was just so stressed and tired by this new job, I didn't think I could fast. And then when my dad started questioning me and just being a bit, not aggressive about it, but you know, he was just irritating me. I kept him quiet by saying I had lady problems and things. For a woman it's the easiest way to get out of it.

Cover stories are also found and pressed into service for explaining away overtly *haram* behavior, like staying out late or drinking. Or eating a non-*halal* lamb and rosemary pie:

On my way back from work, I was walking through the City Centre and I walked past a shop called 'Urban Pie'. I thought that I might try that, so I walked in and ordered a Lamb and Rosemary Pie (which was beautiful might I add). Anyway, I was eating my pie and my cousin who works in a shop nearby saw me through the window and walked in. He saw what I was eating and said 'What you eating that for?!!!'

I think I blagged it, luckily. I said that I had heard so much about this place and I really wanted to try it and I gave in. Then I went on to say that everyone sins. I told him that not eating haram and not drinking are not the only 2 points of being a Muslim and there are much worse sins.

So, somehow, I managed to give him an Islamic lecture while eating a *haram* lamb and rosemary pie!

This is Hanif. I asked him about this—it is an online post he had written—in our interview and he confirmed the veracity of the story. What is especially striking about it is how sensitive Hanif was to the accusation of apostasy, even though this wasn't an accusation levelled by his cousin, who was merely inquiring why Hanif, whom he knew to be observant, was eating non-*halal* food. Hanif could have just said that he had given in to temptation and that, in any case, everyone does it, and left it at that. But he didn't leave it at that. He also added that 'not eating *haram* and not drinking are not the only 2 points of being a Muslim'. He said, in effect, to his cousin: 'do not think that I'm not a Muslim, think instead that I'm prone to weakness, just like all other believers'.

Masood's standard cover story is that he is prone to depression. That's why he would go out drinking and come home drunk. It had nothing to do with Islam. It wasn't a symbol of his lack of faith, still less evidence of apostasy. It was depression: 'I'd pass it off as me being depressed and drinking to drown my sorrows'.

Cover stories are also used in advance of engaging in *haram* behaviour, so as to facilitate it. When Nubia first came to Britain to study for her A-Levels, she was living, at her mother's insistence, in an all-female Muslim dorm. 'I couldn't stand it,' she says. Not only was she made to wear the *hijab*;

There were Quran lessons every day. They'd knock on your door for the early Morning Prayer and you'd have to pray with all the girls in the house. And after the morning prayers a different girl would recite a different part of the Quran. They had verses of the Quran up on the walls. And then every month we'd visit a different mosque. It was just suffocating for me because it was too Muslim.

STAYING IN: CONCEALING APOSTASY

Nubia remembers how on leaving the dorm to go into central London she would take a detour to the women's toilets at the railway station and remove her *hijab* and *abaya*, hoping that 'I wouldn't run into any of the girls from my dorm'. She also says that she had carefully fabricated a cover story in order to enable this errant behaviour and explain staying out late. Her story was that she worked part-time at a local hospital—'a complete lie'—and that from time to time she had to work late shifts.

Cover stories vary in their scale and intricacy: some are bigger and more elaborate than others. The largest are those which are the most impactful: the one's which facilitate an entire *haram* lifestyle. Abdullah, for example, lied about the merits of the university he currently attends. It wasn't necessarily his best option, academically, as he had argued to his parents. It was just very far from his home city and that's why he chose it: so he could live outside the gaze and judgment of his parents and the South Asian community in which his family is embedded. His father supported his wish, believing that 'mentally I'm still a very religious man so I wouldn't do anything out of line'.

Of all Nubia's cover stories, the most impactful was the one she crafted for her mother about the Muslim dorm she used to live in. It was just too far from her university, where she often had to attend lectures until as late as 7pm; it wasn't safe commuting on her own; her dorm-mates were untidy and noisy and unserious about study: this is what Nubia told her mother, arguing that it made far better sense to move to a student residence closer to her place of study. And her mother, after two months of Nubia's insistent lobbying, reluctantly gave in and allowed Nubia to move.

Aisha had similarly lobbied her parents to allow her to live away from home in a university halls-of-residence. She did this not by lying, exactly, but by exaggerating. She said it took over two hours to travel from her home town to her university campus. This was not technically a lie, but it wasn't exactly true either, since Aisha had deliberately taken the most protracted route possible. After months of trying to convince her father that commuting was untenable, Aisha eventually found a breakthrough and her father relented and gave her permission to live away from home.

Masood, whose parents still, despite his advancing years (he is almost forty), expect him to enter into an arranged marriage with a Muslim, says: 'I don't know. I might just tell them that I'm impotent and I don't want to get married or something. I don't like lying to them, but you know.' Masood, who likes to joke, is not joking. Nor is Tasnim when she says she had considered the possibility of entering into a marriage with a gay Muslim man, so that they could both lead double-lives. She has since discarded this idea, owing to its impracticality: 'In Asian culture [in London] everybody knows everybody so they'd know and we wouldn't be able to live separate lives so we'd probably have to move away.'

So it's clearly one thing to lie about eating a non-*halal* lamb and rosemary pie and quite another to lie about a living arrangement, a serious medical affliction or an entire marriage. Whereas the former requires a degree of improvisational intelligence, the latter requires systematic planning and a long-term commitment.

Retreating

'The liar lives in fear of losing control'.[14] This is Adrienne Rich again. But control of what? Control of information, mainly.[15] Having friends, sharing confidences, being part of a community of mutual concern and care: this means opening oneself up, not closing off. This means vulnerability. And vulnerability risks exposure. One way of countering this, or at least minimizing it, is to retreat: to withdraw from existing social networks and relationships, because that way the secret can be protected. That way, the information can be protected—from exposure. As Goffman observes: 'By declining or avoiding overtures of intimacy the individual can avoid the consequent obligation to divulge information. By keeping relationships distant he ensures that time will not have to be spent with the other, for, as already stated, the more time that is spent with another the more chance of unanticipated events that disclose secrets.'[16]

All closeted respondents embarked on a process of retreat. They closed themselves off from their friends and family. This, partly, was a natural consequence of their disinvolvement from Islam. It felt alien to them now, as did many of their relationships with Muslims, with whom they shared little in common by way of interests and understanding. But it was also because they didn't want to expose themselves to exposure. They didn't want their secret to get out. So they withdrew to prevent that from happening, so that they wouldn't give themselves away, because there would be no one around to give themselves away to. Or to be betrayed by. Or even to lie to, which always made them feel wretched, however necessary they thought it was.

Maryam says that she is increasingly distant from her mother. This is deliberate. It is so she doesn't have to lie to her about her double-life with her non-Muslim boyfriend: 'I tell my mum about my life as little as possible now just to avoid having to lie about anything.' And Maryam has come out to her mother. With her father, to whom she has not come out, she is even more distant: partly so she doesn't have to lie to him, but also so as to avoid any possible slips.

Omar also says that he hates lying. Just doesn't have the talent for it. 'I would have to lie, because whenever we used to get together, we would pray and so on. Could I do that? I can't. Have to sit there and listen to non-sense?' So in order to escape the necessity and self-abasement of lying to his friends, Omar has withdrawn from them. He has isolated himself.

Nubia has also deliberately estranged herself from the wider Muslim community: 'I don't really go to Sudanese areas, which is like Shepherds Bush, Acton, [in London] that's where they are. I try to avoid those areas as much as possible.' Not just because she feels alienated from what she sees as their parochial mentality, but also out of fear that someone from the community might see through her cover and recognize her as an apostate. 'If I listened to my mum,' she says, 'and went to all these Sudanese events or whatever I'd be in trouble.'

Ahmed, though more open on the issue of mixing with other Muslims, is certainly cautious and keeps his distance. Speaking of his life away from home at university, he says that:

> when it comes to making Muslim or Arab friends I am always wary. It's almost like they have something more to prove to me that they are okay. Because I know from my own experience that Arabs and Muslims can be closed-minded, so I try to be extra cautious when it comes to making Muslim and Arab friends.

Exposure

What Nubia means when she says that she'd be 'in trouble' is that she would be exposed. That she would be 'outed' as an apostate. And that this exposure would in turn expose her to condemnation, to moral rebuke, to indignation. This is Nubia's big fear: this, and having her mother find out, and all that would unleash. Nubia's fear is exposure. Which is of course precisely why she covers: so as not to expose herself. So as to conceal herself—her apostasy, her 'true' identity.

Exposure is an unavoidable occupational hazard for the closeted apostate: because they are not who they say they are. They are not believers. They are not Muslims. They do not involve themselves in religious practice or ritual. Only if it is necessary, only if it is required. They are withdrawn. Covering all this requires great effort and strength of will. Enormous self-vigilance, too. And self-restraint. It is a hard act to pull off. Especially in front of family members. Because somehow they know, they can sense it.

This is certainly true of Aisha's family. They saw the change in her: 'Like one minute I'm going to the holiest place on earth and then the next I take off my headscarf and so they're really shocked by this.' She was going out a lot, now, too. Aisha credits her mother with the ability to see through her: she 'seems to know everything'. She feels transparent in front of her. Aisha finds this is uncanny, 'weird'. But it isn't: Aisha makes herself transparent in front of her mother and anyone else who cares to look. And for this Aisha is now paying the price—the price of exposure.

First, there was the insistent questioning. The *hijab*: why had she stopped wearing it? What did that mean? What did it signal? An interest in boys? Was that it? Was she trying to meet boys? This is what her mother was thinking: 'Everywhere I go, she's like, "Are you going to meet a boy?, are you going to meet a boy?"' Then the censoriousness, the parental indignation: you are immoral; you are immodest; you are disobeying Islam; you are disgracing yourself. This is what her father had said; her mother, too. Next, more questioning: about the drinking. Aisha had tried keeping it quiet. But she was becoming careless. It all came to a head on New Year's Day. Aisha had gone out the night before. She'd been drinking and partying the whole night:

> I come back at 8am and my mum grabs my face and she's like, 'You smell of alcohol' and I'm like, 'No, I don't.' She goes, 'Yes you do, yes you do' and she starts crying and then I went to bed. And then I wake up and my mum's telling my dad over the phone and my dad's crying too, he's upset, he's like this is probably the worst possible thing that could ever happen to his daughter.

First the *hijab*, and now this—the not coming home and the drinking. This was serious. This required not just condemnation, but something more: action—punitive action, correction. Aisha's mother took the initiative. She enlisted the help of a local *imam*. To exorcise the evil. To return her daughter to the righteous path. To purify her. This is how Aisha recounts it:

> It was a bit weird. Oh God. So basically we [Aisha and her mother] have to wait in this random office and we were waiting for this guy because he has a lot of clients. And so we go into the room and we ended up having a discussion and I said I just want my mum to leave me alone because I don't like being forced to do things, I don't work like that. He was trying to understand and he was like, 'Well, she is your mother, she only wants what's best for you' and I'm like, 'But she's pushing me away'. And then he came to the conclusion that I may have been hit with the evil eye or black magic. And then he said, 'Here's the thing, you are going to go to the grave and you are going die soon'. And he points to a picture of a grave and he's like, 'This is where you are going to end up' and then my mum starts crying. And then she tells him that I've been wearing skirts and that I dress like a prostitute and so he was like, 'Why would you disgrace yourself like this?' Because my mum was telling him about the change in my behaviour and he thought that was really weird for somebody to know the truth and then to abandon it later. It was just completely unheard of and so he didn't understand. He's like, 'There's something you're not telling me, there's something you're not telling me'. And then at one point my mum turns to me and screams, 'You're an atheist, aren't you?' And then the *imam* goes, 'First of all, do you believe in Islam? And I'm like, 'Yes'. 'Do you believe in the Prophet?' And I was like, 'Yes'. 'Do you believe in God?' I'm like, 'Yes'. And then he goes, 'Then why are you acting this way? Most people who have done a lot of sin would feel some remorse, but you don't.' And then I had nothing to say after that and they became really suspicious and my mum started yelling at me, calling me an atheist and she was really, really yelling at me. And then after that I was put on, like, medication. I had to take this weird pill. It gives you the runs, it's supposed to clean out your system from any black magic. And I had to bathe every night in water that the *imam* had read the Quran over. And then I had to put this pure olive oil all over my body. It smelled a bit funny, like incense. My mum did that, put that on me. It was so uncomfortable and so degrading that I actually cried that day and I never cry. And it pissed me off.

In an effort to avoid further corrective punishment, Aisha embarked on a mission: she would, just as Nubia had done, play it confused. She was a Muslim, she told her mother, not an atheist. A Muslim. That is what she was. But she had been misguided. She had fallen in with the wrong crowd. It was those *salafis*—they were the source of her confusion: 'I just said the biggest lie, that I didn't think I was being taught the right brand of Islam and so I blamed them.' As a symbol of her sincerity, Aisha promised to see the *imam* again to better clear up her confusions: 'I was just trying to slowly build things by convincing them that I'm a good Muslim again.'

* * *

Aisha has a long way to go in this. Her parents do not trust her. When she returns home to London on weekends, she is rigorously policed. Indeed, her mother has put her under 'house-arrest' and prevents her from seeing her friends. In vacation periods away from university, she must live with her father, 'so he can have a watchful eye on me'.

Exposure, for Aisha, has been a disaster. The closet she inhabits has become even more confining, even more suffocating. Before drawing all this negative attention, Aisha had room for manoeuvre. It was limited, to be sure, but it was there. Now it isn't. Now, her every move is scrutinized and subject to suspicion, her every wish closely analysed for its propriety or for what it might say about her. And it plainly hasn't worked, all this policing and punishment. Aisha has been subdued, certainly. But she hasn't been reformed. She hasn't returned to the righteous path. On the contrary, she now feels even more estranged from her family and from Islam. And not a little resentful and not a little pissed off, too.

Azhar has been through a comparable experience. He, like Aisha, had once been devoutly religious, although he was never a *salafi* and his devout phase had started earlier: 'I myself took a religious turn around twelve or thirteen and actually I really believed with all my heart.' This phase, though not short-lived, didn't last:

> So I really did believe. I really did hold it dear to myself. It was only when I got to about seventeen and I began to take philosophy more seriously and began to read outside of the Muslim canon that I opened my mind to different ideas and I realized that I don't want to stick to just one way of looking at the world.

By the age of nineteen, Azhar was agnostic. Before this, there had been three tumultuous years of doubting, of trying to find answers, of reading and researching. Three years also of gradual disinvolvement: 'From sixteen to nineteen I had been gradually losing faith, not praying anymore and not fasting and not reading any Islam'. Not only was he not observant in this period, he was also deviant, causally transgressing various Islamic prohibitions: he was drinking, he'd lost his 'pork virginity' and he was smoking weed. More crucially, he had met, via an online forum, Celine. Despite living in two different hemispheres—she was based in Canada, he in London—they'd developed a powerful bond. Powerful enough to want to elope, to run away together. At the time, Azhar was in his second year at university and living at home. But he'd been doing a part-time job and had saved enough money for the flights and one month's rent. So Celine came to London, where she was met at the airport by an anxious Azhar. He was worried she wouldn't turn up. He was also worried about the letter he'd just left for his parents:

> I left them a letter saying I'm leaving, I don't want to upset you and I hope you are not upset. I hope you can understand that I made a decision to start a new life where I will be completely in charge and I wouldn't have to pretend to be obedient to you when I don't want to do that.

What Azhar didn't say in the letter was that he'd apostatized: that he was through with Islam and that his eloping with Celine wasn't just about escaping the restrictions of the family home, but also of Islam: 'I still was pretending, because I couldn't ever say I'm not a Muslim anymore. I couldn't bring myself to say that. I felt as if I would break their hearts and I'm naturally a coward as well.' So in the letter Azhar deliberately 'didn't let it sound as if it was a religious thing—more just that I wanted to explore myself and to see the world'.

The plan: hang-out in London for two days and then fly to Italy to start a new life together. It didn't work; they hung out in London, but they never took that plane to Italy. Their flights had been cancelled. Azhar still doesn't know how this happened, but suspects that his uncle, who is a travel agent, had something to do with it. Neither he nor Celine had the funds to pay for replacement flights. Reluctantly, he called his family and his father and uncle came to collect them. His father was angry, his uncle threatening: 'He's a tough guy, he's a big guy, he likes to throw his weight around and he was saying, "I could chop you up into little pieces and put you in the Thames right now and no one will find out."' Celine was taken to a vacant house owned by the family and Azhar was driven to his family home, where his father demanded that he not 'ruin his life for a girl' and that he return to university. Celine stayed in the house for a week, 'terrified and distraught', and was then driven to the airport by Azhar's father to catch a return flight to Canada. They didn't get the chance to say goodbye to each other, Azhar and Celine. Because the day before she left for Canada, Azhar took a flight of his own: to

Pakistan, with his uncle: 'I allowed my parents to talk me into going to Pakistan and they took me right that day.' 'Allowed' because it was made clear to Azhar that if he didn't go, something bad might happen to Celine.

And the reason for the trip to Pakistan? Correction, Islamic rehab. Soon after landing in Lahore, Azhar's uncle took him to a mosque. This is how it went down:

> So he takes me to this mosque, we go into this room where the *imam* is and I was told to sit down and my uncle's taking this really seriously. I sit down and I don't even know what's going on at this point and the *imam* takes a glass of water and starts praying over it. Then he starts speaking in very broken English and he's not making any sense, just saying random English words. It was kind of like he's almost in a trance, but you could tell he's just putting on a show, trying to talk to someone but he's not really saying anything. So I asked one of the other guys who was in the mosque, who's sitting next to me, I said, 'What's he doing right now?' And he says, 'Oh, you don't know? You have an evil spirit inside your body who's clung on to you in London and the spirit is in love with you and is refusing to leave your body. And he's talking to her right now in English, telling her to leave'. But I said to him, 'He's not speaking English, he's speaking gibberish'. And it was very difficult for me to suppress a laugh at that point. And it was just looking over at my uncle and seeing murder in his eyes that stopped me from laughing. And then the *imam* prays and tells me to drink some water and makes me walk around the room three or four times and tells me, 'Okay, now how do you feel?' And I'm like I feel the same but I lied and said, 'Yeah, I feel better, thank you very much' etc., etc., and then he says to me, 'You know how I know that there is definitely a spirit inside of you? Because your eyes are so red' and I'm thinking to myself that's because I've spent the last few days smoking Afghan hash with my cousin. But obviously I can't say that to him either so I'm like, 'Yeah, you are probably right', and then I get out and obviously I go home and I call Celine in Canada and we spend about three hours laughing about it. I literally didn't stop laughing for about an hour. It was really comical. My uncle, though, took it all seriously and the sad thing is I am pretty certain my mum paid good money to have that exorcism done. I'm sure she spent good money on that.

For one month Azhar stayed in Lahore with his mother's family. And when he returned home to London, he was still an apostate. The devil in him hadn't been exorcised, despite the best efforts of the *imam*. Only now he was angry and aggrieved. And certain: certain that his family would never accept him for who he really was. So on returning he didn't hang about. He left almost straight away: 'I came back on Boxing Day and on

3 January I stole my passport, took my guitar, some clothes and a small backpack and I left for Canada.'

Exposure, as Aisha's and Azhar's experience shows, can be a profoundly dispiriting experience, making life in the closet even more constraining and harder to bear. But it can also serve as a prelude to exiting the closet, because the added encroachment it brings is so intolerable. Aisha, for now, is keeping a low profile and biding her time, but the foundations for her exit have already been laid. The irony of course is that no one has done more to secure these foundations than her own family.

The Costs of Concealment

The ex-Muslim closet, just like the gay closet it so strikingly resembles, is damaging. It is oppressive and stultifying, the enemy of spontaneity and freedom. It is shameful, too, forcing its occupant to lie and to hide and to betray themselves. And it is a place of profound loneliness and isolation, always standing in the way of true and meaningful human connection.

Frustration

What does it feel like to live a closeted life as an apostate? Nubia's preferred metaphor is 'suffocation': that's how she felt in the closet of the all-female Muslim dorm she lived in when she first moved to London. All that piety and all that competitiveness over who could be the most righteous Muslim: 'all that crap', as she described it. She couldn't take it. She felt oppressed by it. And she wanted to call them out on it, all the time, saying, 'this is such bullshit!' But she couldn't.

Farhad uses the word 'trapped'. His family is pious. All his friends are Muslim. The area in which he lives has a large Muslim population. The university he attends is the patron of a visible and highly vocal Islamic society. So Islam is present everywhere in his life, and it drives him crazy, because he doesn't believe, because it's 'just such bullshit' to him, and he can't identify with these people and their faith. But it's there, it's in his face and so he feels 'trapped'.

Farhad's chief source of frustration comes from having always to pretend that he's someone he isn't. And having to pretend to pray. He especially loathes Fridays: the day when he and the men in his family, following a well-established tradition in Islam, go to the local mosque to pray together. 'It's the ultimate feeling of being trapped. I sort of feel like a zombie.'

Abdullah shares this frustration and says that praying, which his family expects him to do when he's back with them during university holidays, makes him feel 'resentful': 'I just hate doing it. I don't know, maybe because of the principle of it.' He remembers it was especially bad during the first Ramadan after he had apostatized, when he was still living at home. He was fasting. That was okay. He could fast. But the praying he found 'hellish', especially the *taraweeh* prayers:

> In the thirty day period they recite the whole Quran, so they do about fifty pages a day, all by standing in prayer. So it takes about two hours a night just standing there in a room with thirty men. And that was while I was depressed and the last place I wanted to be was in my own head, so having two hours a night just to do nothing but think was pretty hard.

Masood's frustration comes from not being able to have the odd drink after work, or always having to look over his shoulder if he does.

> I might go for a pint or two after work, but I'm constantly aware that my parents might smell it on me and so I'll have to go and chew some gum or eat some peanuts or whatever. And it's annoying that I have to do that, that I can't just have a relaxing pint after work and then just go home.

Annoying, also, is this:

> I'd like to be able to walk into a restaurant, maybe order a glass of wine and some pork chops or whatever, and be able to indulge in that without people going, 'Oh my god, aren't you a Muslim?' I want to live my own life in freedom but I've accepted that I can't in some ways.

Hanif, too, has accepted this. And it has been extraordinarily difficult, because, unlike Masood, Hanif doesn't just have an occasional interest in alcohol and pork chops. As he puts it, 'I have a big passion for food and wine and alcohol. So I really know about my food, I know about my wines, I know about my beers.' But Hanif can share none of this with his wife, who is from a tribal area in Pakistan and is devout, nor his relatives, who are also observant. It is a professional interest, too: Hanif is a restaurant manager. He recalls attending various wine-tasting courses for work and lying to his parents that he 'was just taking notes' and didn't consume any. About all this, Hanif says, resignedly: 'So living my own life how I want to live it, it kind of causes a difficult situation in that sense.' And Hanif worries about this. Many respondents said that in the immediate aftermath of their apostasy they had felt angry, especially at themselves: for not having renounced Islam sooner, for wasting time, for missing chances. Hanif's worry isn't about this, not anymore. It isn't about lost time; it's about a lost future. Hanif is worried that in remaining in the closet he is depriving himself of certain joys and opportunities that he will never be able to recapture later on, once it is too late, once his youth has gone. It's not the things he could have done that concerns him; it's the things he can conceivably do, but is not doing, because if he did them it would compromise his cover and lead to exposure.

> It is something that really does concern me and I think about it a lot. I do feel like I'm wasting my twenties a lot of the time. That is probably one of my biggest concerns in this whole not coming out thing. For example, all my mates went on holiday to Paris last year and I couldn't go and I was just thinking, what am I doing? It's little things like that which make me think I might be wasting the best years of my life. My twenties should be the best years of my life.

Farhad similarly worries that 'this is the only life that I will get' and that the longer he remains closeted the less time he has to live it as he would like. Or as Abdullah said of his closeted life: 'I resent it for how much of my life gets taken away from me and how much of the future it's probably going to take away from me'.

As bad as it is for Farhad, Masood, Hanif and Abdullah, it is worse for women in the ex-Muslim closet, because they have even less room for manoeuvre than their male counterparts, less scope for engaging in un-Islamic behaviour. Abdullah, as an addendum to the summary of his own frustrations in the closet, explains it like this: 'I'm very lucky being male. My sister had a very hard job just being allowed to go to the local university which is around the corner from my house. She would never be able to move away to a non-Islamic environment.' Even for those who have been permitted to live away for the purposes of study, the room for manoeuvre is limited. Nubia, for example, is closely policed by her mother:

> She calls me every day. She calls and she asks me to go on Skype or stuff like that. But she has to talk to me every day. She even calls me in lectures. She calls me in lectures and she has my timetable—she just emailed my tutor and he gave it to her. She said, 'Oh, you have blah, blah next' and I was terrified.

I thought, how do you know that? She's a control freak. She has to know everything.

Aisha, sounding like Abdullah, says: 'This wouldn't be that bad if I was a boy, if I was a guy, a man. It wouldn't be as dramatic. I would be able to have the freedom to do whatever I want. And that's what pisses me off the most.' Khadija reinforces this:

> I think for guys, guys don't have to come out as ex-Muslims in order to be able to live reasonably okay. They don't have to. They can continue to pretend to be a Muslim. For girls, especially the ones that are living at home or the ones still in regular contact with their family, it's harder to be an ex-Muslim and keep it hidden. I suppose they're being watched more often. The community reports back on them more often. And they have to dress a particular way. So I just feel that they're trapped more.

Luqman says that the most frustrating aspect of the closet, when he was there, was how it would stifle free expression of thought and feeling:

> It was particularly annoying. I had to bite my tongue basically. Every time they tried to preach to me I was dying to tell them, to shout out I don't believe all this. I completely don't believe it. I had to bite my tongue for many months.

As does Farhad and it drives him nuts:

> I never ever speak out against Islam. I usually keep quiet and mum nags me and I just ignore her. Try and blur it out of my head because it is always the same stuff. You need Islam. You need Islam to go to university. You need Islam to succeed in life, because, obviously, if you don't believe God won't give you anything, so if anything goes wrong in my life, if something has gone bad, it's always because of Islam, always comes back to Islam. Sometimes I do want to lash out verbally, but I always hold it back. It's really frustrating.

Omar, characteristically, is more direct: 'I'm sick to death of always having to watch what I say.'

For Nubia, one of the most maddening things about the closet is how it shapes and limits interactions with others:

> I just hated it because people assumed things about me. For example, at university I wasn't really included in any of the fun things. People just treat you differently. I think it's because they're trying to be respectful. Or they think you have certain lines you don't cross or whatever. But I just found it really suffocating and annoying. Even in discussions I'd go to, like the Atheist and

Muslim Society events, people just assume that I'm on the side of the Muslims. Obviously I can understand where they're coming from, but to me it was really annoying. I remember I was in this lecture and they asked all the Muslims in the room to raise their hands and I had to reluctantly put it up because of my *hijab*.

Aisha, in the last few months of wearing the *hijab*, had also become exasperated by the very misperceptions she had helped create:

Like when you're talking to people and they make some sexual reference. It's like I'm not allowed to hear it because of who I am. And obviously it wasn't who I was and I hated having to be this symbol of Islam. It just really annoyed me, because whenever somebody would talk about the Republic of Iran or how much they hate theocracies people would automatically assume that I support Iran or theocracy but I actually don't.

Sometimes the pressure of constant suppression becomes so intense that there is an overwhelming urge to throw it off and revel in the thrill of frankness. Masood recalls the following incident:

I was at work and some customer came in and said 'Jazakallah' to me, which is basically a way of saying thank you to someone whilst praising God at the same time, and I remember I was having quite a shitty day at the time so I said, 'What makes you think I'm a Muslim?' And he said, 'Your name badge said Masood on there, which is pretty Muslim-sounding'. And I said, 'Yeah, well, there's Christians in Palestine called Abdullah so it doesn't make me a Muslim', and he said, 'Right, sorry' and that was it.

A yet further source of frustration for closeted ex-Muslims comes from always having to be 'on' and in state of self-vigilance. As Abdullah says, reflecting on how his life has changed since moving away from home:

I'm not conscious of the things I do. Before I always had to act a certain way and be a certain way and say certain things and it was annoying. But here just having that sense of freedom to do what I want is sort of liberating and not having to worry about who will see me or what people will say.

Maryam, since moving away from her home town, is similarly less self-conscious about how she acts and the impression she gives off:

I'd say it's less stressful since I've moved to Durham. When I was in Birmingham I would be quite scared because my dad, his shop and his restaurant are in Birmingham. I'd often be scared if I was out with friends just wearing normal clothes, my perception of what is normal to me anyway. That my dad or any of his friends might see me or if I was out with my boyfriend that they might see us as well. And it was quite stressful. Now that I'm here it's not so bad.

But it isn't entirely stress-free, either. Maryam, speaking of a recent weekend visit home, says:

I overheard my dad talking about something and I thought he was talking about me. It was just as I was walking into the sitting room and he was talking about it quite angrily and actually he was talking about one of my cousins. Something to do with her going out and getting drunk and not calling and everyone was quite worried. I can't remember why, but the way he was talking I just felt as if he was talking about me. I was going downstairs and I could hear what he was saying and I was thinking about what to say in my head. What I could say back, I had been drinking and blah blah blah. And then when I got downstairs he was like, 'Oh there you are. Do you know what Nadia did the other day?' And if he hadn't actually said that at that point I might have said something and completely blown my cover when I didn't need to at all.

Farhad similarly worries about blowing his cover. So much so that he can't even buy, much less eat, a bacon sandwich in tranquility.

The buying part is the commitment for me. What if the cashier looks at me, or if they know me? You become paranoid all of a sudden. Even now there is still a sense of paranoia about drinking alcohol, about eating non-*halal* meat, about eating bacon. I've become paranoid, I look around, what if someone here knows me? So I think if there is any possibility of someone knowing me, or even if there isn't any, I still think, what if, what if? Those scenarios pop into your head. So it's always an uncomfortable thing, there's always that paranoia in the back of your head, what if someone finds out?

This is exactly how Nubia felt when she first removed her *hijab*:

In the first few months I took my *hijab* off I wouldn't look at anyone and just walked straight because I thought if I caught someone's eye they're going to recognize me. Plus, I was really paranoid someone would tell someone who knew my mum.

All closeted respondents confessed to feeling vulnerable in this way, although some felt it more deeply than others. Because there are always slip-ups and you never know what might happen or who knows what. Closeted respondents worry about this. And they even dream about it. Nubia, for example, says:

This is funny, because I had a dream last night and, oh my God, basically I went to a CEMB meet-up and on the way back I went into a corner shop for something. And then my cousin called me and she said, 'Where are you?' And I said, blah, blah street and then she said, 'Can I come and see you?' And I thought, oh no, I'm not wearing my *hijab*, she's going to know. And then I thought, you know what, she's actually nice, this will be okay, she's open minded. So then I met her and she was with my mum and my two brothers. And they saw me and it was just a shit storm. It was horrible. And I woke up straight away.

Aisha's closet dreams follow an almost identical script:

It used to be quite frequent, like every night. They'd find my Christopher Hitchens book or they'd find the website for CEMB and this is something I still worry about. It feels horrible lying to my parents, but I haven't got an alternative.

For some closeted respondents, then, there is no escape from the anxiety of the closet. Even when they're asleep and ostensibly 'off' they're 'on'.

Shame

Salman Rushdie, himself a profound guide to the psychology of shame, writes with great insight about his own sense of shame in the early years of the *fatwa*. Recalling an incident in which he had to duck down behind a kitchen counter in a Welsh farmhouse so as to avoid the attentions of an approaching neighbour, he writes:

As he crouched there listening to Michael [Rushdie's host] get rid of his man as quickly as possible he felt a sense of deep shame. To hide in this way was to be stripped of all self-respect. To be told to hide was a humiliation. Maybe, he thought, to live like this would be worse than death. In his novel *Shame* he had written about the workings of Muslim 'honour culture', at the poles of whose moral axis were honour and shame, very different from the Christian narrative of guilt and redemption. He came from that culture even though he was not religious, and had been raised to care deeply about questions of pride. To skulk and hide was to lead a dishonorable life. He felt, very often in those years, profoundly ashamed. Both shamed and ashamed.[17]

Of the various humiliations Rushdie had to suffer in the *fatwa* years, preeminent was his fictitious conversion—'I am able now to say that I am a Muslim'.[18] It was, as he calls it, with hollering capitalizations, the Great Mistake.[19] It 'had made him feel very bad about himself'.[20] It had made him feel 'foolish and weak',[21] cowardly,[22] dishonorable.[23] In a later interview, Rushdie elaborates on this and says 'I felt sick about it then and I feel sick about it now, because it felt like a betrayal of myself'.[24]

This, broadly, is what closeted ex-Muslims say about their own lives into the closet. Farhad says the closet makes him feel weak and cowardly. His mother constantly badgers him about his laxity, 'making me feel horrible for not being religious'. And Farhad takes it. Doesn't say a word. Just tries to screen it out. 'It makes you feel weak,' he says, because he doesn't answer her back, doesn't defend himself, doesn't stand up for himself.[25]

Tasnim's word for it is 'ridiculous'. She pretends to pray, not all the time, but has to during Ramadan, when she also pretends to fast. And it makes her feel ridiculous:

> I do pretend to fast. Or I do pretend to pray when it's Ramadan. Usually I pray downstairs or pretend to pray downstairs. It can take twenty minutes and you hear the guys go out to the mosque and pray. And if my sister's praying and my mum's praying upstairs, I'll go downstairs. Then if I can hear someone coming I quickly go to the prayer mat and pretend to continue praying. It does feel ridiculous but I know if I don't pray I'd hear the whole 'Oh, why aren't you praying? And fast.' I'd rather not hear that. It is really ridiculous. But, yes, it's fine. It's not really. I think it's become easier now than it used to be. Maybe I've done it for so long and I don't know anything else. I don't know any other life.

Nasreen, who has recently divorced and lives on her own, uses an even stronger word to describe how the closet makes her feel: 'horrible'. She is 'out' among her largely non-Muslim friends, but not among her family. She says she doesn't want to hurt her parents nor face all the turmoil of them finding out. So she covers. And for a time, though she had discarded her *hijab*, she continued to wear it whenever she visited the family home:

> It felt horrible. It was disgusting because I remember physically having to go to a tube station or go to a cafe or something and put it on before I'd go to the house. It would feel very, very humiliating because I completely disagree with this scarf, this religion, this whole sexist way women are treated. I just can't stand it at all. And then the fact I have to pretend to be happy with it, the fact that people would think I am that, I am still promoting this religion. It was very damaging psychologically. And then going to visit my parents they'd always think everything was okay, but I'd be very moody with them. And every time I'd go home after I'd be very upset.

Ramesh was similarly self-hating when he was in the closet. Speaking of this period, he says:

> I was one thing at home, acting in a way, and myself when I was out. I had, like, these two personalities. And going to her [his wife's] parent's house and then prayer time comes around and I'm standing there and I'm praying there and I'm standing there thinking what the hell am I doing? I'm just going through the motions, acting. There was that feeling of being an actor and that feeling of being real somewhere else.

In addition to feeling cowardly for not being true to themselves, for not standing up for themselves, for betraying themselves, some closeted respondents said they felt shameful for not being true to others, especially loved ones.[26] Alia, who is certainly not alone on this score among closeted respondents, says she lost count of all the lies she'd told her parents. And this made her feel bad, like she was betraying them.

Loneliness

Closeted respondents live a life of great loneliness. This is for three central reasons.

First, even when they're not alone, even when they're surrounded by family and friends, they feel estranged, distant, emotionally alienated. Farhad sharply captures this when he says, 'I'd see people in headscarves, beards, whatever, and it just made me feel alone.' It is primarily a problem of connection, of 'relating'. And Farhad can't. Can't relate with Muslims, because he isn't one, because he thinks differently and because he's been through so much and they couldn't possible understand. Abdullah also says this, referring to the first few months after he had apostatized: 'I just couldn't relate to anyone that I had been close to before and there weren't very many people anyway. So I just became estranged from everyone.' Aisha similarly says: 'When I had left Islam I distanced myself from most people because all of my friends were Muslims so I distanced myself, I kept myself to myself and basically became a loner for a long time'. According to Omar: 'I don't see my Muslim friends now because, what have I got to discuss with them? What do we have in common now that I'm an atheist? What we had in common was our brotherhood in Islam and it's not there anymore.'

Second, among closeted respondents there is a perception that Muslims in turn will not relate to them; that, indeed, evidence of their apostasy, should it be discovered, would invite condemnation or even outright rejection. Consequently, interaction with Muslims is avoided or attenuated so as to minimize the risks of what David Matza calls 'righteous scrutiny'.[27]

Nubia, for example, is cautious around Muslims, watches what she says and is emotionally closed-off. Farhad, whose closet is far more constricted than that of Nubia's (he lives at home with his family in a Muslim area) is similarly closed-off in the company of Muslims, absenting himself psychologically from conversations that he can't avoid.

Tasnim says that there was 'a part of myself that I couldn't express'. Something very profound has happened to her. One of the defining emotional experiences of her young life. She wants to share this, especially with the people she most cares about and loves. But she can't, because she knows they will be devastated about her apostasy and that they will probably banish her from the family home. So she has to keep her apostasy hidden from them and has to live a lie and this makes her unbelievably lonely and depressed, suicidal even, because most of her friends are Muslims and so, too, is the community in which she lives, and she can't open up to anyone. Recalling the period just after she left Islam, Tasnim remarks:

> It was rough and I could barely pull myself together. I was crying fifteen times a day. I could barely get out of bed in the morning. They noticed that I'd removed myself from them. That I wouldn't participate—I'd keep myself to myself. I'd want to stay in my room. I didn't want to talk to anybody. I just wanted to be by myself a lot of the time. I think deep down because I knew they wouldn't accept me.

Omar links his own depression, which is intermittent, to the fallout from his apostasy. He told his two best friends about his apostasy and they rejected him, something that immensely pains him still to this day. And because he doesn't want to go through the pain and humiliation of further rejection, he keeps his apostasy hidden from his other friends, all devout Muslims. Keeps it hidden by not seeing them, by avoiding them. That's the only way he can do it, because he can't openly lie to them, much less pray with them. 'I've put myself into a bit of an exile because of it,' he says. And it's made him depressed, because there is now a huge void in his life: 'The depression occurred after my apostasy. And it isn't because I am an apostate, it's everything that's gone hand in hand with it. The isolation, not being able to connect.'

STAYING IN: CONCEALING APOSTASY

In Ramesh's case, the person he felt most estranged from wasn't a mother or a father or a brother or a sister; it was his wife. He had apostatized and in the beginning he couldn't tell her. He'd kept if from her, because he wasn't sure how she would react. He'd thought she might leave him and take the children with her. He had changed and this was reflected in his behaviour, too. He started going out more—he could do this because he regularly travels with work. He started drinking and having fun. His wife saw the change and suspected something. But he tried concealing it from her and this created a vast ocean of distance between them and slowly eroded their relationship. As Ramesh explains:

> I kind of did stuff behind her back. I started leading a double life in a way. Because I couldn't come out to her, because I knew if I came out to her it would mean automatic divorce and I'm gonna lose my kids. So I was leading a double life. I started drinking. But it was always outside and I didn't need to tell her about it. When I was out of town I'd have drinks with work colleagues. Eventually she started questioning me. And she kept asking me, 'Are you drinking? Are you drinking?' I kept saying no. But she picked up on the change. Because we were like splitting apart. Our connection was not there anymore.

Hanif is currently in a similar position: closeted and married. His wife, he says, 'knows that I've got no interest in religion', but she knows nothing about his disbelief and this creates an enormous emotional distance between them:

> In terms of interests, and also coming back to the religion thing, it is quite difficult in my marriage. Like she talks about a lot of stuff which I find superstitious nonsense, like the evil eye, she loves that topic basically.

But even more estranging for Hanif is that he can't talk to his wife about his apostasy, can't let her in on this ground-shifting event in his life, can't share his true feelings, let alone include her in his enthusiasms and passions.

Third, there is a fear among closeted respondents that developing decent and emotionally satisfying relationships with non-Muslims will compromise their cover and attract the suspicions of family and friends. Some closeted respondents said that they had deliberately erected barriers to prevent themselves from becoming too closely involved with non-Muslims, because they knew that these *haram* relationships, if not heavily circumscribed, would exact too great a toll on them emotionally, would ask too much of them. Masood, for example, had met a woman and embarked on a relationship with her. She wanted to develop it further. Would he consider moving in with her? Yes, he would. But it was impossible. She wasn't a Muslim. And, in the eyes of his parents at least, he was. If he were to move in with her it would have all come out—the whole story—and he wasn't prepared to face the fallout from this. 'I thought at the time that they [his parents] would probably disown me', Masood remembers, adding, 'and I didn't want to hurt them like that'. So the relationship ended, although 'I'm still friends with her and occasionally she gets maudlin when she gets drunk and texts me saying I wish you'd fought for me'. Tasnim, too, has had relationships, but these have gone nowhere because she very deliberately decided that they would go nowhere. 'I can't be bothered with the heartache,' she says. Of one doomed relationship, she comments: 'There was a friend who wanted more than just friends. He was agnostic and I just said, "It's not a good idea, my family won't accept you. You'd have to be a secret, you don't want that"'. Hence the ex-Muslim closet is not only detrimental to intimate relationships with Muslims; it can also serve to prevent intimacy with non-Muslims.

The Paradox of Concealment

There is a fascinating and rich sociological literature on gay lives in and out of the closet.[28] A central theme in this work is the profound psychological damage of remaining closeted. Closeted gay men and women must lie and deceive others in order to protect their secret. They might have to vigilantly police their every gesture in an effort to pass and to appear fully heterosexual,[29] even colluding in homophobic and sexist bigotry so as not to raise suspicions.[30] And they might seek to distance themselves from others for fear that closeness, emotional intimacy—the foundation of any minimally satisfying life—risks exposure.[31] This all exacts a deep personal cost.

The closeted lives of ex-Muslims strongly echo the closeted lives of gay men and women prior to the emergence and successes of the gay liberation movement in the 1960s. They too, are living a lie, 'betraying the trust' of their family and friends, and also, even more harmfully, 'betraying' themselves and the things they value. All the while they remain closeted—they cannot move on in their lives, cannot properly develop new interests and fully follow their passions, but must remain imprisoned in a life lacking in human connection and true intimacy. And the longer this endures, the weaker and more strained existing relationships become. This is the great paradox of being 'in the closet'. It is endured because it is supposed to preserve and protect relationships with family members and friends. But because of all the deceit required to sustain it and the emotional distance this creates, it ends up imperiling these, as well as fuelling resentment and distrust between loved ones. How ex-Muslims manage their relationships, as well as other obstacles and challenges, post-apostasy, is the subject of the next chapter.

6

HANGING ON

MANAGING APOSTASY

I thought I was the only one.

Maryam

In the end I really did miss belonging to something.

Aisha

I know that whenever they look at me they are going to think he's a fucking apostate.

Omar

I have nephews and nieces. I want to grow up to see the people they're going to be. I want to go to their weddings. I want to know what they're doing. I want all that.

Tasnim

The Post-Apostasy Phase: The Ex-Muslim Jihad

For most respondents, leaving Islam and becoming non-religious was a cumulative process, culminating first in disavowal to self and then disavowal to others. It was also marked and solidified by various disavowal rituals and a gradual disinvolvement from the cultural life-world of Islam. But it was not always marked by full disclosure. Indeed, just over half of respondents had very deliberately resolved not to disclose their apostasy to their parents, other family members and other Muslims in or outside their local communities.

This chapter focuses on what happens next. What happens after the point of disavowal to self and to others? And how does the ex-Muslim negotiate the challenge of completing their disinvolvement from Islam, regardless of whether they have disclosed their apostasy to significant others? My concern, in other words, is to explore the vicissitudes of the 'post-apostasy phase', where the apostate must adjust to the deeper or longer-term implications of their exit from Islam.

In what follows, I suggest that leaving Islam can usefully be understood as a jihad (i.e. struggle) and is waged on two distinct fronts. First, there is the 'jihad of the mind', where the ex-Muslim must address the wider existential and moral meaning of their apostasy. And second, there is the 'jihad of the heart', where the ex-Muslim must manage the emotional task of renegotiating relationships with loved ones. I call these twin-challenges of adjustment 'the ex-Muslim jihad', subdividing them into, respectively, the 'lesser' and the 'greater' ex-Muslim jihad.[1]

The Lesser Ex-Muslim Jihad

As I described the process in Chapter 3, respondents prior to disavowing Islam ruminated carefully on two central questions: 'what do I believe in?' and 'who am I?' On both, they were uncertain and undecided. So they probed, researched, deliberated. They sought to find answers. And they eventually did and this was invariably facilitated by coming into contact with irreligious source-material. So now they were certain. They did not believe in Islamic scripture. Nor could they go along with key aspects of Islamic morality. And they did not feel Muslim. This, after months or even years of deliberation, is what they had decided: they did not believe; and they were no longer Muslim. This all felt immensely clarifying. And satisfying: it felt good to draw a line in the sand and say 'this is what I don't believe in' and 'this is who I'm not'. But the satisfaction was temporary, because it left so much unanswered. If Islam was no longer the central reference-point in their lives, what now was? What should they now believe in and how should they now define themselves? They knew what they didn't believe in, but what was it that they did believe in? What worldview or schedule of values did they subscribe to? And, in addition to not being Muslims, who now were they? How, or in reference to what, should they define themselves? Respondents also had to confront the challenge of resisting and repudiating the efforts of others to decide the question of identity for them. They were not bad people; they had not done a bad thing in leaving Islam. This is what they needed to tell themselves and, where this was possible, others. Deciding how to frame this—how to create a counter-discourse—was a challenge they had to face.

There was also the less abstract question of how respondents should now carry themselves in their post-apostasy lives. They could now date. For many respondents, this presented a host of problems: how do you organize a date?; what should you wear?; how do you signal sexual interest or unavailability?; etc. They could now drink. More problems: what do you drink and how fast and how many? These are just two areas in social life in which respondents had to reorient themselves and create new scripts for acting.

The Greater Ex-Muslim Jihad

Whereas the 'lesser' ex-Muslim jihad is primarily an internal existential struggle, a battle fought with the self over identity, belief and personal orientation, the 'greater' ex-Muslim jihad is primarily an emotional struggle fought with loved ones over issues of self-worth and role expectations. Unlike the former jihad, the latter is about reaching out, not looking in. It is about self-fulfillment in and through relationships with others, not personal self-discovery.

For many respondents, leaving Islam impacted negatively on their relationships with family members and friends. They felt bad about this and even though they wanted to embark on new lives beyond Islam and free of family interference they still wanted to preserve these relationships. Figuring out how best to do this, how best to balance their personal convictions and goals with their obligations towards family and friends, is for almost all respondents one of the greatest challenges they face in exiting Islam.

I classify this as the 'greater' of the two ex-Muslim jihads because of its ongoing nature, because it is a life-long struggle without end and because, more centrally, its consequences for emotional well-being are so profound and impactful. Just what this involves and means is spelled out in the last section of this chapter and is further taken up in the conclusion.

THE APOSTATES

Exit Wounds

In what follows, I describe three core overlapping moral experiences which all respondents encountered—suffered—in the weeks or months after mentally disavowing Islam: disruption, disconnection and discreditation. I try to convey what these experiences felt like for respondents and suggest that, together, they form the basis for a second crisis of the self, whereby the following questions all returned with a vengeance: 'who am I and how should I live my life?', 'where do I belong?', and 'am I wrong?'

Disruption

When the moment of disavowal came and Islam as a source of belief and identity was rejected many respondents felt a surge of excitement. The weight of not knowing what to believe or with what to identify was lifted, for a while, and the world—a world without Islam and the Islamic God—could be imagined anew. That was thrilling. Life didn't adhere to any supernatural plan. Life was boundless and full of mystery and wonder. As Abdullah had put it, 'just having that uncertainty about life and what the purpose of the universe is or how things work, that was very exciting to me.' And enlarging, too: 'Those few months are about the only time that I felt like I grew as a person when I tried to think for myself for the first time'. But Abdullah also felt 'daunted' by the prospect of a godless universe and soon became fixated on the issue of his own mortality and reason for being.

Many respondents had similar experiences. Islam gave them epistemic and moral guidance. Now that they had renounced it, they had to creatively evolve their own sense of right and wrong and truth and falsehood. The big existential questions—'why am I here?' and 'what is my purpose?'—loomed especially large. Amina describes it in these terms:

> That's been a struggle as well, that it feels like there's no purpose and it's kind of depressing at times. There's no evidence for God, there's nothing to really believe in, but how do you feel comfortable in that? It just feels so pointless that we were born and we just die and I know you can do everything in between and you get old and you die and sometimes it's more intense than that but sometimes my thoughts are like that and I feel quite down. I actually feel envious of religious people. They know who they are, they have an identity and they believe in something, they have a purpose and I just feel lost.

Nabilah echoes this, saying that her overwhelming preoccupation in the aftermath of renouncing Islam was: 'Okay, so now what? Do we fill it [the void left by Islam] with Christianity, do we fill it with Buddhism, or do we follow it with Judaism? So now where do I stand?' Ahmed's unclarity on these fundamental questions was even more acute:

> The real struggle came a few years later [after he had apostatized] when I was in my early twenties. I became really, really depressed, where I would just think there's no point in life and I went through this huge stage of depression where I couldn't function, I couldn't work, I couldn't do anything, I couldn't get out of bed. I felt that my life had lost meaning and that there was nothing to live for.

Tasnim had also fallen victim to feelings of depression in the months after leaving Islam. Although it had 'opened up a whole different world to me, because I wasn't restricted by religion any more' and that felt emancipating, it had also aroused a more insistent feeling: unease. 'So where do I go from here? How do I live the rest of my life without a purpose?' She didn't know, not at first. Khadija followed the same path. At first, everything 'felt exciting'. But then, later, the excitement faded and 'everything just seemed pointless' and she became 'very depressed.'

For Tasnim, moreover, as indeed for many respondents, the uncertainty she felt wasn't just a matter of belief. It was also a matter of identity. Now that she didn't believe, how should she now define herself? She wasn't a Muslim anymore, not really. But, equally, she wasn't *not* a Muslim, not really: that is, she still felt culturally tied to Islam in some way. How to reconcile this? How to create an identity which recognized in equal measure her atheism and her cultural Muslimness? For a long time, that perplexed and troubled her.

A second major source of disruption, in addition to uncertainty over belief and identity, had to do with freedom: now, they had it, or so it seemed, and they didn't quite know what to do with it or how to manage it. Before, when they were Muslims, most respondents had tried to act in accordance with Islamic codes of conduct, berating themselves for any lapses or deviations from the righteous path. Hanif, for example, was a voracious drinker at university and felt bad about that, because he knew drinking was *haram* and would shame him if it came to the attention of his family. For Alia, the object of shame was sex. She was a Muslim when she met her partner Stephen and she was still a Muslim when their relationship progressed and they had sex. She, too, felt very bad about that. As did Ahmed for his sexual interest in men, which he knew to be unsound from a conventional Islamic perspective.

But now, post-disavowal, respondents no longer had to square their actions or personal desires with Islamic morality. They were now free to transgress Islamic prohibitions, if they so wished.[2] They could engage in *haram* behaviour, without consequence, without guilt. If they wanted to drink, they could. If they wanted to have sex, they could—theoretically. They were now free to experiment. To be who they wanted to be, or to find out what that was.

For some respondents, this was a profoundly unsettling experience and learning who they were came at a price. Aisha felt a rush of euphoria on renouncing Islam: 'I felt extremely liberated at first...it felt amazing...I could drink if I wanted to. I could listen to songs that I had been avoiding which were quite blasphemous...I could enter a club. I can wear whatever I want. I could date...'. But Aisha also felt bewildered and confused, because, now, she didn't have a script. Confronted with a world of limitless possibility, or so she imagined, she had little sense of how to respond to this and reorient herself to the new challenges it presented: 'What am I supposed to do? Everything I said and everything I did was in accordance to Islam. What am I supposed to do now? That's my whole life shattered, I don't know what to do, even about the little things.'

In his novel *The Pregnant Widow* Martin Amis explores the upheavals and casualties of the sexual revolution in the late 1960s and early 1970s. The central theme of the book is that it was a difficult period of transition and that 'every hard and demanding adaptation' fell to women.[3] Girls, Amis says, were expected to behave like boys and this ushered in 'new and sinister ways of getting everything wrong'.[4] This seems an apt, if slightly dramatized, way of describing how a small number of respondents first reacted to the sea-change of their apostasy: by getting things wrong or, as respondents were inclined to express it, by 'fucking up'. Not the serious things: they didn't go round murdering people and looting and running wild. I don't mean that; nor do they. They were not suddenly without a core moral code, because, as many respondents insisted, they'd always had an elemental sense of right and wrong independent of Islam or religion. I mean primarily getting things wrong—fucking-up— in the twin fields of leisure and personal relationships. Aisha provides a vivid example. On apostatizing, she felt the tingle of possibility. But she didn't act on it straight away. And then, after a while, after a period of just savoring it and imaging it in the abstract, she seized on her new-found freedom. A little too over-zealously: 'I went out a lot but I just had to get this whole new way of living out of my system, I just wanted to experience things.' Her first ever drink quickly led to her second ever drink and before she knew it she was drunk. As she told me, she didn't have any restraint, no idea of what was too much or when to stop. And this—'going out and getting shit-faced and vomiting'—happened a lot.

Another respondent—who shall remain nameless—was similarly unpractised in the ritual of social drinking. Unpractised, too, in the sexual ritual. She recalls the following mortifying experience:

> Losing your virginity is something so intimate and it's a bigger deal in my culture and it was a big deal to me. I felt really guilty about it because it was with somebody I didn't know. And it didn't end well because I like puked-up half-way through and passed out and some people had to carry me back to my room, it's just too much. It took a while for me to get over that.

This person, like Aisha, has had to learn the hard way: through painful and humiliating experience. 'You just have to learn from your mistakes', as she measuredly put it.

For Nubia, the process of adjustment has been far less tumultuous, although in the first few months after moving out of the Muslim dorm in which she was living 'all I would do was go to bars and go to clubs and just try to catch up. I just felt like I was missing out on so much. Now I'm a bit more laid back.' Many respondents charted a similar trajectory, although it was the women among them for whom the learning curve was the steepest and for whom the scope for mishap was the greatest, since, unlike their male counterparts, they had little preparation for dealing with the challenges that their new-found freedoms presented. The boys, the men, prior to their apostasy, had already done a moderate amount of fucking-up: because they could, because, unlike their female counterparts, they were given the scope to fuck-up. The girls, the women, were not; they had been subject to greater social controls, presumably, because, as Aisha pointed out to me, when a woman fucks-up, it marks her with a permanent and unforgivable stigma. The world of partying and getting loaded and doing crazy shit had already been experienced by most male respondents, even the formerly devout among them. So on becoming apostates they were ready for it. They were ready for blandishments of the *haram* world; they had a degree of *haram*-savvy, most of them. But the women, with one or two exceptions, did not have it, and so, to quote

Amis, 'every hard and demanding adaptation' would be falling to them, though some, like the level-headed Nubia, fared better than others.

Disconnection

Islam, as well as being a source of belief and identity, is also a source of community, a way of belonging. Leaving Islam, correspondingly, is as much a way of unbelonging as of disbelieving. All respondents said this, felt this: that not only did they not believe, but that they did not belong, that they had become estranged—from Islam and, more painfully, from Muslims, especially loved ones. They couldn't relate to them, still less open up and speak freely about matters of great personal importance. And that went the other way, too. They had changed and distanced themselves from everybody and were not emotionally available. Their families knew this and didn't like it and intervened to reverse it. But this served only to heighten respondents' sense of disconnection.

Coming out is the single most critical variable in the 'apostasy phase' and can catalyze feelings of estrangement in a very immediate and dramatic way. As we have seen, respondents who disclosed their apostasy to family and Muslim friends were invariably met with censure, opposition, incredulity and much else and while it didn't always end in separation it caused great upheaval for everyone concerned and severely damaged or diminished relationships, despite the best efforts of respondents to mitigate this. Alia's final act of disclosure effectively terminated her relationship with her parents. So did Khadija's. Wahid's disclosure to his mother didn't end their relationship, but it dramatically reconfigured it and for the worse, because there is now a huge distance between them. Many respondents who had disclosed their apostasy to friends lost those friends. Nubia told her best friend and that friend cut her out. Aisha's friends, with one or two exceptions, did the same to her on discovering her apostasy. And so did Omar's on discovering his. There is a lot of pain here and it centres on the irreparable loss or degradation of important and in some cases life-long relationships and bonds.

But not coming out is no less fateful and can also serve to catalyze feelings of deep estrangement. Whereas self-outed ex-Muslims must contend with rejection, ostracism and resistance from family and friends alike, closeted ex-Muslims must forswear intimacy with friends and loved ones, emotionally distancing themselves from them so as to prevent the exposure of their apostasy or their second life as a secular libertine. Although less destructively catastrophic than disclosure, concealment is nonetheless powerfully corrosive of decent and satisfying personal relationships, because the deepest concerns, anxieties, fears, hopes and longings not only cannot be shared, but must be actively hidden.

It is perhaps useful here to refer to Robert S. Weiss's distinction between emotional isolation and social isolation.[5] According to David Riesman, the former 'results from the loss or lack of a truly intimate tie (usually with spouse, lover, parent or child)', whereas the latter is 'the consequence of lacking a network of involvements with peers of some sort, be they fellow workers, kinfolk, neighbours, fellow hobbyists or friends'.[6] Self-outed respondents suffered from both forms of isolation: they had disclosed their apostasy to friends and family members and their social network was severely damaged in consequence, as were the few deep personal ties which existed within or alongside it. For closeted respondents, by contrast, the isolation was primarily emotional. They had not been banished from their social orbit, because they hadn't outed themselves, because they were living the lie. But by remaining closeted they had all experienced a profound deterioration in their relationships with loved ones, because, as one of the characters in *The Human Stain* puts it, 'Where is the intimacy...when there is such a secret?'[7]

Nabilah, reflecting on her apostasy and how far she has come since the point of disavowal, says she doesn't miss the praying and certainly doesn't miss all the piety, but she definitely misses the sense of community and belonging which Islam gave her:

> You know what I miss the most? It's my friendships and the community. And the sense of unity. Not the conformity, just the unity. The sense of belonging to something...Because Islam is wonderful like that, in the sense that every single Muslim is your brother and sister and you don't feel alone. But as soon as you leave Islam you get this overwhelming feeling of loneliness and you don't have all those millions of brothers and sisters anymore.

Omar similarly laments the loss of friendships and the sense of 'brotherhood' that Islam gave him. As does Aisha, who misses what she calls the 'sisterhood':

> I really enjoyed that. I didn't like the judging and the constant advice. But I do miss it because you would meet people and they won't know you, but they'd offer you food and be like, 'Hi my name is this', and they'd supposedly love you all in the name of God and it was quite nice.

For Alia, the biggest and most painful loss has been the support and solidarity of her immediate and extended family:

> I do miss the family a lot. I do miss the big support network and it's, well, we are such a big family. It's not easy. I'm finally free, I can finally be myself. But I do miss them a lot. I miss big gatherings. I miss the food. I miss them. Hopefully one day they will come around but it won't be anytime soon.

This sense of disconnection and isolation is compounded by the fact that there are few people outside of the Muslim community to whom respondents can turn for support and advice. Many had grown up in Muslim communities. Most of their friends were Muslims. With one or two exceptions, they didn't know or hang around with non-Muslims. And, in any case, non-Muslims wouldn't get it. This is sharply expressed in the following post from an ex-Muslim online forum:

> I've been feeling so lonely. I feel like I don't have any friends. I am a pretty friendly person, but since I became an ex, I've lost contact with almost 95% of my friends. College started which should make it easier to make friends, but I can't relate to anyone. I don't drink, smoke or 'party'. I wanna find some friends who I can relate to when it comes to the whole ex-Muslim thing. Thank you.

Masood makes a similar point, although obliquely and by way of a joke: 'Scientific fact: I've had less ass as an apostate than I did as a Muslim!' This is a riposte to Muslims who believe ex-Muslims apostatized for the sole purpose of engaging in *haram* behaviour, especially casual sex. But it also turns out to be true: it *is* a scientific fact that Masood has had markedly less ass since becoming an apostate than when he was a Muslim. Masood, who is by no means an unattractive man and who is certainly not lacking in charisma and intelligence, didn't immediately become less attractive, intelligent or charismatic on leaving Islam, although he did develop colitis. So that isn't it. It is, rather, that his social situation changed. It wasn't just that it was now lacking in sex. It was that it was just lacking. And this, as the above quotation intimates, is because when Muslims become non-religious and leave Islam they do not thereby join a new welcoming community of disbelief, because this community doesn't really exist. It's just too amorphous. And coldly indifferent. As Nubia said of the response of non-Muslims to her apostasy, 'people don't really care'. And nor do they fully understand. 'If you tell a Muslim that you've left the religion,' Maryam says, 'all hell would break loose. But if you tell a non-Muslim, to them they don't quite understand the implications.' Salim corroborates this: non-Muslims 'don't get it in the same way that someone from a Muslim background would'. Alia, too, says as much:

> Stephen said it to me several times, that he's no idea what I'm going through, and he is there when I need him to be and he said he will always be there for me but in terms of giving advice, he is a bit useless, like most people, they don't understand my situation.

Ex-Muslims are thus doubly marginalized. They don't belong to the 'Muslim world', but nor do they quite fit into the secular and predominantly white non-Muslim world. They experience a double un-belonging.

Discreditation

'Leaving your faith is the worst thing that you could do.' So said Tasnim. She meant, from the perspective of her family and the wider *ummah* of believers. Leaving Islam is the worst thing you can do from their perspective. But it also happened to be Tasnim's perspective, too, for a period, even though she felt intellectually and morally that she was in the right in renouncing Islam. It was her perspective because it had been inculcated in her growing up. It was part of the air she breathed. She renounced Islam and this left her feeling immensely guilty, as though she'd committed some terrible crime. So she berated herself for this—especially for the shame her apostasy would inflict on her family should it be made public. And she became depressed, withdrawn and lonely.

Tasnim has not fully disclosed her apostasy. She told her sister, but then, after witnessing the extremity of her emotional response, she soon took it back. She has told a few friends. But she has not told anyone else in her family, from whom she is vigilant in concealing it. Thus Tasnim hasn't experienced the kind of assault on her integrity and sense of self-worth that someone like Alia has. Nor has she experienced the sustained and humiliating punitive interventions to which Aisha has been subjected by her parents. But she knows that she has done something which her family and the wider community in which she lives would regard with great disfavour, even revulsion, that she has indeed become someone to whom they would feel antipathy. It's just that they don't know. But Tasnim knows. And, for a while, this tormented her and she felt intensely ambivalent about it.

Farhad felt the same way in the months following his apostasy. Had he done the right thing or had he done the wrong thing? He was torn on the issue. It felt like he'd done the right thing, but it also felt like he'd done the wrong thing: 'I feel right but at the same time I feel guilty. I know I've done nothing wrong but I feel as though I've hurt my mum even though I know I'm in the right.' Nasreen similarly said of the period just after she had apostatized:

> At that point I was still quite young and out of Islam and I was quite ashamed of being the way I was, even though I realized I was right. It was like, oh my god, why can't you just be religious, why can't you just agree with everything?

Nasreen was in her early twenties at the time. She was studying at university and living away from home 'in a very un-Islamic household'. She remembers the unease she felt at having her sister visit:

> I don't have prayer mats and things around, I have booze around. I don't dress up very religiously. I think it's just the little things and you think, oh my god, if my sister opens up my cupboards she'll see skirts as opposed to long scarves or something. Little details of my personal life and my lifestyle that she would pick up on and I was afraid that she would comment or say something bad or something would get back to my parents.

Nasreen remembers the feeling well: 'I didn't want to show them [her family] that I have become like this, even though it's a dichotomy, on one side I know there's nothing wrong with being the way I was, but to their eyes it is wrong.' So Nasreen felt ashamed. But also, at the same time, not ashamed, because she felt that she was in the right and had done nothing wrong and had nothing to feel ashamed about.

Like Tasnim, Farhad and Nasreen are closeted. And so thus far they have escaped the bruising confrontation which disclosure to their loved ones would in all likelihood bring. They are, to use Goffman's terminology, the discreditable, not the discredited.[8] Still, they know exactly what their family and the wider Muslim community would think of their apostasy and the kind of person they have become.

Anti-Apostate Narratives

And how, in their view, would their apostasy be thought of and accounted for among Muslims? The following five themes are a summary of the views and reactions respondents had come across, directly or indirectly, and draws on additional sources for the purposes of explication:

(1) Ex-Muslims are imposters: they were never 'true' believers in the first place and hence their apostasy is false: they were always outside the bounds of the faith. The implication here is that had they 'really' been 'true' believers—had they fully exposed themselves to the truth and beauty of Islam[9]—they would never have contemplated leaving: 'Never could a man who has tasted the sweetness of Islam think of relapsing into unbelief.'[10] Or, as Sultanhussein Tabandeh put it: A man who deserts Islam by definition 'must have played truant to its moral and spiritual truths in his heart earlier'.[11]

(2) Ex-Muslims are cognitively mistaken, confused or deluded: that is, their leaving is premised on either a lack of knowledge about Islam or a misunderstanding of its beliefs. This echoes the now much derided Marxian explanation for the political passivity of the proletariat: had this class not been living a state of 'false class consciousness'—had its members properly recognized their 'true interests' and not yielded to the delusions of capitalist ideology—it would have risen up against the bourgeoisie and removed them from power. Had ex-Muslims properly understood Islam and appreciated the overwhelming intellectual and moral force of its beliefs and values, they would never have doubted it, let alone departed from it.

(3) Ex-Muslims are unserious: that is, their apostasy is fundamentally frivolous, and above all, temporary or 'phase'-like: a kind of teenage rebellion out of which they will eventually mature, suitably chastened. All of the 'outed' ex-Muslims I interviewed had encountered this response, usually from close family members; and all of them were acutely aware of the implication it conveyed: that they were not really unbelievers or apostates, but merely 'playing at it' and would return to the fold once they had recovered their senses.

(4) Ex-Muslims are morally depraved: and it is this, not Islam, which explains their apostasy. The ex-Muslim's depravity takes two forms. The first is motivational: Islam is discarded precisely because it stands in the way of the fulfillment of base and worthless desires,[12] like fornicating and drinking.[13] The second is temperamental: Islam is discarded because of the weak and depraved moral character of the apostate. Base and worthless desires assail Muslims from all directions.[14] Good Muslims follow the Quran and are able to fight these

off. Apostates cannot or are unable to, since they are morally weak and allow themselves to be seduced by ungodly desires.

(5) Ex-Muslims are crazy: that is, mentally unhinged.[15] Their apostasy is not the result of an active, still less rational or reasoned decision, but has been caused by some affliction (e.g. drug addiction), tragedy (e.g. the death of a family member or close friend) or trauma (e.g. sexual or physical abuse)[16] in the life of the apostate. As a consequence of this, apostates have undergone a kind of intellectual and moral rewiring and this has rendered them incapable of following the faith or appreciating its meaning and truth. Loss of faith—and hence sanity—is in some cases attributed to demonic possession.

As can be seen, these five narrative-accounts (for greater detail, see chapter 4) serve to insulate Islam from negative criticism by either (1) denying the apostate's existence ('you were never a 'true Muslim' anyway'), (2) denying the very possibility of principled apostasy (i.e. apostasy motivated by avowable reasons); (3) ascribing disreputable motives to the apostate ('he did it just to mess around'), or (4) defaming the moral character of the apostate ('he's weak').

By constructing Islamic apostasy in these terms, apostates can be conveniently erased from the empirical record. And, where they can't be so readily marginalized from view, their actions can be discounted as motivationally dubious. In short: ex-Muslims don't exit, and even if they do, they have no right to.

One of the greatest challenges ex-Muslims face is resisting and rebutting these demeaning narratives and advancing an alternative definition of reality which portrays them in a more positive light.

Reclaiming the Self

All ex-Muslims must face and adjust to the three problems outlined above. Below, I describe how respondents went about this.

Reorientation

Islam, for many respondents, had been a fundamental source of belief and meaning and guidance. Renouncing it radically overturned that, because now they didn't believe and that left a void, a deficit of belief and meaning and guidance. So they needed to fill that; they needed to recreate a new pattern of belief and meaning and guidance.

In the opening sentence of Saul Bellow's *The Adventures of Augie March*, the novel's narrator declares 'I am an American, Chicago born...and go at things as I have taught myself, free-style, and will make the record in my own way...'[17] Much like Augie March, the respondents I interviewed—all, with one exception, 'Muslim born' but Muslim no longer—must 'go at things' and 'make the record' *their* way, free-style. They have renounced Islam, and now the world looks different and it is facing them, beckoning them, challenging them, astounding them, thrilling them, terrifying them, and they don't quite know how to approach it. But approach it they must. And free-style, without the guidance of Islam, without the support and sympathy of the wider Muslim *ummah*. They once had a script, but now they don't. And that feels extraordinarily exciting, freeing. But also disquieting, because now they have to create and improvise a new script, a new *modus operandi*, a new set of rules for acting and that feels like a very tall order indeed.

Respondents had to adjust to two central problems: (1) the existence of a world without supernatural custodianship and meaning; and (2) the existence of choices and relationships unregulated by Islamic commands.

Existential Reorientation

This is a post from an ex-Muslim forum:

> We don't need a higher meaning; we just need to have goals in our lives. A higher meaning is just a facade that prevents people from truly having a fulfilling life. I'm quite content with having absolutely no metaphysical meaning in my life. And I really doubt any guide for finding meaning in a secular manner has any metaphysical elements to it.
>
> The fact that people have always sought a higher meaning proves nothing other than that people have been brainwashed into it. Yes, I was so fucking depressed when I stopped believing in religion, but that's because I was used to it; it was my safety net, the thing I always fell back on. I know people who were born into atheist families and never went through existential depression. They were and always are content with their lives.
>
> Plus, even if people really *do* need metaphysical meaning, it doesn't mean a metaphysical meaning exists. That argument is ridiculous. Just because you need something doesn't mean you can have it. How childish. But it's a good thing that we don't actually need it. (Emphasis in original)

The author of this post is Ahmed. There is no 'higher' or transcendent source of meaning in the world, no metaphysical *telos* or point to anything. But life is not thereby pointless or without meaning, for it is our goals, our purposeful activity, which give our existence meaning and a measure of satisfaction. This is what Ahmed now thinks. But he didn't always think like that, as he made clear in our interview, and for a while he was overtaken with the feeling that in the absence of a divine plan everything was pointless and futile. Shaking that feeling was difficult, but necessary and he knew he had to do it to stay sane and healthy:

> So I just had to rebuild everything, because my life-plan was set by my religion and I had to now make my own plan and find myself on a deep level and just occupy myself with all sorts of things for me to be happy and find happiness and be more conscious of my life in this world.

Manzoor had reached a similar conclusion. In the aftermath of his apostasy, he says that he 'went all existential' and was troubled by the question of ultimate ends. What were they? What really was the point of life and all the unrelenting struggle and entanglements it entailed? The point, however notional and abstract, had once been to serve God, to follow his commands and to find salvation in a glorious afterlife. But it wasn't anymore. So what now was it?

> There is one thing that I would point to my struggling with, which is, well, if there is no inherent meaning to life, why live it? And the obvious answer didn't seem that obvious to me at the time—that you're given it whether you want it or not, you either live it or you don't. To me it's the obvious answer, but unfortunately I found myself struggling to get behind it. I ended up accepting it because I don't see anything wrong with that analysis. You've got one life to live, so you might as well live it rather than work for an afterlife that may or may not be there. It is something that I had trouble accepting I suspect because it was drilled into me growing up—that we have been created for a purpose.

Tasnim, like Manzoor, also went 'all existential', although she doesn't phrase it quite like this. She said that renouncing Islam had made her feel lost, 'as though I don't know who I am anymore'. The scaffolding of her identity had collapsed and this made her question not only who she now was, but why she should carry on living and to what end: 'I used to think you live your life to please God and get into heaven, but I don't have that anymore. So where do I go from here? How do I live the rest of my life without a purpose?' For a period Tasnim didn't know and that disturbed her. But then:

I eventually realized you don't need a purpose. You just live and you die. That's just life. There is no point to it. You just continue every day. You're just breathing and then one day you'll stop breathing and you'll be dead. I wasn't okay with not having any kind of purpose, to go from having a purpose in life and getting into heaven to nothing. I think that was a struggle. But I just grew up and accepted it, there's no purpose. You just live your life and that's it. That's pretty much it. There's no big picture.

Salim says something similar, but is somewhat more specific on the period between the commencement of breathing and its termination:

You live and then you die and after that you rot and you become part of the universe and in millions of years the earth as it is will no longer exist and there's no meaning to any of it. I just think that my purpose is just to make my family happy, to improve their lives as much as possible, to be happy myself, to be healthy, to live as long as possible, maybe help others in the world, but when you die you die, that's it. That's your fifteen minutes of fame gone. So I don't have a meaning but I do have an aim in life to try and be a civil person and try and be generous, try to be good.

Ayaan Hirsi Ali writes: 'Death is certain, replacing both the siren-song of Paradise and the dread of Hell. Life on this earth, with all its mystery and beauty and pain, is then to be lived far more intensely: we stumble and get up, we are sad, confident, insecure, feel loneliness and joy and love. There is nothing more; but I want nothing more.'[18] Most respondents, I think, would agree with this. Not necessarily with the last five words—some respondents indicated to me that there was a part of them which, as Amina lamented, 'still wants to believe in something, that there is some kind of creator and some kind of deeper meaning'—but with almost everything else: that there is no heaven or hell and that there is only one life and that it must be embraced and lived as fully as possible.

Once this was accepted—that death is final and that there is no after-life and that human actions and events occur for reasons wholly unrelated to God's plan, because there is no God—the ethos of personal responsibility had to be accepted. Some respondents said that adjusting to this was initially difficult, so habituated were they into thinking that their life's plan was divinely preordained. They themselves would now have to take responsibility for their actions. If things went bad in their lives, it was because of them; it had nothing to do with God. Masood recalls:

There's a kind of fear in that I do have to take responsibility for my own actions. It's not like, well, God will sort shit out for me, it's like, if I am complaining about something in my life it's because of something that I've either done or not done, unless it's something completely out of my control. But if I'm saying I'm rubbish at talking to people it's because I'm not going out and talking to people. It's not that it's God trying to save me from the sin of fornication because if I talk to people it will be a slippery slope to shagging someone outside of marriage.

Masood remembers the time he lost his virginity. He barely knew the woman, 'met her on a work thing', and he couldn't get it up, couldn't get an erection. Masood was a Muslim at the time. So he implored God to help him out, even though he knew that God wouldn't approve and that there would be serious consequences later: 'I remember fervently in my mind saying to God please let me do this. If you do I will deal with the consequences.' Masood was eventually able to raise himself to the task. God had willed it. Or so Masood thought at the time. But he now knows otherwise: that the reason he was unable to become aroused was because it was his first time and he was nervous. And he'd been drinking. It wasn't because God was trying to save him from the sin of fornication.

It didn't come easy, adapting to this new way of thinking. But it has immeasurably improved his life, Masood says, because it has forced him to acknowledge and to confront his own shortcomings, instead of excusing them as part of God's design:

> I'm more aware of the fact that things that I'm doing or not doing are down to me as opposed to God trying to throw in an intervening hand. If I want to make a change I have to do that myself. In that sense it's like growing up I suppose. You're not relying on someone else.

Maryam similarly remarks that for so long she had been accustomed to thinking that 'God will change things at some point' that discarding—'letting go of', as she phrased it—that way of thinking was initially difficult. But it had to be done, she said, because the world, intellectually and morally, made infinitely more sense that way.

Practical Reorientation

In the Afterword to his superb book *Marital Separation*, Robert S. Weiss observes that 'separation seems to me like being packed off to a foreign country in which one is constantly confronted by new customs and new practices, and constantly thrown off balance by the strangeness of others' reactions'.[19] 'But in separation', Weiss adds, importantly, 'there has been no customs shed to warn that the setting will be new, and there is no foreign language to signal the possibility that others may behave oddly'.[20] This is also a useful metaphor for thinking about the post-apostasy situation of non-religious ex-Muslims: they discard Islam, which itself is an intensely tumultuous experience, and they then enter a world which is in many respects foreign. This world is the same world as the one they inhabited before: it is populated by the same people and the same zones of life and interaction continue to shape it. And yet it is a profoundly different world, where there are now new challenges and new rules. And, as we have seen, new ways of getting it wrong, of fucking up, because there is no rule book, no reliable ex-Muslim post-apostasy script, for knowing what to do in the face of the myriad dilemmas and difficulties which befall the person who renounces Islam.

On leaving Islam respondents had to learn, and learn fast, new ways of approaching the various practical challenges and opportunities that the world—the world beyond Islam—had in store for them. These challenges and opportunities were by no means new to them, but they hadn't faced them before, not fully and not so as to have acquired a reliable and personally suitable *modus operandi* for dealing with them. Challenges and opportunities like creating and sustaining personal relationships with non-Muslims, socializing with non-Muslims of all genders, partying with non-Muslims, going on dates with non-Muslims, having sex with non-Muslims, boozing, dressing non-Islamically, dining non-Islamically. Before, as Muslims, they had tended to avoid these sorts of challenges and opportunities, or, on the occasions when they succumbed, dealt with them altogether badly and with serious consequences for their self-esteem. And so they were short on experience and their game was at best rudimentary. That would have to change: their game would need tightening. So they actively worked on that, because they knew that there was no alternative and that the world would not wait for them and would not forgive their inexperience.

Dating and drinking: these were two key areas of personal social life for which tightening their game was definitely required, especially for the women respondents, who had had scant experience in both. About the latter, this is what Amina, who is now in her mid-twenties—had to say:

> Drinking—that's another anxiety, because everyone my age knows how to socialize and I feel like I don't know the customs. I know people sometimes buy people rounds, but how does that work? Do you offer them, are you

supposed to and when? And what drinks are appropriate for what times? Are there drinks that are appropriate for certain times and places, like restaurants? I don't know. That's my worry as well, that I might drink too much and be silly and I don't want to puke or something.

Amina says that she finds socializing difficult, partly because of her natural shyness, but also because she's had very little practice at it. The CEMB forum has helped her with this, because it has provided a social network with which she has connected. She is an active participant of forum 'meet-ups', where online members meet regularly and socialize outside the forum. This gets her out of the house, away from the computer ('I'm an online kind of person'), and has helped her overcome some of her shyness and learn how to interact with people in bars, restaurants and nightclubs, places which had hitherto been unfamiliar to her and a source of much anxiety. Meet-ups, she says, feel safe, 'because some of us are kind of shy and new to the whole drinking thing and there are people there we sort of know from the forum'. Meet-ups, as Amina describes them, offer a kind of training for social engagement beyond the forum community.

Like Amina, Aisha, when she first apostatized, was also baffled about 'the whole drinking game', but that didn't stop her from embracing it as soon as the chance arrived. But for all the humiliations and mortifications and self-recriminations, Aisha in time learned 'that there are limitations and that you can say no'. And that has been an incredibly valuable lesson and not just for regulating her drinking.

Many respondents confessed that they had problems dating: they just didn't know how to do it or how even to organize a date. There are sexual scripts for this[21] and respondents didn't have them. Hitting on people, too: that was another source of bafflement and difficulty, especially for male respondents, because they knew their game here was especially poor and the poverty of it shamed and frustrated them. This is Masood on his nightclub experience:

> The only times I've ever really spoken to women in clubs has been when I'm pissed and quite taken with their glittery trousers and complimenting them on their choice of outfit and coming off as camp or gay or something. And it's weird because if they're a single girl and I talked to them like they're a genuinely interesting and a unique person it freaks them out, like what does he want?

Masood, though taking full responsibility for his own fallings on this front, explains that his ill-preparedness for picking up women is related to his family background: 'I remember when we'd go to relatives and friends we'd be segregated in various rooms, the men would sit in one room and the women would sit in another, and I'd just sit there in silence with the men, listening to them talking about medical ailments or whatever.' That Masood has problems talking with women—outside of family and work—is primarily because he was so unpractised in talking with them growing up.

For Nabilah, the issue isn't picking up men, not least because Nabilah is funny and warm and strikingly beautiful. The issue, rather, is how to indicate sexual interest in men she is attracted to, as well as initiating actual sexual contact. Nabilah, who is in her late thirties, married young, very young. But she is no longer married, having recently divorced. And so for Nabilah, who for nearly the entirety of her adult life has been with one and the same man, the whole dating game is new. But, as she says, it's a learning process.

The Unlearning Process

Just as respondents had to develop a *modus operandi* for dealing with relatively new and unfamiliar challenges, they also had to unlearn certain structures of response and reaction which had defined and guided their former Muslim self. That, too, was part of the reorientation process—to discard certain ingrained reflexes and habitual ways of thinking.

Azhar, for example, said that although he has firmly renounced Islam as a system of belief and morality there are moments when he is overtaken by impulses and urges that had been part of his old Muslim self but which he now finds repugnant. And this shames him, because these impulses and urges are fundamentally anomalous with his new self-image, with the person he has now become. They belong to his past, to his biographical prehistory, not to his present, to the here-and-now, and his conscious mind does everything it can to purge them from his mental landscape. Azhar's atavisms are primarily to do with sex and sexuality:

> I have absolutely no reason to be against or offended by any sort of consensual sexual practice. I'm liberal. I don't care if you have sex with whoever and whatever you want to do, go ahead and do it, but obviously within Islam I was taught that being gay is wrong, that sodomy is wrong, that a man and a

woman shouldn't have sex before marriage and so on. So I can't just switch that off. I can't just wake up one day and be like, it's fine, you can be gay. I have to actively tell myself that it's okay and repress those feelings that have been programmed into me to feel that's it's wrong. And if I come across say a new sexual practice I won't instantly think, oh that's kind of cool, what is that about? I'll be like, oh that's so disgusting. But then why would I think that? It just this Islamic programming and I am trying to ignore it, but it's still there in the background.

Abdullah also made reference to his 'inherent homophobia and misogyny', said that these were hangover traits from his past and that he has had to actively resist their grip, because intellectually and morally he is opposed to prejudice of any kind.

For many respondents, the problem wasn't atavisms related to the practices or proclivities of others; it was very precisely guilt feelings related to their own practices or proclivities: they would do something, were about to do something or would want to do something and suddenly, out of nowhere, a familiar voice would intrude itself and try to crowd out all other thoughts and feelings. It was their old nemesis, the *halal* voice. It would seize them and for a moment, for a second or two, it would beseech them and they'd listen to it and cower, before regaining their balance and telling it to 'shut the fuck up'.

Azhar again:

I also had a sense of guilt. So now if, say, I somehow come across some gay porn, I may still have that sense of guilt looking at it. But I have to tell myself this is stupid, why am I feeling guilty? I should have no problem looking at this, I just have to make sure I tell myself that in the first place, to reason with myself and say this is stupid, I shouldn't feel guilty about this. But sometimes it is difficult to reason with emotion.

Islam, Azhar says, 'sticks with you in your sub-conscious'.

Masood, as we have seen, is dismissive of the idea that ex-Muslims leave Islam solely for the pleasures of the *haram* world and is insistent that 'I could have been out just doing the usual hedonistic thing, just going out and getting pissed, shagging birds but I didn't'. Elaborating, Masood revealingly said that, 'a lot of the accusations were things like you're just doing this so you can get drunk and fornicate but so what if you want to... it's taken me a while to admit that it's okay to do that'.

For Khadija it has also taken a long time—admitting that it's okay to engage in sex outside of marriage. But there are times when she feels that casual sex is, to quote Aisha, reporting the words of her sister, 'an immoral act, filthy' and that to engage in it is to 'have no respect for yourself':

> I still find that deep down I'm unable to shake the way that it [Islam] made me feel about having sex and stuff like that. I'm sexually repressed. Although it doesn't sound like it online, in real life I'm a sexually repressed atheist, which is because of my background. There are these parts that still make me quite unhappy that I can't shake in which I feel that Islam still plays a part in my life. I might not be a Muslim anymore but that hasn't changed the way I relate to men, the way I relate to sex, the way I relate to feelings of shame.

Many other respondents made the same point and said they were concerned that Islam had not been fully expunged from their internal world and that aspects of it continued to hound them, like some demented stalker. Nubia has put this very well:

> Sometimes if I go out and come back late I feel really guilty, what am I doing? What if my mum saw me now? I should be ashamed of myself. Am I bringing dishonour to my name? Stuff like that. I think there's still a feeling of, I'm sinning or I'm doing something wrong, even though deep down I know it's not really wrong. But there's just that lingering feeling that I shouldn't be doing this. But I think that's because my mum focuses a lot on self-image and how you present yourself and things like that. Especially with women, my mum, she's horrible. Like, whenever we'd walk together somewhere all she'd do is comment on the way women are dressed in the street, she'd say, 'oh look at what she's wearing, her jeans are too tight, she's definitely going to hell'. And I never could stand it even as a Muslim, I thought who are you to judge? That's God's judgment. My brother and I had this game we'd play when we were younger and we'd be sitting in my mum's car with our heads out the window and we'd just look around at all the women and decide if they were going to heaven or hell based on how they were dressed. We'd say, 'oh she's not dressed modestly, she'll go to hell'. So I think that's why, because my mum just beat that into us, the whole modesty thing. If I see other people I don't judge, but with me I berate myself a lot. It's like there's an inner Muslim in me still, yelling at me and saying, 'what are you doing?'

Ali has similarly had to fight his 'inner Muslim'. He says that when he first apostatized he was still very uneasy around women, because it had been ingrained in him that women were somehow dangerous and might corrupt him:

> I've certainly become more liberal and I now have more confidence. Just recently I went to a salon and had my hair cut, but four years ago I would

have literally not had my hair cut in a salon. You still have that kneejerk reaction in you, it's a woman touching my hair, she's washing it so you still feel that stigma, oh what is she thinking about me? It's a bit intrusive, but I have more control over this now.

Some respondents said that their 'inner Muslim' manifested itself in the spontaneous invocation of Islamic expressions and that they'd worked hard to expunge these from their lexicon:

Oh yeah, that's big. That's big. '*Inshallah*', '*Alhamdulillah*', all these words. It's because it's so intertwined with the culture itself and it's really hard sometimes to separate the culture from the religion, especially Arab culture. I know some of the people on the forum, they're Pakistani, they're Indian, Somali, Sudanese but being an Arab, it's in your food, it's in the way you eat, your music, everything. So I find myself saying whenever I'm cooking and if I've poured hot water down the sink '*dastoor*' comes out, because the jinn lives in there and I would burn him if I didn't say it, and then I laugh. Because as soon as that happens you recognize it and you laugh and you consciously try not to do it again because you know it's silly. (Nabilah)

For Khadija, as she explains in an online forum post:

It was '*Bismillah*' and '*Inshallah*' which were the hardest for me to shake, but I got over it, it took a while but I don't even feel the urge anymore. I did work on it though, so it is something you would have to actively remind yourself not to say, until you stopped saying it altogether. I think 'salam' is fine, it just means peace, but anything that incorporates the word 'allah', maybe you should try scratching that from your vocabulary. It's all relative though.[22]

Not a few respondents confessed to having difficulties in eating pork products, especially bacon. They just couldn't do it. It repulsed them, the look and feel and smell of it, even the idea of it. And for some, this clearly troubled them, because it contained the implication that they were not fully through with Islam, that it still had a psychological hold on them in some way. Whereas for others, it didn't bother them, because, as they saw it, their revulsion of pig-meat was simply a natural and unavoidable consequence of their upbringing ('because it's drilled into your head very much that it's disgusting, it's dirty': Amina) and held no significance in terms of belief and conviction.

Reference

In Chapter 3 I suggested that that the process of becoming an apostate is marked by a crisis of the self and that this occurs as doubts amass and intensify. This crisis is primarily a crisis over belief and identity and prompts a personal odyssey of self-discovery, culminating in disavowal. But the crisis is not fully resolved, and returns in a second instalment. This is because disavowal itself is not enough: it is not sustaining enough, somehow, to continually define belief and selfhood negatively. Belief and identity, respondents felt, must also be defined positively and not solely in reference to a negation. They needed to move on, but knew that this would be impossible if they were constantly in thrall to the negative. They needed the positive, or at least some semblance of it. So they went in search of that. They also went in search of something else, something even more vital: understanding, solidarity, a sense of belonging. They needed a release from their social and emotional isolation. They needed to know that they weren't crazy, that there were others just like them. They needed the spark of human connection.

They needed reference points: people they could talk with and with whom they could exchange their experiences and learn from. And they found them—in the virtual world of the internet, because it was safer there and because there were so few obvious reference points among the people they knew in their everyday lives beyond that virtual world.

For many respondents, the crucial reference point was the online forum of the Council of Ex-Muslims of Britain. This forum was launched in 2007 and attracts members from all over the globe, although the core of the membership is from Britain and Canada. Members tend to be non-religious, identifying themselves primarily as either agnostic or atheist. The other major forum for ex-Muslims—established and funded by Faith Freedom International—attracts greater numbers of ex-Muslim converts to Christianity and is more overtly political in its concerns, whereas the dominant emphasis of the CEMB forum is on self-help and mutual aid.

The forum itself is multifaceted. It is made up of a diversity of thematically demarcated zones. There are ten in total, ranging from 'News and Events', 'Life, the Universe & Everything' to 'Genders and Sexualities' and 'The Pit of Perdition' (an area explicitly reserved for 'ranting'). Each zone is further divided into specific themes. The site is run by a small group of 'admins' (administrators) and 'mods' (moderators), whose function is to maintain and update the site. Admins and mods also police the content of the site, removing any hateful speech that comes to their attention.[23]

Because the forum is primarily focused on self-help, a good deal of the posting on it concerns the personal experiences of ex-Muslims and the collective problems they face. It is primarily a place for communion, for telling stories, for sharing and for learning. Members take this aspect of it very seriously and the emphasis is on inclusivity. Muslims, for example, are welcome and welcomed. Some of the discussion is solemn, as it must be, but much of it, solemn or otherwise, is enlivened by good humour, especially irony. Advice is freely given and debated. Cautionary tales are exchanged and dramatized. Much of this concerns the twin problems of concealment and disclosure. By way of illustration:

> Sometimes you'll have to be an amazing actor/undercover cop/spy in covering your tracks acting 'as a Muslim' to certain Muslims who don't know you well enough and give you the benefit of the doubt.

> Fake praying is much easier than normal prayers. I can just pretend I'm on the last *rakah* and just chill out. Make sure you say *takbeer* out loudly though.

> Learn the art of peppering your conversations with token '*mashallahs*' and '*inshallahs*' accordingly to blend in depending on how religious the crowd is (this is probably quite easy if you have just left Islam but gets harder as time goes on). However, one thing I categorically refuse to do, even if everyone in the room does it, is murmur 'peace be on him' like a sheep whenever Mo [the Prophet] is mentioned.

> Avoid telling Muslim relatives or friends that you are an apostate unless you are 110% sure they won't tell others. I've made terrible misjudgments in the past about the things that I have told people (they seem to be agreeing with you or seeming to 'see your point of view' at the time, then go and spill the beans to your parents or siblings). Until you are financially independent, it's much better to be someone who is seen as Quran-only or 'progressive' rather than as an apostate.

> My 2 cents:

> Make friends with other ex-Muslims in real life if you can. Find them on this forum or other places around the net if you don't know any already. I've gotten to know a few via Facebook and we have created quite a circle in our part of the world—2 of my good friends have even fallen in love and gotten married (both ex-Muslim atheists). We get together often, have become quite close friends and help each other out with various things like listening to each other, relating, sharing ideas, partying, supporting each other. It's

given all of us a lot of confidence and a sense of community that most of us were sorely lacking. It can be difficult to trust people online, and I'd advise everyone to be very careful as there are all sorts hanging around on the net. But over time, you could meet some awesome people if you proceed slowly and use your best judgment. When in doubt, best to err on the side of caution, but don't isolate yourself completely if you don't have to. It can be great to have even a couple of like-minded people a phone call or text away...I can't put enough emphasis on working on getting yourself financially independent, especially for the ex-Muslim women, but for all ex-Muslims really. It's the #1 advice and it will help you throughout your life to not be financially dependent on anyone for your own survival. Get a career, get a degree, a certification in something you can do that will pay the bills if you need to move away and live on your own. Even if you don't have to, it will make your parents and your partner respect you more than if you are dependent on them for your finances...[24]

Don't go buckwild with the drinking etc...Refrain on calling Muslims idiots and other insulting names. You were one of them once...Be prepared to lose friends and family if you come out...[25]

Goffman says that every stigmatized group has its own lore, its own hard-earned wisdom.[26] The ex-Muslims grouped around the CEMB are no exception.

Among respondents who joined the forum,[27] most said they came across it by accident. 'Stumbled' is the word they commonly used: they stumbled across it. By which they meant that they weren't looking for it. Couldn't have been, because they didn't know it existed, didn't even know that there were 'ex-Muslims', much less that they had their own organizations and forums. In stumbling across it, they were truly startled at what they saw and heard. It was revelatory: they were not alone. And it was vindicating: vindicating just by dint of knowing that there were others like them, who had been through similar experiences, whose families sounded just like their families and whose trajectories and travails echoed their own. Knowing this lessened their sense of isolation; it also helped subdue their private suspicion that they were somehow odd or 'weird'.[28] And that felt good and confirming.

Alia was looking for advice when she found—'stumbled across'—the forum. She was planning her second coming out, but hadn't yet gone ahead with it. And she wanted a sounding board, someone she could share her thoughts with, and wisdom, if she could get it. How should she tell her parents—for the second time—about her apostasy? So Alia turned to Google. There was a link to the website of FFI and she hit it. Alia says she 'lurked' there and on its forum, but not for long, since she felt uneasy about what she saw as its unremitting anti-Islamic bias, detecting also an undertone of racism among some members. She was also put off by the high volume of 'Christians on there, using it to try and convert ex-Muslims into Christianity'. So she went back to Google and tried again, this time discovering a link to the CEMB and its forum. She followed it and was reassured and inspired by what she found: 'It was very helpful to read everybody else's stories, especially successful ones, and it does help you to know that you're not alone and that everybody else has to go through the same crap.' Alia decided to become a member and her first post was a cry for help:

> I made a thread asking them for advice. How on earth am I going to tell my parents that I'm not a Muslim? Yeah, I just came out with that. I didn't mention anything about the boyfriend part first because I was a bit worried they might accuse me of leaving Islam solely for him and that's not a good enough reason. So I didn't mention him straightaway. I just asked them how I'm going to come out.

This is what Alia's first post in fact read:

> Hey everyone, I'm new to this forum. I'm looking for some advice. I am an ex-Muslim and my family and everyone I am related to is a Muslim. I have absolutely no idea how I will be able to tell my parents that I have deconverted as I know it will upset them a lot. They are quite traditional in that they have arranged marriages and the whole family honour thing. I love my parents a lot and I don't want to hurt them or destroy their honour but I cannot spend my entire life pretending to be a Muslim. I really feel like I've betrayed them as they trust me a lot. I would love to hear how everyone else told their parents. I'd also like some advice on how to tell mine.

Someone on the forum suggested that Alia compose a letter explaining her position and send it to her father. This didn't appeal to her: 'I can't do a letter because it's just not me and I thought I don't know when it's going to arrive and the uncertainty of that just put me off using a letter.' Someone else then suggested she send an email—and that did appeal to her.

Nubia discovered the CEMB forum under similar circumstances. She was in need of advice, support. But there weren't many advisers, still fewer supporters, whom she could reliably turn to, certainly no one among her network of friends and family. So she sought out the company of strangers in the online world, because that was the safest option,

because that was her only option. She'd just come out to her mother—
fully this time—and there had been a 'shit-storm' and she was desperate
to talk about it and to figure out what her next move would be.

> I knew it existed. I used to lurk for a long time, for two or three months. But I
> only joined when I told my mum and I didn't know what to do. I had no idea.
> And I wanted some support because I didn't know anyone at all who was an
> ex-Muslim. I just felt alone so I went on the forum and I made an introduction
> explaining what happened with my mum. I was like, help, I don't know what to
> do. Everyone was really nice. And they're all a close community of people who
> understand each other. Because it can get really lonely at times and you start
> thinking, am I the crazy one? Am I wrong? What am I doing?

So Nubia was looking for support and there on the CEMB forum she
found it. And this was a common experience among respondents.
Nabilah, remembering the first time she came across the forum, said:

> I was floored...It's like, whoa, you guys actually exist, oh my god! There are
> ex-Muslims in the world. And I appreciate that, just knowing that ex-Mus-
> lims exist. That's fantastic. It validates us, yes we exist.

Tasnim, on first discovering the CEMB forum, was similarly taken
aback and heartened by the realization that she was not alone:

> I was just typing in Google searching stuff. Then I came across the forum and
> it was so strange because I don't know anyone who went through the same
> things as me. Anyone at all. It was strange reading the bios and to see every-
> one just gathered to talk about the struggles they had and the life experiences
> they had. They were so similar to mine. It was just like, you know what, I'm
> not alone.

Farhad, referring to a YouTube video produced by a CEMB forum
member, says this:

> I joined the forum after I saw a YouTube video of one of the members. He
> chronicled his process of becoming an ex-Muslim. And it was one of the most
> powerful moments in my life because this was the first time I'd actually heard
> another ex-Muslim's voice. And he was saying and repeating what I had in my
> head, a lot of my doubts, a lot of my thoughts about Islam. And it was a really
> powerful moment because it made me realize there were other people like me
> who'd left. Obviously I know absolutely no-one who has left Islam so I felt
> alienated, I didn't really have anyone to talk to. There was no-one who I could
> share experiences with and no-one whose experiences I could learn from.

And this was true for most respondents, which is why the CEMB forum was such a revelation: 'It was good just feeling like there were other people out there who were just like me' (Amina); 'It's good to know that you're not completely on your own' (Maryam); 'It was great having a community of people who could discuss these things openly and with whom you could make a joke about Islam without looking over your shoulder' (Azhar).[29]

But however revelatory it was, the forum was not a comprehensive answer to their loneliness and alienation. It alleviated it, certainly, but it didn't dispel it. And sometimes it became too much, too overwhelming. Too many sad stories, too much upset and heartache. Farhad, who was initially euphoric at discovering other ex-Muslims online, said:

> It used to help but now it brings me down more than anything. That's why I don't really post anymore on the forum or read it much. It's sort of depressing. Sometimes you just want to get away from your problems and reading about other people who have similar problems to you, it brings it back to me.

Wahid similarly said that although the forum helped him and widened his frame of reference ('this is going to sound really bad but knowing that people have had it worse kind of makes me appreciate that I don't have it that bad'), it also made him feel low:

> If anything the forum depresses me more than it makes me feel happy. Because most of the things I relate to are going to make me sad. I can get upset really quickly and the forum doesn't help in that because if somebody posts something and it's about how they feel that will trigger off emotions in me and I can get really depressed.

Robert S. Weiss writes that loneliness is 'the state of being without emotional partnership'.[30] While the CEMB forum is an important source of support for its members, it does not provide the kind of intimate and enduring emotional partnership which can act as a bulwark against lasting loneliness, because only the world of non-mediated face-to-face interaction can offer this. The forum may provide a catalyst for it (I met a few people who had struck up enduring friendships outside of it), but forum-life itself is not an adequate substitute for it. Omar puts it like this:

> We are a social animal. I want some proper bonding. I don't want to be sat behind a fucking computer. I'm a child of the eighties, before all this stuff

came out. I want proper interaction. I want to go to a restaurant. I want to go to a pub.

Khadija, also a child of the eighties and though strongly supportive of the forum, shares the same frustration. She says the forum helps her feel less alone. But only when she's on it. And so when she logs off and goes back to her real life she is instantly returned to feelings of loneliness and depression.

Redefinition

As well as serving as a reference-point for former or wavering Muslims, the CEMB forum also provides a language for self-redefinition, a web of categorizations which former or wavering Muslims can draw on to make sense of their experiences and who they are or are becoming.

With just one exception (Aisha), respondents affiliated with CEMB apostatized before they came into contact with the CEMB website and forum. So the forum didn't facilitate their apostasy.[31] But it undoubtedly coloured its meaning, because it delineated it. It categorized it and gave it shape. It gave them shape—as persons, as moral beings. Made them realize who they were and how they differed from the people they grew up around and became estranged from. It sharpened their self-awareness. It solidified their difference from Muslims. Yasmin, for example, says that in the period between disavowing Islam and coming into contact with the CEMB forum, she defined herself as 'Pagan', because 'I specifically liked that it means non-Christian, Jewish or Muslim and it has a certain deviant quality to it that I liked'. 'I also called myself', she adds, 'a Heathen and an Apostate, again in a sort of defiant way'. But what she didn't call herself was an ex-Muslim, because 'I didn't even know what an ex-Muslim was'. The CEMB forum changed that: it opened up a new world and gave her 'a sort of cohesive vocabulary' with which to express 'a lot of things I had already thought or considered'. And it gave her the term 'ex-Muslim': 'As soon as I heard it, it clicked, like, oh yeah, that makes sense'. Nabilah similarly recalls that 'I didn't even know they existed until I found the forum'. She describes reading the testimonies of ex-Muslims as 'a wow moment' and says discovering the CEMB forum 'helped label me as an ex-Muslim': 'I recognized myself. I said, hey I'm that—that's what I am. I'm that, I'm there, that's what I am. Seeing Mohsin and the rest of the crew on the forum I found myself and where I fit.'

THE APOSTATES

The Dissenting I

A few respondents were emphatic on the matter: they did not want to define themselves as ex-Muslims. They saw Islam in uniformly negative terms. Even the very word 'Muslim' they viewed negatively. So they didn't want it in their self-definition. What they wanted was to eradicate it from their self-definition: to not reference it. In any way. So there would be no calling themselves 'ex-Muslims'. The first two letters were fine; it was the seven remaining ones which furnished the problem. They had to go, had to be erased, so keen was the impulse to dissociate, to cut loose from Islam.

This, however, was unusual, because most respondents on discovering the term chose to adopt it as an identity marker. Not necessarily as their foremost identity marker and not without reservations. But it was undeniable: they were ex-Muslims. That is who they were.

Although most had adopted the term, its meaning and salience clearly varied from respondent to respondent and with the passage of time. Typically, for the newly apostatized it had greater significance and emitted a brighter glow, whereas for those whose apostasy was of an older vintage that significance had waned and the scarlet 'A' with which they had first branded themselves had become less vivid. Salim recalls:

> I wanted to be this apostate, you know, *The Apostate*. It used to be like a badge of honour to me. I used to think I'm the first of many, a maverick. Someone who would make Muslims leave their religion and make non-Muslims realize that this plague is coming and they have to lock the doors and hide their daughters and stuff.

Salim says that in the year after he had apostatized there were bouts of great fervency, of researching Islam and of publicly challenging it, albeit only in the online world and always under the cover of anonymity. In this period, Salim would also visit Islamic-themed forums for the sole purpose of seeking out Muslims whom he could antagonize with his anti-Islamic rhetoric. Salim calls this 'trolling' and admits that for a short time that is what he became: an internet 'troll', his victims all unsuspecting believers of the faith. In opposing Islam Salim says he found a purpose. Playing the role of 'The Apostate' gave his life a meaning. But the role was short-lived and the negative energy required to sustain it petered out. At university he had been exposed to 'critical thinking' and he began to rethink some of his own assumptions, eventually realizing that 'you're not that important and the world isn't black and white and Islam isn't this giant plague on the borders of Europe trying to engulf it'.

Hanif's trajectory is in some respects similar, although he was never militant in the sense that Salim was. Indeed, Hanif has always been resolutely opposed to Salim's former brand of militancy and spoke with lively contempt about FFI and its agenda. Still, the 'ex-Muslim' label, when he had first discovered it, was immensely important to him. And then, after a period, it became appreciably less important as an aspect of his identity:

> If we'd met three or four years ago I could have spoken about scriptures, spoken about *hadiths* and things like that with a really critical eye but now I'm kind of bored of it all. I'm bored of Islam now. So three or four years ago it would have been a major part of my identity being an ex-Muslim and I was looking a lot into it. Now I've kind of mellowed and I don't really care about religion anymore.

Some respondents said that although the term 'ex-Muslim' had less and less salience to them with the passage of time, they did not want to fully erase it from their identity, since they felt it was politically important to publicly profess it, anonymously or otherwise. They didn't want their past to overshadow who they now were or had become. But at the same time they felt it was crucial to acknowledge and to tell the world that they were once Muslims, that it is possible to leave Islam. Over and over they had heard the same thing: that they had never been 'real' Muslims and so were not 'truly' apostates or that their apostasy was just a fleeting and reckless phase or that no sane person actually leaves Islam or leaves of their own accord and for good reasons. These respondents vigorously dissented from all this. 'We are here. We Exist. Get used to it.' This is what they wanted to say. This message was important to them. For sure, it did a degree of violence to their own singularity, but that was a price they were prepared to pay. They had drawn inspiration and validation from finding other lone voices just like their own. And they in turn wanted to give something back and help all those others just like them who hadn't yet found a voice with which to identify and to take solace from. As Yasmin put it, 'I have moved on, but I feel it's a politically expedient thing to do at times'. Jaffar concurs with this. He has major reservations about using the term 'ex-Muslim' to define himself, but nonetheless espouses it publicly in defence of 'the ex-Muslim community'. Azhar similarly says that although he has misgivings over self-identifying as an ex-Muslim, he embraces the term as 'a rallying cry'. 'It's a banner to stand under and I'll proudly stand under it.' Luqman, though he doesn't want it to become a master status, also commends its use, because 'it's showing that, yes, you can leave'.

A small number of respondents reported that although they had 'moved on' and no longer centrally defined themselves in terms of the ex-Muslim label they would summon it and associated and more pungent sobriquets like 'apostate' and '*kāfir*' if the occasion demanded and not just for a political purpose: when, for example, they had encountered belligerent forms of apostate denial or apostate condemnation from Muslims. As Jaffar comments, 'I like using that word [apostate] to piss people off sometimes, more like a fuck you'. Yasmin, as we have seen already, said something very similar, minus the profanity.

The Affirming I

A striking number of respondents said that although they recognized themselves as ex-Muslims, they still felt uneasy about adopting the term as a signifier of personal identity. This, they explained, was because they didn't want to define themselves negatively—that is, in relation to what they were not. They wanted to define themselves positively. They wanted to affirm something and incorporate that, and not a negative property, into their self-definition. Jaffar, for example, remarks:

> As an individual do I want to be called an ex-Muslim and defined by something I'm not? As an individual, I'd prefer to be called something that I am rather than something I'm not. If you're divorced would you rather be known as a single man or an ex-husband? You're not going to go round and tell people, 'Hey, I'm an ex-husband'. You're just going to tell them you're single.

Ramesh expresses the same sentiment:

> I don't like defining myself. I guess I have to in some circumstances. Right now, I am an ex-Muslim talking to you and an apostate because I am. But at the same time I don't want something negative defining who I am. I don't want to be defined by something that I'm not. I want to be defined by something that's positive. If anything I'd probably say that, if I could have a big title, I'm a humanist, maybe. Something positive. Something that is not ex-anything. Something that is positive in its own right. And then underneath that I could be an atheist or agnostic, ex-Muslim, apostate. Under there. But my main title should be something that's positive and something that isn't an ex-anything else.

Azhar endorses this almost word for word:

> I guess I would say that I'm an apostate or ex-Muslim, but I don't like defining myself as a negative. I don't want to be 'I'm not that'. I don't want to go down that road. It's true that I was a Muslim and I'm not anymore but I don't really want to be labelled as anything.

For a few respondents, the affirmative project of self-identity involved not just looking forward and beyond their past for new sources of identification, but also looking back in an effort to selectively disentangle the good from the bad in their former lives as Muslims. Tasnim says that although she has apostatized and adopted an atheist outlook, she still feels culturally tied to Islam in some way. She had grown up with and among Bengali Muslims and feels that this core biographical experience has indelibly shaped her as a person. Certain attitudes and ways of acting in her culture she likes and admires. There are other aspects she doesn't like or value. Regardless of this, Bengali Muslim culture, as she experienced it in the city she has lived her whole life, was, is, an elemental part of her. So she wants her self-definition to reflect that:

> My friend was like, 'Oh, you don't'—this was back when I didn't drink—'You don't drink, you don't eat pork. You don't fuck around, you're still a Muslim.' But I'm like, 'I don't believe in God'. She's like, 'but you still act like a Muslim'. I think that's what started me thinking about being a Muslim atheist. It sounds like a contradiction, but it's like the journey from Muslim to atheist and how you can combine the culture of Muslims with the belief of atheists. Putting it into one to see how it could work despite it being an oxymoron.

For Omar, the emphasis is the other way round. It is atheist first, Muslim second:

> If somebody says, 'Come on, it's time for prayer, we've got to pray', then no I can't do that. Everything else, Eid, for example, I see that as part of my culture. I identify with that on a cultural sort of level because culturally what else do I know? What, do I suddenly become a Chelsea fan and make football my religion? Atheist Muslim. That's how I would define myself. You get secular Jews don't you? So I don't see a problem with identifying with a culture that I've grown up in because, right okay, I reject everything, what do I do, what's left?

THE APOSTATES

The Irreducible I

In *The Human Stain* Nathan Zuckerman, the book's narrator, describes Coleman Silk, a disgraced former classics professor and a black man who passes as a white man, as 'the greatest of the great *pioneers* of the I'.[32] Silk's overwhelming drive and ambition is to be himself, to live life on his own terms, 'to become his own man'.[33] Even if it means lying and passing as a white person, even if it means renouncing his family ('murdering' his mother, as Zuckerman describes it)[34] and cutting all ties to the entirety of his past. He has allegiance to neither the black world nor the white world. He has allegiance only to the singular Coleman Silk:

> At Howard he'd discovered that he wasn't just a nigger to Washington, D.C.—as if that shock weren't strong enough, he discovered at Howard that he was a Negro as well. A Howard Negro at that. Overnight the raw I was part of a we with all of the we's overbearing solidity, and he didn't want anything to do with it or with the next oppressive we that came along either. You finally leave home, the Ur of we, and you find *another* we? Another place that's just like that, the *substitute* for that?...No. No. He saw the fate awaiting him, and he wasn't having it. Grasped it intuitively and recoiled spontaneously. You can't let the big they impose its bigotry on you any more than you can let the little they become a we and impose its ethics on you. Not the tyranny of the we and its we talk and everything that the we wants to pile on your head. Never for him the tyranny of the we that is dying to suck you in, the coercive, inclusive, historical, inescapable moral we...Instead the raw I with all its agility... Singularity. The passionate struggle for singularity. The singular animal.[35]

Most respondents, I think, would be able to identify with Silk and his struggle against the overbearing we and its we talk and we morality. They had felt estranged from Islam because it didn't reflect who they really were. They rebelled against what they saw as its unthinking group mentality, because this radically undermined their deeply felt sense of personal autonomy. So when they renounced Islam it would not be for an alternative totalist system of belief, religious or otherwise. And when it came to redefining themselves they would not be exchanging the grip of one tyrannical signifier for that of another. They were trying to work out who they were and what they discovered was that they were not one thing, but many things. They were irreducible, boundless. They were singular individuals. Check out, for example, Nabilah's take on this:

> Okay, so I'm an ex-Muslim, but I'm also this and that and I work at the Women's Shelter and I'm so proud of myself for doing that and I'm learning

and there's so much more to it than that. So here I am and that's what I am, sure, and we can discuss that but we can also discuss so many other different things and if you see me as so many other different things and not just that you'll connect with me on something else. You will. Okay, you're against me on this but that's fine, that's only one part of me.

Amir was similarly keen to stress that he was far more than the sum of his apostasy: 'Yes I am an ex-Muslim. I am an apostate. These terms describe a side of me, but not the whole me.' Salim put it in this way: 'So if I was to say I'm an apostate, that's along with seventy or eighty other labels I am which could include fan of *Pulp Fiction*, you know?' Says Ramesh, hitting on the same theme: 'I'm not a believer in God. I'm not a follower of Islam. But at the same time I'm also a father, a graphic designer and so on. There's all these things that I am.'

Reaffirmation

About apostates, the Quran is unequivocal: unequivocally severe, that is. 'God rejects those who disbelieve', it says.[36] But what about those 'who, having believed, then increase in their disbelief...'?[37] What does it say about this category of unbeliever? What does it say, in other words, about the ordinary men and women at the centre of this book? It says this: they 'will not be saved even if they offer enough gold to fill the entire earth. Agonizing torment is in store for them, and there will be no one to help them.'[38] Agonizing torment not in the here-and-now, but in the hereafter: 'If any of you revoke your faith and die as disbelievers, your deeds will come to nothing in this world and the Hereafter, and you will be inhabitants of the Fire, there to remain'.[39] Interminable agonizing torment, then.

All respondents were aware that in apostatizing they had crossed a line, aware that, from the perspective of Islam, they had done a very bad thing indeed. But they knew it instinctively, because it was implanted into their very DNA that disbelief was bad and that, of all the variants of disbelief, atheism was not just bad, but abominable and dangerous. They had assimilated it because that is what their parents had taught them: to have faith, to stay on the straight path, to fight temptation (the Greater Jihad), and not to question or doubt the word of God. So when they began to question Islam and explore their doubts more systematically and in an open spirit many respondents felt guilty. And not a little ashamed, which is in part why they kept their doubts hidden from others. Even after the point of disavowal some respondents continued to feel ambivalent, as though they had done something wrong, even though intellectually they knew (except when they were besieged by fleeting moments of doubt) they were in the right. But as they exposed themselves to more and more irreligious material and as they took greater and greater emotional distance from Islam they grew in confidence and became less and less ambivalent.

Everyone I interviewed was clear on the matter. They had done the *right* thing. They were as unequivocal about this as the Quran is unequivocal about the wrongs of apostasy. Some felt bad, certainly: bad for disclosing their disbelief, because of all the pain this inflicted on their family, and bad for disappointing familial expectations and, in a few cases where it had occurred, for damaging family reputation. But they all felt sure that they had done the right thing in renouncing the epistemic and moral claims of Islam. They hadn't always felt like this, but now they did. So they were not, on the face of it, in need of self-justification. But they were in need of justification all the same, because they were constantly being called to account, questioned, doubted, indeed vilified, by other Muslims. And so they had to defend themselves from all the accusatory rhetoric, because it stung and because, as they saw it, it was fundamentally untrue. Defend themselves and set the record straight: this is what they were required to do, felt that they *had* to do, because their integrity demanded it. And because they wanted to be understood, to not be judged or misjudged and because ultimately though they were through with Islam they were not through with Muslims. They had once been Muslims. Their families were Muslim. Some still maintained friendships with Muslims. The regard of these people continued to matter to them. Which is why their disregard hurt them so. And which is why they invested so much effort into the project of defending themselves against it. They wanted to be not merely understood, but accepted. Accepted by Muslims, especially their families.

Azhar is no longer active on the CEMB forum, but he used to be. This is one of his many posts:

> I was back in London for a few weeks recently and I was confronted by an old friend of mine. He used to have a beard and be religious and we would go to mosque together in our mid-teens. So, I find out he can deliver me some mary j [marijuana] and I go to see him. It was a bad idea.
>
> 'What are you doing in Canada?'
> 'Living with my wife.'

'You're married?? Is she Muslim?'
'No, she doesn't want to be.'
'Yeah, but you have to convert her bro, you're Muslim, innit.'
'No, I'm not.'
'What the fuck?'

It's pretty awful being in that situation. I suppose I could have lied to him, conducted the business and been off on my way but I didn't really want to lie. In the end, quite ridiculously, I had to apologize for hurting his feelings and robbing him of his brother just to get away.

I spoke to Azhar about this and he corroborated it. Other ex-Muslims on the forum tell similar stories. The stories are obviously dramatized, amplified for greater emotional affect and poignancy. Some in part resemble 'atrocity tales'.[40] But most are like the story above: stories of everyday confrontations with intolerance and obtuseness.

One of the greatest sources of annoyance for respondents is the accusation that they had never been 'true' believers in the first place and hence their apostasy is fundamentally bogus, a non-event, and hence not to be taken seriously. The implication is that had they 'truly' believed, had they fully exposed themselves to the truths and beauty of Islam, they would never in a million years have abandoned it. The implication is that they were 'playing' at being Muslims and that emotionally and intellectually they had little or no understanding of Islam and its 'true' meaning.

Masood, as noted already, was particularly vexed by this suggestion. But also very obviously profoundly hurt by it, because Islam had meant a great deal to him in his former life, because he had once taken it very seriously and because he had invested so much of his former self into it. To say that he had never been a 'true' Muslim was to erase his past. It was also to simultaneously trivialize his present, implying that he hadn't had to face any challenges in renouncing his faith and adapting to a godless world, because he had always been essentially disbelieving.

As well as interviewing Masood on two separate occasions, I also retraced some of his online footprint.[41] The following is from an exchange in an Islamic forum which occurred in the year after Masood's apostasy. The subject of the exchange concerns Masood's reasons for leaving Islam.

Mujahida:

Pazuzu [one of Masood's numerous online pseudonyms]—I still don't understand how you could leave Islam. I just don't get it. To me it's like you never had Islam in your heart, because if someone understands the true meaning of Islam (and this life) and the beauty of Islam, they will not be able to leave it.

You can give me an explanation and all that, but like I said—I will never understand.

Pazuzu bin Hanbi:

Thanks for your honesty, female warrior! For me, however, it comes as a tired old game now. I encounter this reaction all the time from muslimuun. In fact, I used to think this way myself when I believed. I have, though, seen people react like this to an intense and enthusiastic muslim who followed Islam for more than 40 years before rejecting it.[42] He even taught at the school founded by Yusuf Islam. People still claim he didn't truly believe or understand Islam. That he has no knowledge. SO not the case.

In fact, reading a lot of muslim sources eventually turned me away from Islam, and the absence of god turned me away from theism altogether.

Mujahida:

Pazuzu—A muslim can be a muslim and have knowledge for 40 years yes, but that doesn't mean he has it in his heart.

If a person truly loves someone, you don't just leave the one you love. To me, it is the same thing with Islam. If a person truly has faith and love in his heart, he is not going to leave Islam because he knows the purpose of this life and what is going to happen in the next life. And if the Hellfire and punishment in the grave doesn't scare him, then I don't know what else will.

There is a great difference in having knowledge and faith stuck in the heart.

Pazuzu bin Hanbi:

Mujahida wrote:

Pazuzu—A muslim can be a muslim and have knowledge for 40 years yes, but that doesn't mean he has it in his heart.

If a person truly loves someone, you don't just leave the one you love.

You can do. I don't know if you've ever fallen in love and had to part ways, or know someone to whom this has happened, but it can and does happen. Same with friends, and same with god. I suppose when your imaginary friend stops talking to you and it hits you with force that it never did speak to you in the first place...you *know* the time has come to part ways!

For another example of obtuseness, observe this:

People are converting to Islam in their millions. Islam is the truth...But you're not interested in the truth, are you?

HANGING ON: MANAGING APOSTASY

You said you've read the Quran. You haven't touched it, man.

You've studied atheism, you haven't studied Islam. Islam has proved itself.
We know it's the truth. You have to research and understand Islam from the
right sources. You are stupid and narrow-minded...and if you die tomorrow
you will go to hell.[43]

Many other respondents encountered the same accusation—that they
didn't know enough about Islam, that they hadn't understood it properly,
that they hadn't opened their hearts to it, that had they known better
they surely wouldn't have made the rash decision to abandon it. They
encountered this accusation and many more, most typically that their
apostasy was frivolous and temperamental, that it was merely a phase,
that they must be confused or mentally impaired in some way (due to
either demonic possession or corruption by unbelievers), and that their
motives for leaving Islam must have been dubious (i.e. they jettisoned it
out of misplaced fidelity to worldly and base attractions, like sex and
alcohol).[44] In addition to this, respondents were critically interrogated
about what they now believed in, which was neither God nor religion,
which was irreligion or non-religion. For adopting this position, they
were assailed, variously, for being arrogant and immoral, even nihilistic.
So as well as having their moral character impugned, respondents also
had their non-religious beliefs subject to critical attack and ridicule.

'How do I convince them,' Nasreen asks, 'that I'm not wrong, that I
am right?' This is one of the key challenges of the post-apostasy phase.
How can ex-Muslims convince Muslims, especially their parents (the
subject of Nasreen's inquiry), that their apostasy is legitimate? How,
more specifically, can they overturn the stigma attached to it and redefine
it in decidedly more positive terms? How, indeed, can apostates convince
Muslims that they themselves are not wrong, that they are not bad or
immoral persons? This is a monumental task and partly explains why the
CEMB forum is such attractive place for the ex-Muslims who congregate
on it. The forum provides, among many other things, an alternative definition of reality from the definition promulgated by Muslims. It provides
a set of justifications for leaving Islam. These are constantly repeated and
refined by members, creating a vast legitimizing vocabulary—indeed an
entire counter-discourse—for exiters. Members explain to each other
why they renounced Islam, citing their reasons. All members do this.
Indeed, it is a condition of acceptance on the forum that they do this:
that they introduce themselves, share aspects of their personal biography

and explain why they left Islam. Some members compile and circulate passages from the Quran and the *hadith* books and explain why they find them morally objectionable.[45] A common theme in many forum posts is the hypocrisy of Muslims. The rhetorical point is obvious: hypocritical Muslims are in no position to sit in judgment, since they routinely fail to live up to the standards by which they condemn ex-Muslims. All this helps ex-Muslims repress vestigial feelings of ambivalence over their apostasy. They discover the forum, they immerse themselves in the personal testimonies of others just like them, they read the various critiques of Islam and of religion and, after having formally introduced themselves to other members via an introduction post, they are warmly embraced and praised for their courage and wisdom.[46] This reinforces their decision to leave. It gives them reassurance.

Masood speaks for all respondents when he says, 'I'd like people to be able to accept me for who I am'. Spelling this out in more detail, he adds:

> I used to believe something, I don't any longer, this is who I am, so deal with me as I am now. If I'm going to have a pint of beer and you're going to have a coke or whatever that's fine, don't keep quizzing me on what went wrong, because that's how they generally tend to see it, that something went wrong.

Masood is convinced that nothing went wrong and he has expended a vast amount of effort on explaining to his former co-religionists why nothing went wrong. The legitimizing project, in other words, has loomed very large in his post-apostasy landscape, as it has for all respondents. But it has now become tedious and tiresome having constantly to explain, to rebut, and to correct all the critical comments and misconceptions. Indeed almost as tiresome as the critical comments and misconceptions themselves.

Masood's is a clear case of apostate burnout: after years of engaging Muslims in critical dialogue, if it can be called that, he has become jaded and disillusioned with the whole legitimizing project, not because he doesn't believe in it, but because it seems so futile, trying to persuade believers to see it his way or even to credit that he may actually have a case which deserves to be taken seriously.

This seems to be the standard trajectory among respondents: in the first few weeks and months of their apostasy, the legitimizing project feels immensely important and necessary. Above all, it feels urgent. Obtuseness abounds everywhere and for those newly apostatized there is a keen vigilance to counter it, to even look for it so as then to counter and repudiate it. But the vigilance fades, because at some point it becomes apparent that the obtuseness is so fiercely impervious to change or rational argumentation and that ex-Muslims and Muslims are in fact speaking two different languages, inhabiting two different and ultimately irreconcilable worlds of discourse. Or at least that is how it feels or looks. As Masood's online interlocutor put it, 'I will never understand'. But it wasn't just a question of comprehension; it was also a question of tolerance. Of not being tolerated. Not accepted. This was just as common a reaction to their apostasy as incomprehension. So there is obtuseness and there is intolerance, and countering both starts to feel like a losing struggle. Feels exhausting. And wholly dispiriting, too, because the ex-Muslim in time learns a difficult and altogether unpalatable truth: that they will never be fully accepted by Muslims and that even moderate Muslims will regard them with a degree of suspicion and indignation.

The Jihad of the Heart

Blood and Belonging

This is Tasnim, speaking about her family:

> I'm grounded with them, and I feel as though if I don't have them then I have nothing. They're my constant. They're my foundations. I guess I'd be lost without them. I don't think right now I'm willing to give that up.

Most respondents would go along with this. They didn't care for Islam, that's one way of putting it. They had renounced it as a system of belief and identity, refused to see the world and themselves through its all-encompassing prism, but they hadn't renounced their families. They *love* their families. They don't necessarily love the dynamic within them, they resent the interference of family members in their private lives and they recoil from the weight of parental expectation, but their mothers and fathers, brothers and sisters, aunts and uncles, nieces and nephews—these are the people they are tied to, for better or worse. These are the people they love, can't help caring about, can't help but love.

The CEMB forum is one thing, and it can be a great thing, an enormously important facilitator of identification and understanding and support. But forum life is not an adequate substitute for real life, for true emotional companionship and intimacy. There is a certain degree of artificiality about it, about life as it is lived and shared on the forum. Members know this, even try to resist it,[47] and despite their investment in the forum would readily acknowledge its limitations.

So forum life is one thing and family life quite another, a source of deep attachment and belonging. But the family is not without its limitations, too. Indeed, for nearly all respondents, family life could be a source of profound frustration and unhappiness, because they felt alienated within its confines and couldn't be themselves with family members, felt too different, felt judged also, not accepted. This caused them immense pain, the pain of not being understood, the pain of rejection. Parents in particular were the source of much torment for respondents. They could be distant, infuriatingly narrow-minded, grudging, judging, and yet, for all that, also supportive, loving. Respondents spoke about them with affection and disaffection in equal measure. And despite all that they had been through together, and many respondents had been through a great deal with their parents, a lot of pain and hurt on both sides, they still wanted their affection, their love. So they fought for that as best as they knew how.

The Clash of Expectations

What do respondents want? Or, more manageably, what do respondents not want? They do not want to live their lives in accordance with the commands and prohibitions of Islam. They do not want to marry Muslims; they want to pursue relationships with non-Muslims, with, specifically, the non-religious. They do not want to raise their children as Muslims. Among those already married with children, they want to minimize the role of Islam in their lives and the lives of their children. They also want to reconfigure their relationships with family members, so that Islam doesn't overly intrude into the texture of these relationships.

But what of respondents' families? What is it that they want? Or what is it that they do not want? They want the respondent to be a 'good Muslim', to marry Islamically, to raise their children Islamically and to create decent and upstanding Muslim families of their own. What they do not want is for them to become a '*kāfir*', because this will bring great shame on the family, to say nothing of divine retribution.

What happens when these expectations are not met or are indeed openly flouted? Invariably, and as we have seen, there is great upset. And then resistance, where family members or custodians of the family embark on their own jihad to win the hearts and minds of the errant family member, so that they 'return to their senses' or, in the case of respondents who have not openly disclosed their apostasy to their families but nonetheless disinvolved themselves from Islam, take more seriously their religious obligations. How did respondents react to this jihad of resistance on the part of their families? There were three major categories of response: *submission, resistance* and *détente*.

Submission

As we saw in chapter 5, a significant number of respondents just can't do it: they can't tolerate the idea of openly flouting their parents' expectations. They had bravely confronted their demons on the question of belief, had faced down their fears of eternal punishment in hell, but they couldn't face the prospect of defeating their parents' hopes, of provoking their disaffection, even rejection. They have, in other words, submitted to the power of expectation, even though privately they are in revolt against it and in practice, outside of the parental gaze, mock it.

Hanif, for example, reluctantly agreed to the marriage arranged for him: 'After a lot of relentless nagging from my parents I kind of gave in and said fine and I knew it was something that my parents really wanted.' But it was emphatically not what he wanted. He barely knew the woman, although he knew she was non-Western and religious, which made him feel all the more uneasy. What, after all, would they have in common, what would they talk about, how would they get along? But he decided to enter the marriage anyway, despite all this, because that was what his parents wanted, what they expected, and he didn't want to disappoint them by not meeting their expectations.

Wahid has similarly deferred to his mother's wishes on the question of marriage. She wants him to marry a Muslim woman, even though she knows that her son has renounced his faith. And Wahid will do this, has resolved to do this, because he doesn't want to cause his mother any further pain—coming out to her, he says, has caused her pain enough. He will do it, even though the idea of marriage and having children doesn't remotely appeal to him,[48] even though he is sure that marriage to a Muslim woman will make him unhappy and more suffocated than ever.[49]

Both Amina and Tasnim are also resigned to the reality of entering an arranged Muslim marriage, even though they have grave misgivings about this. Tasnim says, 'I hate to admit to myself, but I will always choose them [her family] knowing that they'll never choose me.' Discussing the issue of marriage, she tellingly remarks, 'I'm not all that fussed about happiness. I think I'm preparing myself for the worst.' Amina similarly admits that 'at times I think I'll just give up' and accept an arranged marriage, 'as long as he's fairly liberal and not too strict a Muslim', explaining that 'I don't want to upset my family or break it up because my parents aren't bad, they were just raised in a certain way'.

Resistance

A few respondents were adamant: they could not tolerate the prospect of submitting to the wishes of their parents. Their future was theirs and theirs alone and they would not live their lives according to the standards of their parents. That would be intolerable, impossible. Neither could they live a lie and pretend to satisfy parental wishes, because that would also be intolerable, having to lie and deceive all the time. So they outed themselves to their parents and immediate family, making it clear that Islam no longer had any purchase on their lives and that they were now free to be who they wanted to be, even though they were not quite sure who that was. In most cases, this caused great turmoil in the family. And the family did not take it lying down. The family resisted and tried to reason with the respondent to rethink their apostasy and return to Islam. And the respondent in turn tried to reason with their family, explaining why they couldn't believe anymore, why they had to distance themselves from it, and how none of that meant that they wanted to jettison their family, whom they continued to love and respect.

Even when respondents had moved out of the family home, whether by choice or coercion, their apostasy was still met with resistance from family members. Manzoor's father, for example, won't let it go. He cannot accept his son's disbelief, nor can he accept his son's marriage to an atheist woman. Even though he has had a few years in which to adjust, he can't reconcile himself to this new reality, so he resists it. Manzoor told me that only recently his wife had received a gift from his father: a book of testimonies of women converts to Islam. About this, Manzoor says: 'I did ring home later to say, "look, this really isn't on", at which point my mum said, well you did have to go off and marry an atheist, maybe you shouldn't have done that, you've strayed quite far, was the general gist.'

Azhar's father similarly refuses to see his son as a lost cause and has been active in trying to persuade Azhar's wife to convert to Islam, thinking that this will cause Azhar to reconsider his apostasy:

> He actually called us last year and he didn't want to speak to me, he spoke to Celine. And he said to Celine, 'I know Azhar does everything you tell him, so I need you to tell him to be a Muslim, because he will do it if you say it'. So Celine said, 'why would I tell him that, that's his choice'. And he said, 'well I need you to be a Muslim too, otherwise I won't accept you guys into my family'. And that's where we are right now, that's the point we have reached, where we are basically saying, 'look, we're sorry, we can't force ourselves to believe something we don't'.

Azhar is in regular contact with his mother via telephone (rarely does he converse with his father), but it is difficult and strained: 'I try to make as much small talk as possible, because otherwise I know she is just going to start crying. She is just going to start blaming me for leaving, for not staying around, for not being a Muslim.'

Luqman's father has also reached out, if it can be described as that, sending his son text messages 'saying things like, you'll never get any happiness. Happiness is only with Allah's *deen*, Allah's religion. Things like that to annoy me, to control me, even though he's no longer able to control me'.[50] And so, too, has Alia's father (through the intermediary of his sister, Alia's aunt)[51] and so, too, has Khadija's (through the intermediary of his wife, Khadija's stepmother).[52] They've all reached out, and although the continued interference of family members is unsettling and vexing for resisting respondents, it at least provides powerful evidence of the enduring importance of their family bond and is a way of maintaining the relationship, of preserving contact.[53] And as long as there is contact, any contact, there is at least the hope, however faint, of rapprochement, the hope that, as Alia said of her own family, 'one day they will come around'.

Détente

The most common response among respondents to family intransigence over expectations is neither submission nor resistance, but aspects of both. I call this 'détente', because there is a readiness on the part of the respondent to engage with family members and negotiate a compromise around the issue of faith and the familial expectations associated with it.

This is done either explicitly, in the form of an open pact or implicitly, in the form of a silent pact.

Among closeted respondents, a common silent pact with family members was that in return for observance of Ramadan and pious attendance of other important religious events, like funerals and weddings, they could expect to be given some slack around the issue of daily prayers and mosque attendance. This wasn't discussed in the open, but an understanding of sorts had somehow tacitly evolved over time. Outed respondents made similar pacts with their families, but openly, explicitly delineating the terms of the bargain. Omar, for example, wouldn't be fasting and he wouldn't be praying anymore under any circumstances and both his wife—'she believes in God, she believes that Islam is the truth'—and immediate family accept this. But Omar would have to make some concessions, too: he would have to keep his apostasy hidden from the wider community, from other Muslims outside the family home, and he would have to pass as a Muslim at weddings and funerals and on Eid celebrations. On the matter of alcohol Omar's wife tolerates his drinking, but never in the house, where she will not permit alcohol to be kept. The same goes for non-*halal* food. And on the more decisive issue of their children's education and upbringing, Omar and his wife have agreed to adopt an inclusive approach:

> We've made a pact. I don't discuss my atheism, although the kids know that I'm an atheist. And she doesn't stress about Islam either. I said, 'you know what, you've got to keep your end of the bargain'. 'If you don't want me to talk about atheism, you're not going to talk about Islam in this house. I want the kids to make up their own minds'. And she agreed. She said, 'let the kids be, let them grow into their own skins'.

Ramesh, too, has had to make compromises, as has his wife, because their marriage was in the balance ('we were drifting apart, our connection was not there anymore and we were fighting a lot'), and if they were to save it, they would have to meet each other half way. They would have to negotiate, because the marriage had changed, because, after a decade of marriage, Ramesh had changed. And so, with the help of a marriage counselor, they thrashed out a compromise, a way forward agreeable to both:

> So we had to come up with some rules for how to make this work. One rule was that I can't come out to her parents. That's why even now on Facebook I'm not saying I'm not Muslim, but I don't say I'm Muslim either. And the

other rule is that there's no pork or alcohol in the house and I can't do it [consume either] in front of the kids. And she doesn't want me drinking openly in Ottawa, in case her Muslim friends see me, but then I don't really go out in Ottawa anyway.

The issue of their children's religious education remains divisive and difficult and for the time being Ramesh has ceded to his wife's wishes: 'They have Quran lessons twice a week. I told her I'm not having anything to do with this. I don't agree with it. But I'm hoping they will start using their brains as they get older.'

Ali says of his family that 'I think I've fought enough with them to be able to have a certain degree of freedom. At the same time catered to some of their things.' In particular, Ali has agreed not to discuss religion with his family and certainly not to openly criticize it: 'My father has drawn a line. He says you can say whatever you want as long as it doesn't cross into religion, and I definitely try my best to follow that.'

And so this is how it goes for many respondents: they cover or pass when it is necessary, when not covering or not passing would be unnecessarily bloody-minded or even gratuitous and in return their family cuts them a break and contrives to interfere less in their private lives. And it doesn't always run smoothly, there are strains and rifts, but at least it keeps the relationship going and intact.

Respondents may balk at the suggestion, but there is no 'beyond Islam'. Respondents have moved past it and they haven't moved past it. I don't mean that they're still susceptible to its spiritual message or that they haven't really got over it, like some first love. I mean very precisely that Islam won't let go of them. Less abstractly: the response of family members to disclosure of apostasy or to evidence of serious disinvolvement from Islam is such that it locks respondents into an endless engagement and struggle with Islam in the form of either submission, resistance or accommodation to familial expectations surrounding faith. I take up this theme in the next and final chapter.

7

BEYOND ISLAM?

For most people, to say I've stayed in my childhood my whole life would mean I've stayed innocent and it's all been pretty. For you to say I stayed in my childhood my whole life means I stayed in this terrible story—life remained a terrible story. It means that I had so much pain in my youth that, one way or another, I stayed in it forever.

Philip Roth, *Exit Ghost* (London: Vintage, 2007), 193

Losing...taught you more profound lessons than winning did...The losers had to re-evaluate everything they had thought to be true and worth fighting for, and so had a chance of learning, the hard way, the deepest lessons life had to teach.

Salman Rushdie, *Joseph Anton*, p. 284

You're always an ex-Muslim as long as they don't accept you.

Nubia

I was defined as a Muslim all my life, but now I can't be defined as an ex-Muslim all my life either.

Nabilah

This is going to be an on-going struggle for me.

Aisha

THE APOSTATES

The Never-Ending Story

Here is how Martin Amis concludes *The Pregnant Widow*, his novel about the sexual revolution:

> The old order gave way to the new—not easily, though; the revolution was a velvet revolution, but it wasn't bloodless; some came through, some more or less came through, and some went under. Some were all right, some were not all right, and some were somewhere in between.[1]

This is an apt description of how it went with the thirty-five respondents I interviewed: some were all right, some were not all right, and some were somewhere in between. But it is not entirely apt, because, though their revolution was indeed a velvet revolution, the old order from which they were rebelling has not given way but remains, uneasily co-existing with the new and preventing it from fully divesting itself from the old. As Manzoor economically puts it, sounding not unlike Michael Corleone in the third—and least satisfying—instalment of *The Godfather*, 'You may leave it but it never leaves you.' Never leaves you because it is always everywhere present. Among closeted respondents, this was true; and among those who had outed themselves it was true. In the case of the former it was true because of the voracious demands of concealment, of always having to be 'on' and vigilant against the perennial threat of exposure. And in the case of the latter it was true because of the doggedness with which their families resisted their apostasy on discovering it. And for a few respondents, closeted or otherwise, Islam never left them because leaving it had been so difficult and so traumatic that they never fully recovered from it.

And so the conclusion that some were all right, some were not all right, and some were somewhere in between can only be at best provisional, because the story is not over, their stories are not over, and because, more crucially, the logic of their exiting very precisely means that they will remain in the story—for as long as apostasy from Islam remains a stigma or mark of shame to be resisted.

What is painfully clear, however, is that respondents desperately want the story to be over. Many said that they were uneasy about continuing to self-identify as ex-Muslims, uneasy because they felt that they had 'moved on' or wanted to move on, and the 'ex-Muslim' label stood in the way of that. It was backward-looking (to the person they had been) and they wanted to look forward (to the person they wanted to be). They were not in denial that they had once been Muslims; they were just now adamant that it—their ex-status—was an element of their past, an aspect of the self they had now become or were becoming, an element in a larger constellation of traits and identities that defined them.

Masood, for example, is insistent that 'there's more to me than being someone who used to be a Muslim', elaborating:

> Nowadays I try not to refer to myself as an ex-Muslim. If it comes up in a conversation online I will mention that I am from an Islamic background but I'll say I'm not Muslim and that's to completely new people in new forums I'm posting at as opposed to the CEMB forum. I suppose in a way it ties me to it, saying I'm an ex-Muslim. At the end of the day, I want people to take me as I am as opposed to how I was. So although at one point I did want people to understand that I am no longer a Muslim and that I don't believe in that anymore, it's not something now that I want to keep revisiting as it were. And I certainly I don't hate Islam because that in itself is a form of devotion, because you're spending all your time thinking about it, getting pissed off. I just want to live my life. I don't want it to constantly be brought up all the time.

Many respondents were similarly insistent that they'd moved on. 'Moved on': that was the preferred expression. Ahmed said it, that he had moved on and no longer felt it necessary to define himself 'via religion'. Luqman said it, 'I've moved on', adding that he was now 'bored' of Islam as a topic of discussion. And Omar said it, clarifying that he didn't want his past status as a Muslim 'to be a big deal', adding, in common with Luqman, that he has become 'sick and tired' of Islamic-themed discussions:

> I went to an ex-Muslim meeting once and all they talked about was Islam. That's all they talked about and I want to get away from that. I don't want to talk about something that I've left behind now. I mean, how long can you whip a dead horse? Move on. Haven't we got other things in common? Apart from being apostates. Apart from being ex-Muslims.

So they had moved on: that was the gist of what many respondents were telling me. But it was clear from everything they said that they hadn't moved on, that the state of having moved on was not a fully con-cretized reality, but an aspiration, an ideal. They had moved on in the sense that they didn't believe anymore, but not in the sense that Islam had ceased to be a central reference-point in their lives, because it plainly was and there was no way of getting away from that.

Nabilah says that 'You realize that being an ex-Muslim is just one tiny aspect of the rest and if you make it all who you are then Islam still has that hold on you in a way.' Ramesh similarly comments that 'I don't want that [the ex-Muslim label] to be my overall definition', explaining that 'because then it's almost like it still has a hold on me'.

So respondents want the story to end, but it doesn't end, they remain in the story, because everyone else who truly matters in their lives wants the story to carry on. As long as ex-Muslims submit to the sensitivities and expectations of their families; as long as they experience resistance and interference from family members and friends after disclosing their apostasy or disinvolving from Islam; and as long as they are engaged in trying to preserve familial relationships in the face of intense strains, they will remain in the story.

Leaving a closely-knit religious group, observes Stuart A. Wright in the context of cults, is like leaving a marriage:

> The disentanglement of affective bonds, the disillusionment that accompanies renunciation of an intense loyalty or sacred commitment, the sense of personal failure, the feelings of confusion, anxiety, anger, frustration and the diminished ability to function following the break-up are characteristics of marital disengagement that may be aptly applied to departures from new religions.[2]

And departures from Islam, too. But the analogy, while illuminating in certain key respects, is deficient in others, not least because there is a point at which most marriages end and the former martial partners adjust to a life beyond the marriage, step out of its shadow and move on.[3] In *After Divorce*, William J. Goode writes:

> The post-divorce adjustmental process is one by which *a disruption of role sets and patterns, and of existing social relations, is incorporated into the individual's life pattern, such that the roles accepted and assigned do not take the prior divorce into account as the primary point of reference*: In more common-sense terms, the woman is no longer 'ex-wife', or 'divorcee' primarily, but first of all 'co-worker', 'date', or 'bride'.[4]

Later on in the book, Goode remarks that adjustment to divorce

is the integration of the divorce experience into her total life experience, such that the individual lives by the daily and future demands of his or her *new* social position rather than by constant reference to the ties defined by the previous marriage. That is, she has adjusted, even if not remarried, if her usual self-image is no longer 'ex-wife of Y—' or 'formerly married to Y—'; if her economic position (even if not pleasant) is not the simple result of having lost the family breadwinner; if her problems with her children are no longer to be traced primarily to internal or overt conflicts about or with their father; if her friendship ties whether new or old are threatened only by the ordinary problems between any friends, not by the strains of loyalty decisions for or against one of the spouses. We do not expect them 'to forget the past'. We are simply asking whether they are solving the problems of their new position or status, rather than reliving the old.[5]

Most among the separated move on, but this cannot be said of the respondents I interviewed: most clearly hadn't moved on, despite their best efforts in that direction. And it wasn't because they were still reliving their past; it was because there were very much in the present and the present wasn't letting go of them.

What the Apostate Knows

So the revolution was a velvet revolution, but it wasn't without its repercussions. Pre-eminent among these was the loss of innocence. Respondents discarded Islam as a mode of belief and identity and that process was difficult and hard but also deeply instructive. They all learned something from it. And what did they learn? What was the knowledge they acquired from their exit journeys? Negative wisdom, mainly: the knowledge you acquire from all the shit and jeopardy and failure and difficulty that life throws at you. Specifically, the negative wisdom which says that blood is thicker than water but not thicker than faith;[6] that love is always conditional and will wither in the face of the imperatives of family reputation and communal honor; that not only are you likely to hurt and exasperate the ones you love but that they are likely to hurt and exasperate you in turn; that the family is not a refuge from the harshness of the outside world—a *Haven in a Heartless World*, to cite the title of Christopher Lasch's 1995 book[7]—but is itself a war zone and a source of harshness and pain;[8] that neither family members nor friends can be fully trusted and will in fact abandon you over matters of faith and honor;[9] that you are expendable and trust no one; and that whatever you do you can't win because someone will be hurt. And so this, briefly and approximately, is the sum of their negative wisdom.

It is conventional among religious converts to speak excitedly of 'seeing the light', by which they mean that in embracing their newly found religion they have shed their illusions and discovered the truth. No one I interviewed used this metaphor. Perhaps this was no accident. Perhaps it was because from where they are standing reality doesn't look so luminous.

Religion and Religious Freedom

Throughout this book I have tried to avoid the politics of apostasy, focusing instead on the subjective experiences of my respondents. But it would be disingenuous to avoid the political altogether and to pretend that the material collected in this book has no implications for political debate and policy.

Preeminently, this study has important implications for current debates over the meaning and role of religion in contemporary society. All too often, these debates are polarized between those who argue that religion is a force for ill in the world and those who insist that it is a force for good. This study points to a more nuanced understanding of religion, showing that it can simultaneously be a force for good *and* ill. Listening to the voices recounted in these pages, it is clear that religion has been a source of division and unhappiness. But it is also clear from what respondents said that in renouncing religion they have encountered multiple losses. And it is possible to infer from these the numerous benefits which religion offers, most notably a powerful sense of community, belonging and identity. The thesis that, as Christopher Hitchens phrases it in the subtitle to his anti-theist tract, *Religion Poisons Everything*,[10] is clearly one-sided and unwarranted.

This study also challenges prevailing assumptions about Islamic apostasy on both the right and left of the political spectrum. Broadly speaking, for the liberal-left apostasy is No Big Deal. Apostates do not live in fear for their lives and are not hounded. The apostasy laws in the *shariah* are rarely, if ever, enforced and the Quran is actually a document of religious freedom. And if apostates do run into problems it is invariably because they are open and unhelpfully trenchant about their renunciation of Islam. Furthermore, concern about apostasy is often a mask for Islamophobic hostility against Muslims. Do now change the subject.[11] So much for the liberal left. What about the right? The right, by contrast, tends to portray Islamic apostates as courageous dissidents living under threat of death. Whose persecution is proof-positive of the essential intolerance of Islam and its radical incompatibility with secular 'western' values.

Both positions, I think, are misconceived. Apostasy, to be sure, is a fundamental human rights problem in Muslim-majority counties, where in some states the punishment for apostasy is death and violent vigilantism against apostates and religious minorities goes unpunished.[12] But not in western secular societies. As Tasnim put it, 'some people have been through worse. I could be living in an Islamic country.' Or as Nabilah said, 'Nobody's trying to kill me; I don't have a *fatwa* on my head or anything like that'. Indeed, no one I interviewed has been subject to physical violence *because* they renounced Islam. But this does not remotely mean that apostasy from Islam is not a problem in western secular societies. On the contrary, it is problematic: problematic for apostates themselves, because of the moral stigma attached to Islamic apostasy within Muslim communities and families and, connectedly, the myriad emotional difficulties and challenges involved in leaving (or rather not leaving) Islam. It is also necessary to add that just because no one I interviewed has experienced violence in retaliation for their apostasy it does not mean that they had not been threatened with violence for leaving Islam. Some, indeed, had been so threatened—although for most the threats came in the form of online hate speech and so it was hard to know how seriously to take them. It must also be made clear that still many other respondents reported feeling uneasy about fully publicly disclosing their apostasy, in large part because they didn't want to hurt their families or have them shamed, but also because apostasy provokes such intense reactions in people and you never can tell what may happen. As Masood put it, 'I've always had this fear of being open not just because it would hurt my family but because it might result in somebody knifing me, you know, it's the old Salman Rushdie thing.' And so although the ex-Muslims I interviewed were not living in fear for their lives they were not exactly living in a state of complete and unfettered religious freedom either, because most felt profoundly uneasy about speaking openly about their apostasy in public.

Islamic apostasy in the secular west is perhaps best understood not as a legal or political problem, but as a moral issue within Muslim families and communities. Steven Seidman, writing about gay men and women in contemporary American society, suggests: 'The struggle to reclaim a place in our families is a battle less for rights than for respect and emotional caring. It is less a struggle led by a movement than a deeply personal battle waged by each of us in our own families.'[13] This is also true of ex-Muslims in the west, for whom the biggest struggle is to reclaim a place in their families and to salvage their respect and love.

The crucial policy issue is how to effectively challenge and change illiberal attitudes within Muslim communities in the west and how to provide better support for wavering and ex-Muslims in moral jeopardy. This may involve questioning conservative theological interpretations of Islam,[14] but also, no less importantly, challenging traditional notions of duty, honor and shame which have little or nothing to do with Islamic theology. It may also involve better educating social workers and mental health-care professionals not only about the intricacies of the Islamic faith but also the difficulties and dilemmas involved in leaving it—and providing public financial aid for ex-Muslim self-help groups like the CEMB and its forum.

One way of challenging intolerance toward ex-Muslims is to create pathways to empathy. This book is offered as a small gesture in that direction. To paraphrase the epigraph with which it began, the stories recounted in these pages are really about you. They are about all of us.

ACKNOWLEDGEMENTS

First and foremost, I would like to thank all the interviewees, without whom, of course, this book would not exist and all those ex-Muslims who were not part of the sample but who spoke with me and shared their experiences. In *Faith No More*, Phil Zuckerman finds that (non-believing) apostates are—this is from the book's dust-jacket—'life-affirming, courageous, highly intelligent and inquisitive, and deeply moral'. Although it has not been my concern to offer a profile of ex-Muslims, Zuckerman's portrayal certainly rings true of the ex-Muslims I interviewed, who awed me not only with their intelligence and articulacy but also with their humanity.

I am very grateful to the Economic and Social Research Council for funding this research (RES-000-22-4308), to Wellesley College, USA, for hosting me on several occasions during the course of my fieldwork and to the Council of Ex-Muslims of Britain, for its openness and assistance.

Many people have helped me generously at various points in the work and I am greatly in their debt: Christopher Hitchens (RIP), Bryan S. Turner, Howard Davis, Martina Feilzer, Stefan Machura, Sioned Wyn Davies, Gareth Jones, Ian Rees Jones, Michael Jones, Bruce Hoffman, Alessandro Orsini, Robin Simcox, Neil Vidmar, Martin Herrema, Dan Burrows, David Redmon, Roger Matthews, Phil Carney, Caroline Chatwin, Jonathan Ilan, Chris Shilling, Balihar Sanghera, Anna Billingham, Judith Oliver, Hersh Mann, Laura R. Olson, Gerardo Marti, Aslihan Arslan, Mohammad Almaawi, Maryam Namazie, Adam Barnett, David Henshaw, Nick Cohen, Ryan T. Cragun, Daniel Dennett, Halima, Sulaiman, Arsheen, Zafar, Razi, Haroon, Lana, Hafsa, Mustafa, Nonna Grazia, Liz Griffith, Hassan, Steven Cottee, Stephen Byers,

ACKNOWLEDGEMENTS

Kodanshi, Billy, Nadia and the late Irtaza Hussain, to whom this book is dedicated.

I should like particularly to express my gratitude to Andrew Anthony for his advice and encouragement and to the late Norm Geras for his friendship and for helping me to think more clearly about almost everything.

Thanks are also due to my dear friend and once mentor Stephen Hester, who sadly died just before I completed this book.

I owe a special debt of gratitude to my friends in Canada: Mia, Zain, Kiran, Nesrin, Ali and Baz.

At Hurst, I should especially like to thank Michael Dwyer, for believing in this project from the beginning and for providing sound advice throughout, and David Lunn for his judicious copy-editing and valuable comments.

At the *Sunday Times*, I would like to thank the awesome Sarah Baxter, Mark Edmonds and James Palmer, for showing me how it's done.

I would like to thank Stacy Baig for her assistance and for her friendship over many years; Alexander Sedlmaier, for helping me to rethink some of my own assumptions; Memona, for sticking by me; Arben Kita, for being a dude and a brother and a world-class ball breaker; and Hasina, for her interest and moral support and for so much else.

I owe a very special thanks to Keith Hayward, a superb colleague and stalwart friend. For nearly a decade now, Keith has been a constant source of intellectual inspiration, advice and good humour.

My greatest and most persistent debt in writing this book has been to the brilliant and fearless Thomas Cushman, for first sparking my interest in this subject and for his originality of insight and force of encouragement.

Finally, I would like to acknowledge the unconditional support and forbearance of Francesca, who also read and commented on the manuscript, and my wonderful and inspiring mother, who didn't read the manuscript but has had to listen to me banging on for a while now.

Simon Cottee   *Canterbury*
                                               November 2014

NOTES

References to *The Quran* relate to The Quran, trans. M. A. S. Abdel Haleem (New York: Oxford University Press, 2004).

PREFACE

1. I draw on Irtaza's interview testimony at various points in the main text, but, as with all respondents, I have anonymized this and given him a pseudonym.
2. Irtaza's father, Sabir Hussain, whom I interviewed in mid-January 2014 for a feature-article on Irtaza for the *Sunday Times* Magazine, denies this (Simon Cottee, 'The Apostate,' The *Sunday Times* Magazine, 30 March 2014).

1. INTRODUCTION

1. Armand L. Mauss, 'Dimensions of Religious Defection,' *Review of Religious Research*, 10 (1969), p. 128.
2. Stuart A Wright, *Leaving Cults: The Dynamics of Defection* (Society for the Scientific Study of Religion Monograph Series: Washington, D.C., 1987), p. 4.
3. David G. Bromley (ed.), *The Politics of Religious Apostasy: The Role of Apostates in the Transformation of Religious Movements* (Westport, Conn.: Praeger, 1998).
4. Bob Altemeyer and Bruce Hunsberger, *Amazing Conversions: Why Some Turn to Faith and Others Abandon Religion* (Amherst, New York: Prometheus, 1997); Mordechai Bar-Lev and William Shaffir (eds.), *Leaving Religion and Religious Life* (Greenwich, Connecticut: JAI Press, 1997); Leslie J. Francis and Yaacov J. Katz (eds), *Joining and Leaving Religion: Research Perspectives* (Leominster: Gracewing, 2000); Lynn Davidman and Arthur Greil, 'Characters in Search of a Script: The Exit Narratives of Formerly Ultra-Orthodox Jews,' *Journal for the Scientific Study of Religion*, 46/2 (2007) pp. 201–216. Moojan Momen, 'Marginality and Apostasy in the Baha'i Community', *Religion*, 37/3 (2007) pp. 187–209.

5. Wright, 1987, p. 4.

6. See, for example, Ali Köse, *Conversion to Islam: A Study of Native British Converts* (London: Kegan Paul, 1996); Stefano Allievi, *Les Convertis à l'Islam: Les Nouveaux Musulmans d'Europe* (Paris: l'Harmattan, 1998); Anne Sofie Roald, *New Muslims in the European Context: The Experience of Scandinavian Converts* (Leiden: Brill, 2004); and Kate Zebiri, *British Muslim Converts: Choosing Alternative Lives* (Oxford: Oneworld Publications, 2008).

7. Ian Buruma, *Murder in Amsterdam: The Death of Theo van Gogh and the Limits of Tolerance* (London: Atlantic Books. 2006), p. 33.

8. James A. Beckford, *Cult Controversies: The Societal Response to New Religious Movements* (London: Tavistock, 1985), p. 139.

9. See especially Olivier Roy, *Secularism Confronts Islam*, trans. George Holoch (New York: Columbia University Press, 2007).

10. *The Quran*, trans. M. A. S. Abdel Haleem (New York: Oxford University Press, 2004), p. 29.

11. Mustafa Akyo, *Islam without Extremes: A Muslim Case for Liberty* (New York: W.W. Norton & Company, 2011), pp. 274–5.

12. Ibid., p. 277.

13. Quoted in Sarah Morrison, 'Allah vs Atheism: 'Leaving Islam was the hardest thing I've done',' *The Independent*, 19 January 2014.

14. I use this word not as a term of censure, but simply to capture the vehemence with which many prominent secularists, like for example Richard Dawkins and Christopher Hitchens, mount their anti-theist case.

15. Sam Harris, *The End of Faith: Religion, Terror and the Future of Reason* (London: The Free Press, 2004), p. 115.

16. Ibid., p. 116.

17. Ibn Warraq, *Leaving Islam: Apostates Speak Out* (Prometheus Books, Amherst, N.Y., 2003), p. 424.

18. Yohanan Friedmann, *Tolerance and Coercion in Islam: Interfaith Relations in the Muslim Tradition* (New York: Cambridge University Press, 2003), p. 4.

19. Ibid., p. 5.

20. See Yusuf Al-Qaradawi, 'Apostasy: Major and Minor' in Patrick Sookhdeo, *Freedom to Believe: Challenging Islam's Apostasy Law* (McClean, Virginia: Isaac Publishing, 2009), pp. 101–18). 'The duty of the Muslim community,' Al-Qaradawi writes, 'is to combat apostasy in all its forms and wherefrom it comes, giving it no chance to pervade in the Muslim world.' (Ibid., p. 102).

21. See Jeffrey Goldberg, 'New Chapter, Old Story,' *New York Times*, 11 October 2013; and Hassan Hassan, 'Hatred, violence and the sad demise of Yusuf Al Qaradawi,' *The National*, 28 January 2014.

22. Susan Crimp and Joel Richardson (eds.), *Why We Left Islam: Former Muslims Speak Out* (Los Angeles, CA.: WND Books, 2008), emphasis added.

23. See esp. Ali A. Rizvi, 'The Phobia of Being Called Islamophobic,' *Huffington Post*, 28 April 2014.

24. See Brian Whitaker, 'False Prophets,' *The Guardian*, 5 June 2006.

25. See Paul Marshall and Nina Shea, *Silenced: How Apostasy & Blasphemy Codes are Choking Freedom Worldwide* (New York: Oxford University Press, 2011), pp. 19–172. At the time of writing a court in Saudi Arabia has sentenced Raif Badawi to 10 years imprisonment and 1,000 lashes. Badawi, who started the 'Free Saudi Liberals' website, was arrested in June 2012 and was initially charged with apostasy, which carries the death penalty in Saudi Arabia. Badawi's website included articles critical of senior religious figures in Saudi Arabia and allegedly insulting to Islam. This sentence comes just after the Kingdom introduced a series of new laws which define atheists as terrorists. See Heather Saul, 'Saudi Arabia orders 1,000 lashes and ten-year sentence for editor of website that discussed religion,' *The Independent*, 8 May 2014.

26. On the life-history method, see Norman K. Denzin, *The Research Act*, 2nd ed. (Chicago: Aldine, 1978). I draw on aspects of this text and even more heavily on the excellent practical advice in Robert S. Weiss's *Learning from Strangers: The Art and Method of Qualitative Interview Studies* (New York: Free Press, 1994).

27. In the course of this study I collected and coded just over 1,000 discussion-threads over a five-year period (2008–2013) from the CEMB forum.

28. Henry De Montherlant, *Costals and The Hippogriff*, trans. John Rodker trans (New York: Alfred A. Knopf, 1937), p. 157.

29. Philip Roth, *Sabbath's Theatre* (New York: Houghton, 1995), p. 247.

30. See C. Kirk Hadaway and Wade Clark Roof, 'Apostasy in American Churches: Evidence from National Survey Data', in David G. Bromley (ed.) *Falling from the Faith: Causes and Consequences of Religious Apostasy* (Beverly Hills, Calif: Sage, 1988), pp. 30–1; and Phil Zuckerman, 'Atheism, Secularity, and Well-Being: How the Findings of Social Science Counter Negative Stereotypes and Assumptions,' *Sociology Compass* 3/6 (2009), p. 949.

31. The authors of *Silenced* evidently felt that it was prudent to do this, enlisting the heft of Kyai Haji Abdurrahman Wahid (Marshall and Shea, 2011, pp. xvii–xxii). Abdurrahman Wahid, in the opening paragraph of his foreword, entitled 'God Needs No Defense', declares that 'God has no enemies' and approvingly invokes a quotation from a 'revered Muslim intellectual' in which the entire planetary species of human beings is disparaged as 'no greater than a speck of dust'. That this sort of highly moralized discourse is deemed a fitting introduction to a serious, and otherwise excellent, book on apostasy and blasphemy is regretful.

32. The decision to interview ex-Muslims from Canada was entirely pragmatic. The CEMB has a good number of members from Canada, some of whom offered to be interviewed. I happily accepted, not for the purposes of comparative research but because at the time I received these offers I was struggling to find a decent sample of interviewees. In total, I made three research trips to Canada.

33. William James, *The Varieties of Religious Experience* (Cambridge, MA: Harvard University Press, 1902/1985).

34. See Wade Clark Roof and J. Shawn Landres, 'Defection, Disengagement and Dissent: The Dynamics of Religious Change in the United States', in Mordechai Bar-Lev and William Shaffir (eds.), 1997, p. 82; and Frank L. Pasquale, 'Unbelief and Irreligion, Empirical Study and Neglect Of' in Tom Flynn (ed.), *The New Encyclopedia Of Unbelief* (Amherst, N.Y.: Prometheus Books, 2007), p. 760.

35. See, for example, Bromley, 1998.

36. See Ryan T. Cragun and Joseph H. Hammer, "One Person's Apostate is Another Person's Convert': What Terminology Tells Us about Pro-Religious Hegemony in the Sociology of Religion,' *Humanity & Society* 35 (2011), p. 154.

37. Here I am indebted to Ned Polsky's classic work on hustlers and beats. Polsky writes: 'Insofar as I treat of social problems, they are not the problems posed by the hustler but for him; not the difficulties he creates for others, but the difficulties that others create for him as he pursues his career.' Ned Polsky, *Hustlers, Beats and Others* (New Brunswick, NJ: Aldine Transaction, 1967), p. 42.

2. ASPECTS OF APOSTASY

1. Cited in Stephen G. Wilson, *Leaving the Fold: Apostates and Defectors in Antiquity* (Minneapolis: Fortress Press, 2004), p. 67.

2. Yusuf Al-Qaradawi, 'Apostasy: Major and Minor' in Sookhdeo, 2009, p. 113.

3. Quoted in S. A. Rahman, *Punishment of Apostasy in Islam* (New Delhi: Kitab Bhavan, 1996), p. 115.

4. I have plagiarized this formulation from Ken Plummer's excellent 1975 study *Sexual Stigma*. Plummer writes: 'Every homosexual who attempts to return to the heterosexual world constitutes a threat to the stability of other homosexuals. If one person can be reconverted to heterosexuality, why not all?' Ken Plummer, *Sexual Stigma: An Interactionist Account* (London: Routledge & Kegan Paul, 1975), p. 152.

5. Friedmann, 2003, p. 5.

6. Cited in Edward Fram, 'Perception and Reception of Repentant Apostates in Medieval Ashkenaz and Premodern Poland,' *AJS Review*, 21/2 (1996), p. 299. See also Saeed and Saeed, 2004, p. 35.

7. Georg Simmel, *Conflict*, trans. Kurt H. Wolff (New York: The Free Press, 1955), p. 44, emphases in original.

8. Ibid., pp. 47–48.

9. Lewis A. Coser, *The Functions of Social Conflict* (London: Routledge and Kegan Paul, 1956), p. 69.

10. Ibid.

11. Ibid., p. 70.

12. Ibid.

13. Muhammad Muhiy al-Din al-Masiri remarks that apostasy 'causes skepticism as to its [Islam's] truth' (quoted in Rudolph Peters and Gert J. J. De Vries, 'Apostasy in Islam,' *Die Welt des Islams*, 17/1–4 (1976–7), p. 17). It is thus not surprising to learn that, according to Stephen G. Wilson, religious associations in the ancient world were 'unlikely to publicize tales of defection'. 'To outsiders', Wilson writes, 'it would be a sign of weakness and to insiders an unfortunate example' Wilson, 2004, p. 8.

14. Equally, it is thus not surprising to discover that religions in the ancient world were keen to publicize tales of conversion: 'Conversions served to enhance their self-image and promote their cause.' (Ibid.)

15. Coser, 1956, p. 70.

16. Ibid., p. 169. Kai T. Erikson's *Wayward Puritans*, a study of the Salem witch trials, provides strong empirical support for this claim, revealing that the trials of witches and heretics came at a moment of great social upheaval and uncertainty in Puritan society. Kai T. Erikson, *Wayward Puritans: A Study in the Sociology of Deviance* (New York: John Wiley, 1966).

17. Coser, 1956, p. 169.

18. Neil Vidmar, 'Retributive Justice: Its Social Context', in M. Ross and D.T. Miller (eds) *The Justice Motive in Everyday Life* (New York: Cambridge University Press, 2002), p. 300.

19. Emile Durkheim, *The Division of Labor in Society*, trans. George Simpson (Glencoe, Ill.: The Free Press, 1960), p. 102. For a useful synopsis of this thesis, see Erikson, 1966, pp. 3–5. Erikson writes that 'like a war, a flood, or some other emergency, deviance makes people more alert to the interests they share in common and draws attention to those values which constitute the 'collective conscience' of the community'. Coser suggests that this essential point applies to *all* forms of conflict behavior: 'Conflict brings into the conscious awareness of the contenders and of the community at large norms and rules that were dormant before the particular conflict.' (Coser, 1956, p. 127).

20. Emile Durkheim, *The Rules of Sociological Method*, trans. S. A. Solovay and J. H. Mueller (Glencoe, Ill: The Free Press, 1958), p. 67.

21. In his excellent account of the 'social situation of the single parent', Robert S. Weiss writes that 'separation and divorce almost always are attended by feelings of having been misused' Robert S. Weiss, *Going It Alone* (New York: Basic Books, 1979), p. 5.

22. This was the defense of Mariam Yahya Ibrahim, who on Thursday 15 May 2014 was convicted of the 'crime' of apostasy and sentenced to death by a court in Sudan. At her trial, Ibrahim insisted that she hadn't committed apostasy, since, as she told the court, she was never a Muslim to begin with—her mother is a Christian, as is she, and her father, though a Muslim, was absent throughout

much of her childhood and didn't raise her. Ibrahim's defense was unsuccessful. Jehanne Henry, 'Dispatches: Sudanese Judge Sentences Pregnant Woman to Death and Whipping,' *Human Rights Watch*, 15 May 2014.

23. In the case of coerced apostates this sense of personal transformation is absent, unless they come to embrace the identity of the group into which they were forcibly converted.

24. Diogenes thought that the best life is a self-sufficient life and that a self-sufficient life necessitates the rejection of arbitrary social norms. See esp. Raymond Geuss, *Public Goods, Private Goods* (Princeton, N. J.: Princeton University Press, 2001), pp. 22–7.

25. Ibid., pp. 12–21.

26. Robert K. Merton, 'Social Structure and Anomie', *American Sociological Review*, 3/5 (1938), p. 677, emphases in original.

27. Georg Simmel, *On Individuality and Social Forms: Selected Writings*, edited by Donald N. Levine (Chicago: University of Chicago Press, 1971), p. 148.

28. See Chapter 5.

29. Daniel C. Dennett and Linda LaScola, 'Preachers Who Are Not Believers,' *Evolutionary Psychology*, 8/1 (2010).

30. His behavior, Merton writes, 'represents a departure from the cultural model in which men are obliged to strive actively, preferably through institutionalized procedures, to move onward and upward in the social hierarchy. Robert K. Merton, *Social Theory and Social Structure* (New York: The Free Press, 1968), p. 204.

31. Ibid.

32. Ibid., p. 205, emphasis in original.

33. Hadaway and Roof, 1988, p. 29. For a similar view, see David Caplovitz and Fred Sherrow, *The Religious Dropouts: Apostasy Among College Graduates* (Beverly Hills, CA: Sage, 1977); Dean R. Hoge, 'Why Catholics Drop Out' in Bromley (ed.), 1988, p. 82; and Roof and Landres, 1997, p. 82.

34. A 'none' refers to someone who, when asked in a survey what his or her religion is, stated 'none' (Zuckerman, 2009, p. 950). 'Nones,' Roof and Landres note, 'are people who reject an institutional religious affiliation...their doing so may or may not correspond with a personal affirmation of faith.' (Roof and Landres, 1997, p. 82) 'Nones', in others words, encompasses both atheists and believers.

35. Hadaway and Roof, 1988, p. 29.

36. Ibid.

37. David G. Bromley, 'Sociological Perspectives on Apostasy: An Overview', in Bromley (ed.), 1998, p. 5.

38. Stuart A. Wright, 'Exploring Factors That Shape the Apostate Role', in Bromley (ed.), 1998, p. 96, emphases in original.

39. Ibid.

40. Ibid., p. 97.

41. Anson Shupe, 'The Role of Apostates in the North American Anticult Movement' in Bromley (ed.), 1998, p. 209.

42. See Lewis F. Carter, 'Carriers of Tales: On Assessing Credibility of Apostate and Other Outsider Accounts of Religious Practices' in Bromley (ed.), 1998, p. 227; and Cragun and Hammer, 2011, pp. 153–4.

43. In the sociological vernacular people who do this are known as either 'converts' or 'switchers' (see Cragun and Hammer, 2011, pp. 156, 158).

44. It is indeed common for ex-Muslim converts to Christianity to self-identify as 'apostates from Islam' (see, for example, Crimp and Richardson, 2008; see also the testimonies in Ibn Warraq, 2003).

45. Cragun and Hammer's preferred term for those who return to their former religious group after having joined another is 'reaffiliate' (Cragun and Hammer, 2011, p. 157).

46. Wilson, 2004, p. 2. See also Maurus Reinkowski, 'Hidden Believers, Hidden Apostates: The Phenomenon of Crypto-Jews and Crypto-Christians in the Middle-East', in Dennis Washburn and A. Kevin Reinhart (eds.), *Converting Cultures: Religion, Ideology and Transformations of Modernity* (Leiden: Brill, 2007), p. 414.

47. Scot McKnight and Hauna Ondrey, *Finding Faith, Losing Faith: Stories of Conversion and Apostasy* (Waco: Baylor University Press, 2008), p. 7. This conflation between apostasy and conversion is also implicit in Bromley's definition of apostasy, according to which the apostate undergoes 'a total change of loyalties by allying with one or more elements of an oppositional coalition.' David G. Bromley, 'The Social Construction of Contested Exit Roles: Defectors, Whistleblowers, and Apostates', in Bromley (ed.), 1998, p. 36.

48. See Cragun and Hammer, 2011, p. 157.

49. See Wilson, 2004, pp. 18–19.

50. Coser, 1956, p. 70.

51. Albert O. Hirschman, *Exit, Voice and Loyalty: Responses to Decline in Firms, Organizations and States* (Cambridge, MA: Harvard University Press, 1970).

52. Coser, 1956, p. 71.

53. Ibid., p. 101.

54. See Lester R. Kurtz, 'The Politics of Heresy', *American Journal of Sociology* 88/6 (1983), p. 1088.

55. G. K. Chesterton, *Heretics* (New York: Dodd Mead, 1923), p. 11.

56. Stan L. Albrecht, Marie Cornwall and Perry H. Cunningham, 'Religious Leave-Taking: Disengagement and Disaffiliation among Mormons', in Bromley (ed.) 1988, pp. 63–4. 'Dropping out', a term also in wide currency in the sociology of religious exiting, is broadly synonymous with disengagement. Hoge, for example, uses it to refer to 'the cessation of Catholic Mass attendance' (Hoge, 1988, p. 82). Yet another widely used synonym for disengagement is 'disinvolvement'. Bromley, for instance, uses it to refer to 'distancing and pulling back from invest-

ment of self in the group' (David G. Bromley, 'Falling from the New Faiths: Toward an Integrated Model of Religious Affiliation/Disaffiliation', in Bar-Lev and Shaffir (eds.), 1997, pp. 48–9). I draw on this term in the closing section of chapter 3.

57. See Albrecht, Cornwall and Cunningham, 1988, pp. 70–71. Hoge prefers the term 'disidentification', since disaffiliation, he argues, 'has to do with being on formal membership lists', which renders it inapplicable to the many religious groups—including the Catholic Church—which do not keep them (Hoge, 1988, p. 82).

58. Albrecht, Cornwall and Cunningham, 1988, p. 63. This is also true of large numbers of Protestants (see Everett L. Perry, Ruth T. Doyle, James H. Davis and John E. Dyble, 'Toward a Typology of Unchurched Protestants,' *Review of Religious Research*, 21/4 (1980)), pp. 388–404, Jews (see Bernard Lazerwitz and Michael Harrison, 'American Jewish Denominations: A Social and Religious Profile,' *American Sociological Review*, 44/4 (1979), pp. 656–66) and Catholics (see Hoge, 1988, p. 81–99). In an illuminating study of gay Christians who had 'completely withdrawn from participating in the Church', Andrew K. T. Yip found that 'almost all still maintain their Christian identity.' Andrew K. T. Yip, 'Leaving the Church to Keep My Faith: the Lived Experiences of Non-Heterosexual Christians', in Leslie J. Francis and Yaacov J. Katz (eds.), 2000, pp.130, 129.

59. See Albrecht, Cornwall and Cunningham, 1988, p. 77: 'the norms of Mormonism much more than the doctrines of Mormonism' were the cause of disaffiliation from it.

60. See especially Paul Hollander, *The End of Commitment: Intellectuals, Revolutionaries and Political Morality* (Chicago: Ivan R. Dee, 2006).

61. See esp. Coser, 1956, pp. 68–9, 103.

62. As Vidmar and Miller explain: 'Punishment reactions against a rule violator may be more intense if the reactor assumes that similar others should know better or have a higher level of morality.' (Vidmar and Miller, 'Social-Psychological Processes Underlying Attitudes Toward Legal Punishment', p. 589) See also Wilson, 2004, p. 107; and Susan Rothbaum, 'Between Two Worlds: Issues of Separation and Identity After Leaving a Religious Community', in Bromley (ed.), 1988, p. 211.

63. From the testimony of an ex-Moonie: 'They had to understand where I was coming from and that I could not function in that situation anymore... At first they tried to talk me out of it, but at the end of that meeting I'd say they finally saw my point of view...I didn't want to be there any longer. I wasn't happy...and other people were going to see that, and that wasn't going to help anyone. So they said, "Okay, you can leave."' Quoted in Stuart A Wright, 'Reconceptualizing Cult Coercion and Withdrawal: A Comparative Analysis of Divorce and Apostasy', *Social Forces*, 70/1 (1991), p. 135.

64. Referring to Jewish apostates in pre-modern Poland, Edward Fram writes that 'when apostasy did take place, it did not always cut off familial feelings and ties, and efforts to entice the apostate back were not unknown' (Fram, 1996, p. 321). Fram alludes to a case in which the parents of an apostatized son 'wanted to bribe' him 'to return to the Jewish Community' (Ibid.).

65. History is depressingly replete with examples of apostasy at the point of the sword (see Wilson, 2004, p. 129).

66. Reflecting on the scarcity of ancient source-material on Jewish, Christian and Pagan apostates in antiquity, Wilson suggests that 'it is probable that those who accepted that they were defectors/apostates would normally have preferred not to draw attention to themselves...Some defectors no doubt carried with them a lingering sense of guilt or did not want to call down the wrath of their community. They saw no need for public renunciation or similar grand gesture but preferred to slip away anonymously into the crowd.' (Ibid., p. 9)

67. Stuart A. Wright refers to the phenomenon of 'sudden deconversion', but remarks that it is 'improbable' that it is a common occurrence Stuart A. Wright, 'Leaving New Religious Movements: Issues, Theory and Research', in Bromley (ed.), 1988, p. 161.

68. Wright categorizes this as 'the declarative mode of leave-taking': 'a confrontational but nonnegotiable type of exit usually accompanied by anger and the release of bottled-up sentiments.' (Wright, 1991, p. 134).

69. Rothbaum observes that many ex-members of totalistic religious groups 'hope for the impossible: that the leader and group will listen to, understand and finally approve their reasons for leaving' (Rothbaum, 1988, p. 218).

70. It is precisely in these terms that James A. Beckford characterizes the experiences of 'self-instigated' or voluntary defectors from the Unification Church (UC): see Beckford, 1985, especially p. 142. Here we may speak of the 'reluctant apostate', a term Beckford himself uses. James A. Beckford, 'Talking of Apostasy or Telling Tales and 'Telling' Tales', in N. Gilbert and P. Abel (eds.), *Accounts and Action* (Aldershot: Gower, 1983), p. 90.

71. See Hadaway and Roof, 1988, pp. 34–46.

72. In their study of disengagement and disaffiliation from Mormonism, Albrecht *et al* found that 'difficulties with church doctrines' did not play a major role in the exit process. Indeed, 'for the most part, because of their marginal status, respondents indicated they didn't know very much about the Mormon religion. They never got into things enough to know whether or not they disagreed with the doctrines' (Albrecht, Cornwall and Cunningham, 1988, p. 76). Beckford's *Cult Controversies* materializes a similar finding: 'the grounds advanced by ex-Moonies in Britain for their decision to leave the UC have very little to do with belief or other cognitive matters.' (Beckford, 1985, p. 153) For many ex-Muslims, by contrast, the reverse holds true: Islamic doctrines are indeed very much a 'deal-breaker'. And Islam is broken with from a position of knowledge: see Chapter 3.

73. Hans Toch writes of the '*instrumental* believer', a person who joins a movement or group 'to obtain security or social support or material rewards or other fringe benefits, and who remains a member on this basis' (Hans Toch, *The Social Psychology of Social Movements* (London: Methuen, 1966), p. 194, emphasis in original). This person is very different from the '*belief-centered*' member, who 'belongs to the movement primarily because he agrees with what it stands for' (Ibid., emphasis in original). In a similar way, one can make a distinction between the 'principled apostate', whose apostasy is intellectually motivated, and the 'pragmatic apostate', whose apostasy is materially motivated.

74. Selim Deringil, '"There Is No Compulsion in Religion": On Conversion and Apostasy in the Late Ottoman Empire: 1839–1856,' *Comparative Studies in Society and History*, 42/3 (2000), p. 548.

75. Ibid., p. 547.

76. Bob Altemeyer and Bruce Hunsberger refer to these 'travellers' as 'amazing apostates' (Bob Altemeyer and Bruce Hunsberger, *Amazing Conversions: Why Some Turn to Faith and Others Abandon Religion* (Amherst, New York: Prometheus, 1997), pp. 12, 21–7).

77. Thus Phil Zuckerman makes a distinction between '*transformative* apostasy' and '*mild* apostasy': the former refers to 'individuals who were deeply, strongly religious who then went on to reject their religion', whereas the latter refers to those 'who rejected religion but weren't all that religious in the first place.' Phil Zuckerman, *Faith No More: Why People Reject Religion* (New York: Oxford University Press, 2012), p. 7, emphases in original.

78. Toch, 1966, p. 175. See also Zuckerman, 2012, p. 7.

79. Roy F. Baumeister, Arlene Stillwell and Sara R. Wotman, 'Victim and Perpetrator Accounts of Interpersonal Conflict: Autobiographical Narratives About Anger,' *Journal of Personality and Social Psychology*, 59/5 (1990), pp. 994–1005.

80. Ibid., p. 994.

81. See Roy F. Baumeister, *Evil: Inside Human Violence and Cruelty* (New York: Henry Holt, 1997), p. 46.

82. See, for example, Davidman and Greil, 2007, p. 204.

83. See Rothbaum, 1988, p. 218.

84. See Wilson, 2004, pp. 130, 134.

85. Howard S. Becker, *Outsiders* (New York: Free Press, 1963), p. 9, emphases in original.

86. Ibid., pp. 11–12.

87. Ibid., p. 13.

88. See also Kai T. Erikson's classic essay, 'Notes on the Sociology of Deviance,' *Social Problems*, 9/4 (1962), especially at p. 308; and John I. Kitsuse 'Societal Reaction to Deviant Behavior: Problems of Theory and Method,' *Social Problems*, 9/3 (1962), pp. 247–56. Becker cites Kitsuse's position as 'very similar' to his own (Becker, 1963, p. 9).

89. See Ibid., esp. pp. 121–63.

90. John M. G. Barclay explores the relevance, more broadly, of interactionist deviancy theory to the issue of apostasy in John M. G. Barclay, 'Deviance and Apostasy: Some Applications of Deviance Theory to First-Century Judaism and Christianity', in Philip F. Esler (ed.) *Modelling Early Christianity: Social-Scientific Studies of the New Testament in Its Context* (London: Routledge, 1995), pp. 114–27. See also the acute and balanced discussion in Wilson, 2004, pp. 11–13, 110–118.

91. For a detailed and expertly nuanced discussion of apostasy in classical Islam, see Friedmann, 2003, pp. 121–59; and Peters and De Vries, 1976–7.

92. Friedmann, 2003, p. 121. The *shahada* is the Muslim declaration of belief in the oneness of God (*tawhid*) and acceptance of Muhammad as God's prophet. The declaration in English and in its shortest form reads: 'There is no god but God, Muhammad is the messenger of God.'

93. Ibid., pp. 122–3.

94. See Sookhdeo, 2009, p. 49. Sookhdeo remarks that this interpretive flexibility renders the charge of apostasy acutely susceptible to abuse. See also Frank Griffel, 'Toleration and Exclusion: al-Shafi'i and al-Ghazali on the Treatment of Apostates,' *Bulletin of the School of Oriental and African Studies*, 64 (2001), pp. 341–2; and Saeed and Saeed, 2004, pp. 44–50, 167.

95. Sookhdeo, 2009, p. 50.

96. See Mohammed M. Hafez, 'Tactics, *Takfir*, and Anti-Muslim Violence', in Assaf Moghadam and Brian Fishman (eds), *Self-Inflicted Wounds: Debates and Divisions within al-Qa'ida and its Periphery* (Washington: Harmony Project, West Point, 2010), p. 30.

97. In what follows I draw heavily on Marshall and Shea, 2011, pp. 76–7; Susanne Olsson, 'Apostasy in Egypt: Contemporary Cases of *Hisbah*,' *The Muslim World*, 98/1 (2008), pp. 104–6; and Kilian Bälz, 'Submitting Faith to Judicial Scrutiny through the Family Trial: The 'Abu Zayd Case',' *Die Welt des Islams*, 37/2 (1997), pp. 135–55.

98. On Abu-Zayd's work and methodology, see especially Charles Hirschkind, 'Heresy or Hermeneutics: The Case of Nasr Hamid Abu Zayd,' *The American Journal of Islamic Social Sciences*, 12/4 (1995), pp. 463–77; and Nasr Abu Zayd, 'The Case of Abu Zaid,' *Index on Censorship*, 4 (1996), pp. 30–9.

99. See Friedmann, 2003, pp. 161–2, 170–2; and Peters and De Vries, 1976–7, pp. 19–20.

100. Michel Balivet, *Romanie Byzantine et Pays de Rum Turc. Histoire d'un espace d'imbrication gréco-turque* (Istanbul: 1994), p. 187, cited in Deringil, 2000 p. 550. Damascinos was a Christian revert (or reaffiliate) and in all likelihood had been coerced into Islam (Ibid., p. 570).

101. Ibid., pp. 551, 557.

102. This lenient attitude was by no means uncommon at the time. Indeed, Deringil reports that 'in the years leading up to and immediately after the Reform Edict of 1856 it became state policy to look the other way when Muslims who claimed to be crypto-Christians openly declared loyalty to their old faith' (Ibid., p. 551; see also p. 561). It was only later, toward the end of the nineteenth century, that this attitude shifted: with the empire 'very much on the defensive, indeed...fighting for its life, it became a matter of vital interest that there should be no defection from its ranks' (Ibid., p. 568).

103. Related to this is the 'heresy hunt': see Kurtz, 1983, pp. 1085–115.

104. Beckford, 1985, p. 139, emphasis in original.

105. See Ibid, pp. 13–20.

106. See David G. Bromley, 'Preface' in Bromley (ed.), 1998, pp. vii–viii.

107. Bromley, 'Sociological Perspectives on Apostasy', p. 4.

108. 'From the perspective of their opponents, subversive organizations embody quintessential evil and are considered to pose a maximum degree of threat to the established social order': Bromley, 'The Social Construction of Contested Exit Roles,' p. 24.

109. Bromley, 'The Social Construction of Contested Exit Roles,' pp. 19–21: 'Apostates have been a significant component of the campaign to invoke social control measures of various kinds against NRMs over the last several decades... apostate testimony has been pivotal in enforcement actions by social control agencies and in civil litigation initiated against NRMs.' See also James T. Richardson, 'Apostates, Whistleblowers, Law and Social Control', in Bromley (ed.), 1998, pp. 171–89; and James R. Lewis, 'Apostates and the Legitimation of Repression: Some Historical and Empirical Perspectives on the Cult Controversy,' *Sociological Analysis*, 49/4 (1989), pp. 386–96.

110. Lewis A. Coser, 'The Age of the Informer,' *Dissent* 1 (1954), p. 250.

111. Max Scheler, *On Feeling, Knowing and Valuing*, Harold J. Bershady (ed.) (Chicago: Chicago University Press, 1992), p. 131.

112. Bromley, 'The Social Construction of Contested Exit Roles', p. 20.

113. Wright, 1998, p. 97.

114. Ibid. See also Eileen Barker, 'Defection from the Unification Church: Some Statistics and Distinctions' in Bromley (ed.) 1988, p. 177. This is the dominant paradigm through which the liberal-left tends to view Ayaan Hirsi Ali. Ian Buruma, for example, intuits in Hirsi Ali 'hints of zealousness, echoes perhaps of her earlier enthusiasm for the Muslim Brotherhood, before she was converted to the ideals of the European Enlightenment' (Ian Buruma, *Murder in Amsterdam*, p. 158). Referring to Hirsi Ali's impassioned defense of Enlightenment values, he detects 'a spark of almost religious fervor in her eyes' (Ibid., p. 168). Timothy Garton Ash, in a similar vein, depicts Hirsi Ali as a 'slightly simplistic Enlightenment fundamentalist' Timothy Garton Ash, 'Islam in Europe: A Review of

Murder in Amsterdam by Ian Buruma and *The Caged Virgin* by Ayaan Hirsi Ali,' *New York Review of Books*, 5 October 2006.

115. This term was popularized by Eric Hoffer's book *The True Believer: Thoughts on the Nature of Mass Movements* (New York: Harper & Row, 1951). Hoffer's basic contention is that every social movement is made up of a core of fanatics who are broadly indifferent to issues of ideology.

116. Hans Toch, *The Social Psychology of Social Movements* (London: Methuen, 1966), p. 123.

117. Shupe, 1998, p. 209.

118. See Bromley, 'Sociological Perspectives on Apostasy,' p. 5; see also David G. Bromley, 'Linking Social Structure and the Exit Process in Religious Organizations: Defectors, Whistle-Blowers and Apostates', *Journal for the Scientific Study of Religion*, 37/1 (1998), p. 153.

119. See Stephen A. Kent, 'Deviance Labelling and Normative Strategies in the Canadian 'New Religions/Countercult' Debate,' *Canadian Journal of Sociology*, 15/4 (1990).

120. See Harold Garfinkel, 'Conditions of Successful Degradation Ceremonies,' *American Journal of Sociology* 61/5 (1956), pp. 420–24.

121. See David G. Bromley, Anson D. Shupe and J. C. Ventimiglia, 'Atrocity Tales, the Unification Church, and the Social Construction of Evil,' *Journal of Communication* 29 (3) (1979), p. 43; Bromley, 'The Social Construction of Contested Exit Roles,' p. 37; Wright, 1998, p. 100; and Daniel Carson Johnson, 'Apostates Who Never Were: The Social Construction of *Absque Facto* Apostate Narratives' in Bromley (ed.), 1998, pp. 131–2.

122. Lewis, 1989, p. 387.

123. Wilson, 2004, p. 106.

124. Anson Shupe, *Six Perspectives on New Religions* (New York: Edwin Mellen, 1981), p. 214. See also Richardson, 1998, p. 173.

125. See Bromley, 'The Social Construction of Contested Exit Roles,' p. 37; Wright, 1998, p. 98; Beckford, 1983, p. 88; and Lewis, 1989, p. 394.

126. Joel Sirkes, *Bayit hadash*: cited in Fram, 1996, p. 320. This is reminiscent of Philo's views on Jewish apostates from the ancient world: these 'rebels from the holy laws', Philo thunders, 'sold' their faith for 'delicacies, strong liquor, sweetmeats and the enjoyment of another's beauty' (cited in Wilson, 2004, p. 36).

127. Rothbaum, 1988, p. 211.

128. Stephen A. Kent, 'Deviance Labelling and Normative Strategies in the Canadian 'New Religions/Countercult' Debate,' *Canadian Journal of Sociology*, 15/4 (1990), p. 409.

129. Ibid.

130. On the sociology of stories, see Ken Plummer, *Telling Sexual Stories: Power, Change and Social Worlds* (London: Routledge, 1995).

131. Salman Rushdie, *Joseph Anton: A Memoir* (Toronto: Random House, 2012), p. 19.

132. See Quentin Skinner, *Visions of Politics (Volume 1): Regarding Method* (Cambridge, Cambridge University Press, 2002), p. 148.

133. See John Dunn, 'Practising History and Social Science on 'Realist' Assumptions', in C. Hookway and P. Pettit (eds), *Action and Interpretation: Studies in the Philosophy of the Social Sciences* (Cambridge: Cambridge University Press, 1980), p. 152.

3. BECOMING AN APOSTATE: FROM ISLAM TO UNBELIEF

1. See Jack Katz, *Seductions of Crime* (New York: Basic Books, 1988), p. 7.

2. According to Weiss, the interviewer should say as little as possible so as not to unduly influence what the respondent says, so as, above all, to let the them talk and relay their experiences (Weiss, 1994). I strictly adhered to this, often adopting Nick Broomfield's excellent advice to aspiring documentary filmmakers: when your subject stops talking and a lengthy silence follows, repeat the last three words they uttered.

3. Katz, 1988, p. 7. On self-justifying rhetoric, see C. Wright Mills, 'Situated Actions and Vocabularies of Motive,' *American Sociological Review* 5/6 (1940), pp. 904–13; and Gresham M. Sykes and David Matza, 'Techniques of Neutralization,' *American Sociological Review* 22/6 (1957), pp. 664–70.

4. Stephen Holmes, 'Al-Qaeda, September 11, 2001', in D. Gambetta (ed.), *Making Sense of Suicide Missions* (New York: Oxford University Press, 2005), pp. 132–3.

5. Michael Cook correctly points out that 'commanding right and forbidding wrong', a phrase firmly rooted in the diction of the Quran, are really the same activities. Michael Cook, *Forbidding Wrong in Islam: An Introduction* (Cambridge: Cambridge University Press, 2003), p. 3.

6. There is an amusing variation on this in Salman Rushdie's memoir. For Rushdie, the deciding issue wasn't God's sadistic depravity, but rather his poor aesthetic judgment: 'The last traces of belief were erased from his mind by his powerful dislike of the architecture of Rugby Chapel... As a schoolboy he thought it hideous, deciding, in that science-fiction-heavy time of his life, that it resembled nothing so much as a brick rocket ship ready for takeoff; and one day when he was staring at it through the window of a classroom in the New Big School during a Latin lesson, a question occurred. 'What kind of God,' he wondered, 'would live in a house as ugly as that?' An instant later the answer presented itself: obviously no self-respecting God would live there—in fact, obviously, there *was* no God, not even a God with bad taste in architecture.' (Salman Rushdie, 2012, pp. 31–2, emphasis in original) As should be obvious, this passage, like the entirety of Rushdie's memoir, is written in the third person.

7. The Quran prohibits sexual activity outside of marriage: see 23: 5, 6 (2004, p. 215).

8. In the interviews conducted with South Asian males, a recurrent motif was the

emotional well-being of the mother. As Wahid said, 'I wanted to be a good Muslim because that made my mum happy'. This wasn't the case with the South Asian women I interviewed, who on the whole tended to speak about their mothers with less feeling and intensity of emotional concern.

9. Interestingly, most of the women I spoke with reported that their fathers were relatively liberal on the *hijab* question, whereas their mothers had been insistent that it should be worn.

10. This is from Mohsin's online memoir, a document he wrote to 'help me make sense of my life'.

11. In stark counterpoint, Nabilah says: 'Some ex-Muslims say 9/11 did the trick. It did *not* do the trick for me. 9/11 was when America got what it deserved. That's how I saw it then.'

12. Cited in Christopher Hitchens, *Letters to a Young Contrarian* (Oxford: Perseus, 2001), p. 29.

13. Sura 4: 56 (2004, p. 56).

14. Sura 6: 70 (2004, p. 85).

15. Sura 22: 19, 20, 21, 22 (2004, p. 210).

16. Among many Muslims, 'atheist' is a term of potent censure. This was made very apparent to me when Omar, a fit and muscular man, said that 'if you went back in time and said to me seven years ago that I'd become an atheist, I would have thrown you out of that window'. Omar was exaggerating. But only a bit.

17. Here is a methodological note of caution to first-time researchers: *always* double-check the audio against the transcript. To the torpid ears of my transcriber, 'Schopenhauer and Nietzsche' were 'shopping and pedicure'. I am not making this up.

18. Ali Sina is a prominent activist ex-Muslim. His work can be found here: http://www.faithfreedom.org/Author/Sina.htm (accessed 11 January 2013).

19. This is similar to what (the wonderfully named) Helen Rose Fuchs Ebaugh calls 'the vacuum', a period in which the 'anchors of social and self-identity are suspended for the individual, leaving him or her feeling rootless and anxious.' Helen Rose Fuchs Ebaugh, *Becoming an Ex: The Process of Role Exit* (Chicago: The University of Chicago Press, 1988), p. 145.

20. *South Park* is an animated television series known for its irreverence. One episode, broadcast in 2010, featured a character said to be the Prophet Muhammad. He was wearing a bear costume. This prompted an Islamic group based in New York to issue a 'prediction' that the show's creators 'will probably wind up like Theo Van Gogh' (see Dave Itzkoff, "South Park' Episode Is Altered After Muslim Group's Warning,' *New York Times*, 22 April 2010).

21. WTF is an acronym: 'What The Fuck?'.

22. Mary Douglas, *Purity and Danger* (London: Routledge, 1966), p. 80.

23. See, classically, Arnold Van Gennep, *The Rites of Passage*, trans. M. Vizedom and G. Caffee (Chicago, IL: The University of Chicago Press, 1960).

24. The Quran is very clear and trenchant in prohibiting its consumption: see esp.
6: 145 (2004, p. 91): '[Prophet], say, "In all that has been revealed to me, I find
nothing forbidden for people to eat, except for carrion, flowing blood, pig's
meat—it is loathsome—or a sinful offering over which any name other than
God's has been invoked."'

25. This is how one respondent described it to me in passing.

26. See Raymond Geuss, *Public Goods, Private Goods* (Princeton: Princeton University
Press, 2001), p. 17.

27. Bromley, 1997, pp. 48–9.

4. COMING OUT: DISCLOSING APOSTASY

1. Alexander Herzen, *From the Other Shore*, trans. Moura Budberg (London: Wei-
denfeld and Nicolson, 1956), p. 124.

2. This is from Rock's 2004 HBO show *Never Scared*.

3. The British novelist Martin Amis is good on this. In *Yellow Dog* one of the pro-
tagonists realizes that 'after a while, marriage is a sibling relationship—marked
by occasional, and rather regrettable, episodes of incest.' Martin Amis, *Yellow Dog*
(New York: Vintage, 2003), p. 8.

4. See Michael Ignatieff, *The Lesser Evil: Political Ethics in an Age of Terror* (Princeton, N.
J.: Princeton University Press, 2004).

5. See Michael Ignatieff, *Isaiah Berlin: A Life* (New York: Henry Holt, 1998), pp. 229,
245, 257, 285, 291.

6. This is from the last essay written by Isaiah Berlin published in *The New York
Review of Books*, XLV, 8 (1998).

7. This is from a CEMB online forum post.

8. Wahid also said that 'I could not live with the thought that I would ruin a Muslim girl's life by marrying her only to later void the marriage by revealing my
apostasy'.

9. When Masood sent this text he was in a pub and drunk ('I think I was pissed
actually').

10. In the event, Amina didn't dispatch her letter and has put her coming out on
hold for now.

11. I use the term 'account' to mean 'a linguistic device employed whenever an action
is subjected to valuative inquiry' (Marvin B. Scott and Stanford M. Lyman,
'Accounts', *American Sociological Review* 33(1) (1968), p. 46). Accounts are 'routinely
expected when activity falls outside the domain of expectations' (Ibid).

12. Cook, 2003, pp. 27–43.

13. Shame, C. Fred Alford, helpfully observes, 'is about what others think of us',
whereas guilt 'is about what we think of ourselves' (C. Fred Alford, *Whistleblowers: Broken Lives and Organizational Power* (Ithaca: Cornell University Press, 2001),

p. 74). Shame, more specifically, as Jon Elster points out, 'is triggered by the contemptuous or disgusted disapproval by others' (Jon Elster, *Alchemies of the Mind: Rationality and the Emotions* (Cambridge: Cambridge University Press, 1999), p. 149). Shame, more specifically still, involves 'failing to live up to the standards of the group through which one gains one's self-identity' (Robert C. Solomon, *A Passion for Justice: Emotions and the Origins of the Social Contract* (Lanham, Maryland: Rowman & Littlefield Publishers, 1995), p. 294).

14. Erving Goffman writes of 'the tendency for a stigma to spread from the stigmatized individual to his close connexions' (Erving Goffman, *Stigma: Notes on the Management of Spoiled Identity* (London: Penguin, 1963), p. 43). This, Goffman explains, is why the stigmatized are ritually separated from the 'normals': to prevent contamination.

5. STAYING IN: CONCEALING APOSTASY

1. Goffman, 1963, p. 13.
2. Ibid., p. 57. This is not so in the case of the 'discredited person': a person whose stigma is 'an undesired differentness' which 'normals' can readily see, such as a physical deformity (Ibid., p. 15).
3. Ibid., p. 57.
4. For an illuminating theological discussion of 'clandestine apostasy', see especially Frank Griffel, 'Toleration and Exclusion: al-Shafi'i and al-Ghazali on the Treatment of Apostates', *Bulletin of the School of Oriental and African Studies* 64, 3 (2001): pp. 339–54.
5. See Goffman, 1963, pp. 57–128.
6. William Ian Miller, *Faking It* (New York: Cambridge University Press, 2003), p. 148.
7. Salman Rushdie, 'Now I Can Say, I Am a Muslim', *New York Times*, 28 December 1990, available at: http://www.nytimes.com/1990/12/28/opinion/now-i-can-say-i-am-a-muslim.html (accessed 30 April 2013). This article was first published in the London *Times*.
8. See Christopher Hitchens, *Unacknowledged Legislation: Writers in the Public Sphere* (London: Verso, 2000), p. 109.
9. See esp. Selim Deringil, *Conversion and Apostasy in the Late Ottoman Empire* (Cambridge: Cambridge University Press, 2012), pp. 111–55.
10. See Marshall and Shea, 2011.
11. Adrienne Rich, *On Lies, Secrets and Silence: Selected Prose 1966–1978* (New York: W. W. Norton, 1979), p. 191.
12. Goffman, 1963, p. 60.
13. On how humor can be used as a 'vehicle of cautious opposition', see, insightfully, Toch, 1966, p. 166.

14. Rich, 1979, p. 187.
15. See Goffman, 1963, pp. 57–128.
16. Ibid., p. 122.
17. Rushdie, 2012, p. 147.
18. Rushdie, 1990.
19. Rushdie, 2012, p. 304.
20. Ibid., p. 285.
21. Ibid., p. 277.
22. Ibid., p. 276.
23. Ibid., p. 294.
24. Mark Medley, 'Faux Joe: Salman Rushdie confronts his past in *Joseph Anton*,' *National Post*, 18 September 2012, available at: http://arts.nationalpost.com/2012/09/18/faux-joe-salman-rushdie-confronts-his-past-in-joseph-anton/ (accessed 22 May 2013).
25. To feel shame, as Jon Elster suggests, is to feel small (Elster, 1999, p.153).
26. Robert C. Solomon correctly observes that 'shame involves the sense of seriously failing those around you, violating their norms, falling short of their expectations, letting them down' (Robert C. Solomon, *True to Our Feelings: What Our Emotions Are Really Telling Us* (Oxford: Oxford University Press, 2007), p. 95).
27. David Matza, *Becoming Deviant* (Englewood Cliffs, N. J.: Prentice-Hall, 1969), p. 151.
28. See especially Steven Seidman, *Beyond the Closet: The Transformation of Gay and Lesbian Life* (New York: Routledge, 2002); and Plummer, 1975.
29. This, as Matza makes clear, discussing passing in general, can be exhausting work: 'Few things are more difficult to achieve than the certainty of possessing a poker-face.' (Matza, 1969 p. 151) See also Seidman, 2002, pp. 31, 38.
30. 'When jokes were made about "queers" I had to laugh with the rest, and when talk was about women I had to invent conquests of my own. I hated myself at such moments, but there seemed to be nothing else that I could do. My whole life became a lie.' This from Peter Wildeblood, *Against the Law* (New York: Julian Messner, 1959). Commenting on this very extract, Goffman says of the passer that 'he will suffer feelings of disloyalty and self-contempt when he cannot take action against "offensive" remarks made by members of the category he is passing into against the category he is passing out of—especially when he finds it dangerous to refrain from joining in this vilification' (Goffman, 1963, p. 109).
31. As Seidman remarks, closeted gay people 'are often emotionally distant from the people they are closest to—kin and friends' (Seidman, 2002, p. 30; see also pp. 46–8, 123).

6. HANGING ON: MANAGING APOSTASY

1. In classical Islamic discourse there is a firm distinction between the 'lesser jihad' and 'the greater jihad'. Whereas the former refers to physical struggle against external aggressors, the latter refers to mental struggle against self-capitulation to worldly/un-Islamic desires.

2. This is from an online forum post: 'Do not hold back. Fuck everything in sight, drink everything in reach, smoke everything you can get your hands on. No mercy. You won't get these years back ever again.' This piece of advice, offered by one hardened ex-Muslim to fledgling apostates, wholly neglects to consider the possible perils of the excess it promotes, especially for those with scant experience of the activities it mentions.

3. Martin Amis, *The Pregnant Widow* (London: Jonathan Cape, 2010), p. 371.

4. Ibid., p. 26. The deeper theme in Amis's book is in fact one of the central themes of classical sociology: namely, anomie—'the pathological mental state of the individual who is insufficiently regulated by society' (Steven Lukes, 'Alienation and Anomie', in Peter Laslett and W.G. Runciman (eds), *Philosophy, Politics and Society*, 3rd Series, (Oxford: Basil Blackwell, 1967), p. 404). Anomie, according to Durkheim, thrives in conditions of social upheaval, where moral codes become irrelevant and outmoded, thus creating a moral vacuum in which individual passions are liberated from all restraint.

5. See Robert S. Weiss, *Loneliness: The Experience of Emotional and Social Isolation* (Cambridge, MA: The MIT Press, 1973).

6. David Riesman, Foreword to Robert S. Weiss, 1973, p. ix. See also Robert S. Weiss, *Marital Separation* (New York: Basic Books, 1975), p. 56.

7. Roth, 2000, p. 178.

8. That is, their stigma 'is not immediately apparent' (Goffman, 1963, p. 57).

9. The idea that 'Islam is the most perfect and complete religion' (Hasan Ahmad Abidin, cited in Saeed and Saeed, 2004, p. 16) is, as Abdullah Saeed and Hassan Saeed observe, 'ancient' and wholly taken-for-granted among the classical Muslim scholars (Ibid., p. 15).

10. This is from the proceedings of Al-Azhar's Fourth Conference of the Academy of Islamic Research, held in 1968: cited in Sookhdeo, 2009, p. 44.

11. Cited in Saeed and Saeed, 2004, p. 15.

12. Apostates, the Quran declares, 'love the life of this world more than the one to come' (The Quran, 16: 107, 2004, p. 173).

13. Hence the subversive quality of Masood's joke about getting more and not less ass as a Muslim than as an apostate.

14. The closing sentence of the Quran cautions Muslims to take 'refuge with the Lord of people' and to be on their guard against 'the slinking whisperer—who whispers into the hearts of people' (The Quran, 114: 1–6 (2004, p. 446)).

15. Saeed and Saeed mention this account in a short discussion of 'reasons for apostasy'. 'To the average Muslim', they write, 'the truth and validity of Islam and the falsity of all other religions must be apparent to anyone'—to anyone, that is, of sound mind. Hence 'if a person converts from Islam, the argument goes, they must be insane' (Saeed and Saeed, 2004, p. 110).

16. Ayaan Hirsi Ali has expressed irritation at the suggestion, advanced by both her Muslim and secular liberal interpreters, that her apostasy is explicable in terms of the traumatic experiences—she was a victim of genital mutilation and other violent abuses—she suffered in her childhood.

17. Saul Bellow, *The Adventures of Augie March* (New York: The Viking Press, 1953), p. 3.

18. Ayaan Hirsi Ali, 'How (and Why) I Became an Infidel' in Christopher Hitchens (ed.), *The Portable Atheist: Essential Readings for the Non-Believer* (Philadelphia: Perseus, 2007), p. 480.

19. Weiss, 1975, p. 310.

20. Ibid.

21. See John H. Gagnon and William Simon, *Sexual Conduct: The Social Sources of Human Sexuality* (Chicago: Aldine, 1973). See also Ebaugh, 1988, pp. 163–4. Ebaugh remarks that the ex-nuns she interviewed were 'very insecure about sexual scripts' and didn't really know how to relate to men and often 'found themselves in embarrassing situations in which the man [they were on a date with] interpreted cues very differently from the way they had intended'.

22. This post is a direct response to the following inquiry, 'I still say salam...it feels strange! I cant kick that habit...shud i?'

23. As one of the mods told me: 'The role of admins and moderators is basically to ensure the forum remains a safe and comfortable place for ex-Muslims to express themselves. Trolling, racism, bigotry, etc, is not tolerated. We do sometimes delete offending posts but that doesn't happen often. We support free speech, but our primary concern is the safety and welfare of ex-Muslims.'

24. This, by the way, is Yasmin.

25. And this is Ramesh. All comments here have been annexed from the same comment-thread, entitled 'Advice to 16–22 years old Ex-Muslims'.

26. Goffman, 1963, p. 106.

27. Of the total number of respondents interviewed, the vast majority—33—were CEMB forum members. A small number of these members were also active on other forums, including that of FFI.

28. Wahid, for example, confessed that growing up he felt different from all his Muslim peers, felt that 'there's nobody else out there like me', that 'something happened with me that hasn't happened with everybody else', that 'I grew up in some weird way'. He still feels this way and it still troubles him.

29. And not just joke, but also to 'vent': to fully and unrestrainedly express feelings and thoughts which cannot be communicated in face-face interaction with Mus-

lims. 'Venting', as it is commonly referred to in this virtual world, is especially important to closeted apostates, since it represents a release from all that tongue-biting and covering recounted in Chapter 5. As one ex-Muslim remarked of the CEMB forum in an online post, 'This forum is a place to vent a secretive life.'

30. Weiss, 1979, p. 194. See also Weiss, 1973, pp. 17, 227 ('loneliness is a deficit condition'). Thomas Dumm similarly observes that 'to be lonely is to be without recourse to others' (Dumm, *Loneliness as a Way of Life* (Cambridge, MA.: Harvard University Press, 2008), p. 51).

31. 'It did help', says Aisha, but only 'a little bit, a little bit'.

32. Roth, 2000, p. 108, emphasis in original.

33. Ibid., p. 126.

34. Ibid., pp. 138–9.

35. Ibid., p. 108, emphases in original.

36. The Quran, 2: 89 (2004, p. 11).

37. Ibid., 3: 90, p. 41.

38. Ibid., 3: 91, p. 41.

39. Ibid., 2: 217, p. 24.

40. See Bromley, Shupe and Ventimiglia, 1979, pp. 42–53. An 'atrocity tale' is 'a presentation of [an] event (real or imaginary) in such a way as to (a) evoke moral outrage by specifying and detailing the value violations, (b) authorize, implicitly or explicitly, punitive sanctions, and (c) mobilize control efforts against the alleged perpetrators.' (Ibid., p. 43)

41. I did this with most respondents, where this was possible.

42. Masood here is referring to Mohsin.

43. This is Luqman's brother, from the audio recording to which I made reference in Chapter 4 (p. 78).

44. Remarks Nubia: 'The funny thing a lot of Muslims say to me is, 'oh you just did it so you could take off the *hijab* and go to the pub and do all that stuff'. And I say, 'No, actually for a full year and half I wore the *hijab* and I didn't do any of that.'

45. Alia, for example, has produced an 8,000-word compendium entitled 'Unethical/questionable hadiths and surahs'.

46. This welcoming embrace is the exact reverse of what Garfinkel calls a 'status degradation ceremony' (see Garfinkel, 1956). The subject of the embrace is not made 'strange', as he is in the rituals of exclusion or 'othering' which Garfinkel describes. On the contrary, he is unmade strange; he is normalized. And far from having his status lowered 'in the local scheme of social types', it is raised. Indeed, he is lauded, for seeing through the illusions of religion and for breaking free of the chains of group-think and superstition.

47. There is a thread on the forum in which members are invited to record their voice, so that other members can know what they sound like. There is also a thread in which members are invited to post pictures of themselves, which is risky, since many members do not want to publicly reveal their status as apos-

tates. Some members get around this by 'cartoonifying' themselves, transforming real photographs into cartoon-like renderings.

48. Referring to his mother, Wahid says that 'she knows I don't want to get married, that I don't like that concept of marriage and she knows that I don't like children either.'

49. Wahid admitted to me that 'no matter what happens I know I'm not going to be happy' and that makes him feel depressed, 'empty', 'like there's a void'. Wahid concludes that 'the best I can do is try and make the people around me happy and that's kind of like my mum', seemingly incognizant to the possibility that that the central cause of his unhappiness is his mother and the weight of her expectations.

50. This is compensated by the supportive texts Luqman receives from one of his sister's inquiring about his welfare.

51. 'My auntie stayed in touch with me to make sure I'm okay, but she's trying to convince me to come back but I've told her it can't happen, I can't be a Muslim.'

52. 'She invited me over for Eid just gone and I didn't go'. Didn't go, because it's the same dynamic, the same deal every time: 'I'll go round there and sit down and listen to all of that bullshit and I can't, I can't listen to it without arguing and if I argue what's the point? What's the point in going?'

53. The idea that conflict may 'serve to maintain a relationship' is illuminatingly explored in Coser, *The Functions of Social Conflict*, pp. 47–8.

7. BEYOND ISLAM?

1. Amis, 2010, p. 393.

2. Stuart A Wright, 'Reconceptualizing Cult Coercion and Withdrawal: A Comparative Analysis of Divorce and Apostasy', *Social Forces*, 70/1 (1991), p. 127.

3. See Weiss, 1975, pp. 235–6, 240–1.

4. William J. Goode, *After Divorce* (Glencoe, Illinois: The Free Press, 1956), p. 19, emphasis in original.

5. Ibid., pp. 241–2, emphasis in original. See also Ebaugh, 1988, pp. 150, 160–1. Ebaugh argues, in line with the above, that the ex must find a way of incorporating their past identity into their future identity and that an important moment in the exit process occurs when the ex becomes, in the eyes of friends, family and co-workers, someone as *other* than an ex. A potential problem for the ex, Ebaugh contends, is if other people continue to view them through the prism of their previous identity, making the process of adjustment—'moving on'—all the more difficult and protracted.

6. Kareem put it like this: '"Friends come and go, but family is for life", that's what I used to think. Sadly, it's not true. In my family, the imaginary infinite friend is more important to them than me, their own son, their own brother, their own

flesh and blood.' Nasreen similarly remarks with great sadness that 'if it weren't for this religion I'd probably have a nice relationship with my parents. But because of this imaginary god I can't ever have a good relationship with my parents.'

7. Christopher Lasch, *A Haven in a Heartless World: The Family Besieged* (New York: W. W. Norton & Company, 1995).

8. Or in Edmund Leach's famous dictum: 'the source of all our discontents' (Edmund Leach, 'Runaway World: Lecture 3: Ourselves and Others', Transmission: 26 November 1967, BB Radio 4, available at http://downloads.bbc.co.uk/rmhttp/radio4/transcripts/1967_reith3.pdf, p. 7 (accessed 26 October 2012)).

9. As Omar says of the experience of having his two life-long friends desert him: 'Because what actually hurts, what does bother me inside, is that they knew I was going through depression, that I wasn't well, and as a human being they could have rang me and asked me, "Omar, are you OK?" But they're so blinded by their adherence to the faith that they can't see beyond that.'

10. Christopher Hitchens, *God is Not Great: How Religion Poisons Everything* (New York: Twelve, 2007).

11. For an illustrative example, see Whitaker, 2006; Nesrin Malik, 'Death for apostasy?', *The Guardian*, 17 October 2008, available at http://www.guardian.co.uk/commentisfree/2008/oct/17/islam-religion1 (accessed 15 July 2013); and Nesrin Malik, 'In Islam, there's more than one way to be an 'atheist'', *The Guardian*, 5 May 2014, available at http://www.theguardian.com/commentisfree/2014/may/05/islam-atheist-saudi-arabia-terrorists-faith-muslim-world#start-of-comments (accessed 16 June 2014).

12. See Marshall and Shea, 2011.

13. Seidman, 2002, p. 97.

14. See Irshad Manji, *The Trouble with Islam Today: A Muslim's Call for Reform in Her Faith* (New York: St Martins Press, 2003).

INDEX

INDEX

INDEX

INDEX